SHAPING A WORLD ALREADY MADE

SHAPING A WORLD ALREADY MADE

LANDSCAPE AND POETRY OF THE CANADIAN PRAIRIES

CARL J. TRACIE

University of Regina Press

Printed and bound in Canada at Marquis.

COVER AND TEXT DESIGN: Duncan Campbell, University of Regina Press
COPY EDITOR: Correy Baldwin
INDEX: Judy Dunlop
PROOFREADER: Colleen Biro
COVER ART: "Untitled" by Cara De Gennaro

LIBRARY AND ARCHIVES CANADA CATALOGUING IN PUBLICATION

Tracie, Carl J. (Carl Joseph), 1939-, author
Shaping a world already made : landscape and poetry of the Canadian Prairies / Carl J. Tracie.

Includes bibliographical references and index.
Issued in print and electronic formats.
ISBN 978-0-88977-393-6 (paperback).—ISBN 978-0-88977-395-0 (html).
—ISBN 978-0-88977-394-3 (pdf)

1. Canadian poetry (English)—Prairie Provinces—History and criticism.
2. Prairie Provinces—Poetry. I. Title.

PS8159.5.P72T73 2016 C811.009'9712 C2016-901402-9 C2016-901403-7

10 9 8 7 6 5 4 3 2 1

U OF R PRESS

University of Regina Press, University of Regina
Regina, Saskatchewan, Canada, S4S 0A3
tel: (306) 585-4758 fax: (306) 585-4699
www.uofrpress.ca

We acknowledge the financial support of the Government of Canada. / Nous reconnaissons l'appui financier du gouvernement du Canada. We acknowledge the support of the Canada Council for the Arts for our publishing program. This publication was made possible through Creative Saskatchewan's Creative Industries Production Grant Program.

Canada

Canada Council for the Arts
Conseil des Arts du Canada

creative SASKATCHEWAN

Dedicated
to all those who love the prairies

Contents

Acknowledgements

It seems immodest to claim authorship for a book that rests on the work of so many—geographers, poets, literary critics—whose perspectives and insights have been critical to this study. To some, however, I owe particular thanks. John Warkentin encouraged me at the beginning of this endeavour, and his continued wise counsel and astute commentary have enhanced the depth and reach of these essays. He also kindly agreed to write the introduction which provides a context for my work. Brian Osborne and Laurie Ricou generously shared their geographic and literary insights in response to my many questions; both helped to shape the early stages of this work. The poetry of Lorna Crozier and Patrick Friesen stimulated my first forays into the interface between geography and poetry. Lorna has been a constant source of encouragement throughout this project, and her love of the prairie has stimulated my own. Patrick's poetic insights over many years have been both enlightening and encouraging. Through personal contact and e-mails, I have come to value their art and their friendship. Di Brandt directed my attention to relevant readings in the early going and in later discussions expanded my understanding of her work. Jan Zwicky enlarged my understanding of metaphor and resonance and their application to geography. I owe special thanks to Dennis Cooley. His lively mind, close reading, and engaging e-mails have quickened and tightened both content and expression of these essays. His friendship over the past four years has been a source of great delight. He also kindly agreed to write the foreword. Lynn Szabo, poet and Thomas Merton expert, guided and informed my thinking on matters poetic, in particular on the place of mystery and silence. Emma LaRocque kindly reflected on my treatment of Abòriginal poetry and provided valuable and necessary clarification.

I am grateful for the enthusiastic support of the University of Regina Press. Director Bruce Walsh and his staff have brought the best of their expertise to bear on this project. I wish to thank especially Karen Clark, Scholarly Acquisitions Editor, for her indefatigable spirit and support in working through various drafts of the manuscript and for her assistance in navigating the complexities of permissions. I have appreciated the careful reading and helpful suggestions of Senior Editor Donna Grant. My thanks to Duncan Campbell and David McLennan who used the striking landscape painting of Cara De Gennaro to design a memorable cover.

I would like also to acknowledge the helpful comments of three anonymous reviewers.

Finally, and above all, thanks to my wife Darlene, my friend and stay.

Foreword

No one has ever written a book on Canadian prairie poetry—not until now, that is. We have books on Canadian poetry, and we have books on the Canadian prairie, but none on the poetry from the prairie. Even essays on the poetry are scarce. That alone would make *Shaping a World Already Made* a signal event.

It certainly is timely. Dozens of able and dedicated poets have been writing out of and about the region for decades, and those numbers have increased in the last 20 years. There are now scores of accomplished writers, many of whom have gone unread. Carl Tracie's bold and sensitive work will do its part to increase our knowledge.

Tracie, a geographer, has done what no other researcher of any ilk has attempted. The result is an important and engaging document. It summons a scholar's care for evidence, and a poet's desire for what can be said. The book is informed by an intimate knowledge of the literature on land and landscape. What makes it new is its engagement with contemporary understandings of language, cultural studies, and poetry. Tracie writes with special scruple and painstaking patience, but he speaks also in the rhythms of his own kind of poetry. The book's awareness of ethnicity and gender, of generational and cultural divergence, of popular work and little-known writing devolves eloquently from prairie landscape. A geographer's interest in landscape is expected, but the focus on poetry—that terrain of shifty meaning and fancied understanding—seems a wonderful new move. Yet there is nothing slight about Tracie's interest. He is intrigued by what it is in the writers that relates so powerfully to a landscape that they carry intimately in their mind's eye and in their body's pulse. He is at once careful to observe a language of "truth," and to respect a language of vision. The double move generates striking readings of landscape.

Tracie has studied a large number of prairie poets, including many authors only now coming into their own. He has read far more poets than has almost any reader, I would guess, and he has done so with diligence and tact. To work with unstudied material, to be one of the first into the field, is surely risky and demanding. Yet Tracie proffers analyses and advances arguments with clarity, his writing always nuanced and allowing. *Shaping a World* offers insights without insisting on them and balances the need for cogency with a reluctance to foreclose on an argument. Tracie works with what can only be called humility. A true student, he believes it is he who is learning.

The research that has come closest to what Tracie has done has also come from another geographer. A quarter century ago, in 1988, Ronald Rees published *New and Naked Land: Making the Prairies Home,* which read the prairie landscape as it was induced through imported notions of order, and as it later emerged in the counter understandings of prairie painters. Tracie's book turns to another art form. It considers the differences between the poetry of settler-invaders and their successors, who have often responded to the land with fear or aggression, and that of (especially) Aboriginal and female authors, who have sought and championed more reciprocal relationships with the land.

Reading the manuscript has been a special pleasure for me. I found myself struck again and again by the power, the sheer sudden rightness of the poets' language in Tracie's so judiciously chosen passages, and Tracie's own invigorating responses to that language, stirring in brevity and grace. Yes, that's it! That is how sunlight sits in the pasture, how the creatures move through the grass and the parklands. Tracie finds and shares with us what many of us have known without knowing, and what it is we most need and perhaps want to know—how it is we might begin to inhabit a place and respond to it with some glimmer of understanding. What Tracie says, and what the poets say as he selects and meditates on their work, can catch your breath. Northrop Frye has spoken of an imagination that occupies a land but does not love it. Tracie shows what an educated imagination might discover and what it might movingly celebrate.

Dennis Cooley
Winnipeg, Manitoba

Introduction

THE GREAT PLAINS
Soil poor, herbage scanty, no wood except on Northern exposures.
Very Arid
Broken Country, rich soil & pasture, partially wooded.
Cree Ind. Camp
Blackfoot Camp
Great herds of Buffalo
Rich & beautiful country
Vast open undulating Prairie.[1]

settlers I have heard on the Canadian prairie
moved into a huge silence wavered
on air there like birds in a desert
& emptiness not to be believed
tumbled past[2]

The first quotation above is from a few of the many descriptive phrases printed on various parts of the map that accompanied Captain John Palliser's report on his scientific and resource exploration of the Canadian prairies in the mid-nineteenth century. The phrases record what they saw. The second quotation is from poet Dennis Cooley, writing over a century later, imagining the experience of pioneer farming settlers encountering prairie space. Why

1 John Palliser, *A General Map of the Routes in British North America Explored by the Expedition under Captain Palliser, During the Years 1857, 1858, 1859, 1860* (London: Stanford's Geographical Establishment, 1865).

2 Dennis Cooley, "this only world," in *this only home* (Winnipeg: Turnstone, 1992), 130–31.

is a geographer such as Carl Tracie moved to write a book on prairie poetry? These quotations help tell us why: there are many ways of perceiving a region, and the creative artist can provide new insights and stir our own imaginations.

Here, I will briefly reflect on some profound transformations that have occurred in the prairie landscape through human intervention in the past two centuries—changes to the prairie landscape that affect the lives of the poets who are from the prairie and who write about it.

Canada has two extensive treeless areas: the vast tundra across the north and the prairie of the southern interior plains. Until the last half of the nineteenth century, both regions were thinly occupied. The tundra remains so today. Only a few small communities are scattered widely in a land little changed by humans. By contrast, the prairie has been almost completely transformed by farmers and ranchers, together with a widely spaced urban system that includes large cities. A new landscape has been produced, and two foundational maps of Canadian geography show the beginning of this profound revolution.

In 1865, just two years before Canadian Confederation, the Palliser scientific expedition produced a great map of the land stretching from Lake Superior to the Pacific Ocean. Of the prairies this elegant map revealed a free flowing land, the home of First Nations peoples. The gentle curves of nature filled the region: rivers, a few small lakes, low hills, and the limit of true prairie land. In actuality this was a land in motion—the home of moving bison herds on which First Nations and Métis depended. The few trails shown on the map wind cross-country. A few trading posts are marked, as well as Selkirk Settlement. People had made little imprint on this land, hardly altering it since they had first arrived. A remarkable harmony had been achieved. (See Map 1.)

The second seminal map, of the land extending from Manitoba to the Rocky Mountains, is from just fourteen years later, 1879—twelve years after Confederation. Prepared by Engineer-in-Chief Sandford Fleming for his wide-ranging Canadian Pacific Railway surveys, it shows a proposed transcontinental railway route across the prairies. What makes Fleming's map imaginatively useful for us today is that, although Palliser's earlier map provides much of the background, it starkly superimposes on those curving contours of nature two harsh, disruptive, straight-line geometric intrusions—both harbingers of a new agricultural and commercial machine age that would destroy the existing society. The first is the stern, uncompromising gridiron of the rectangular land survey, commonly called the section survey, shown spreading across southern Manitoba, heading inexorably westward. This represents the new underlying industrial age of property, section lines, homesteads, and farms that imposed a new face on the open commons landscape. It looks as if the land is being caged. The second, thrust right across the region, is the firm, unswerving route of the coming transcontinental railway, marked in long, straight segments. Adding to the railway's heavy mark, placed methodically every 16 kilometres at right angles to the line, are the names of proposed villages and towns, printed on the unsettled land from just east of Winnipeg to just west of Battleford. Like repetitive hatchet blows, the names cut sharply into the sinuous landscape, accentuating the fact that powerful new forces are entering the prairies. (See Map 2.) In 1881 the route was significantly changed, and when the main CPR line was built it went directly west from Winnipeg through present-day southern Saskatchewan and Alberta.

Two worlds meet on Fleming's 1879 railway surveys map: one of movement across the commons of First Nations, Métis, bison, and a few traders, and that of commercial cultivation, in which farmers are fixed on their homesteads and it is their products that move on rails to distant markets. Once farmers, ranchers, villages, and towns arrived, the commons quickly were gone. In this settlement process the most brutal change of all was that nomadic Indigenous peoples were placed on reserves, not yet shown on this map.

This shattering revolution began not even a century and a half ago. A new society, made possible by the Homestead Act, the new land survey, railways, and an immigration policy inviting agricultural settlers to resettle the region, destroyed the existing society and created a new landscape. Jan Zwicky describes this landscape as it appeared many years later:

> you can see for thirty miles:
> sheds, dugouts, the gridlock
> of stubble and summerfallow, windbreaks
> paralleling the section lines, and the road
> like some edict of connection,
> empty.[3]

3 Jan Zwicky, "Highway 879," in *Songs for Relinquishing the Earth* (London: Brick Books, 1998), 75.

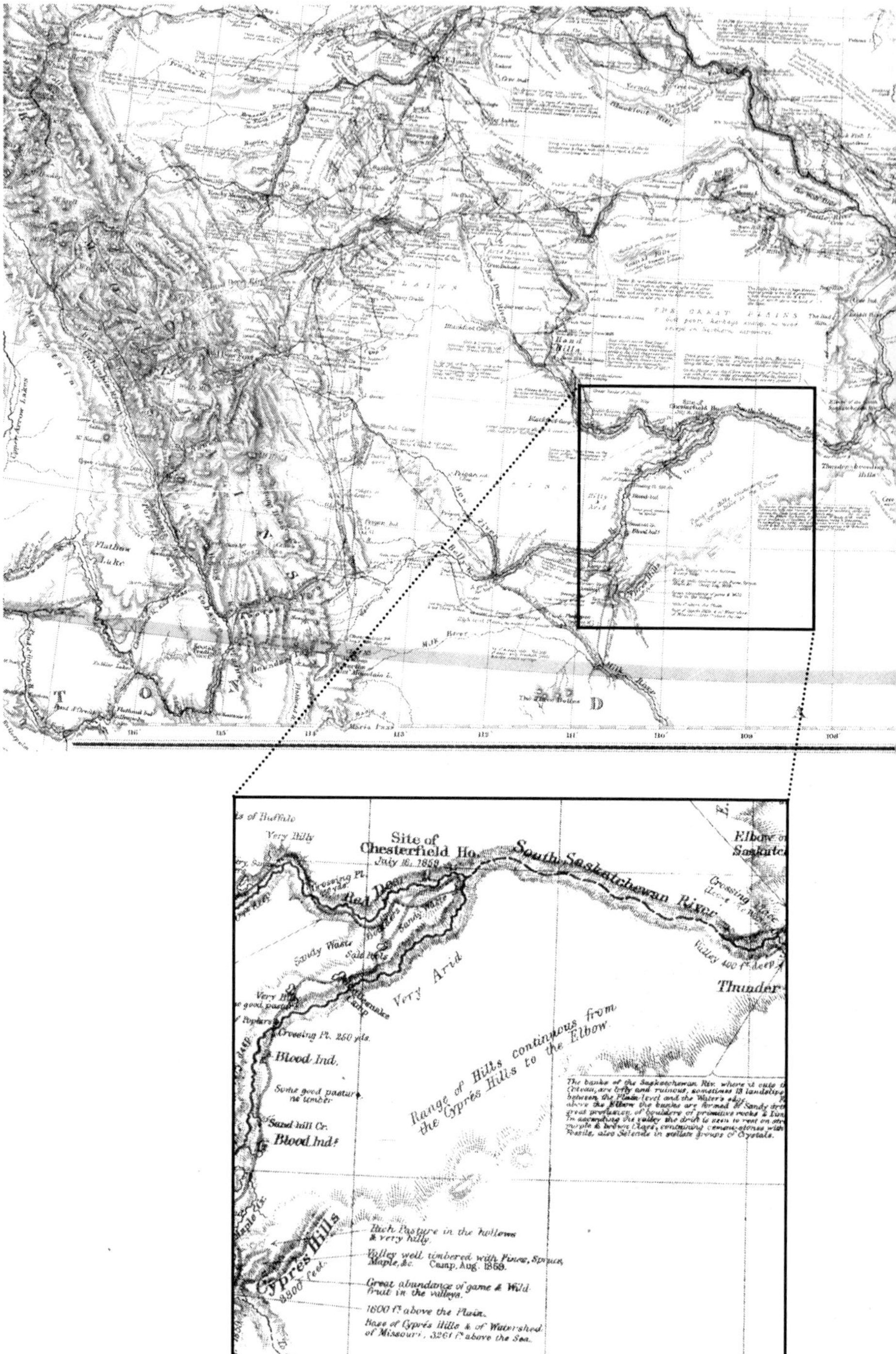
Flatbow Lake
Site of Chesterfield Ho.
July 16, 1859
South Saskatchewan River
Very Hilly
Sandy Waste
Very Arid
Crossing Pt. 250 yds.
Blood Ind.
Some good pasture no timber
Sand hill Cr.
Blood Inds
Range of Hills continuous from the Cyprés Hills to the Elbow
Thunder
Cyprés Hills
Rich Pasture in the hollows & very hilly.
Valley well timbered with Pines, Spruce, Maple, &c. Camp, Aug. 1859.
Great abundance of game & Wild fruit in the valleys.
1600 ft above the Plain.
Base of Cyprés Hills & of Watershed of Missouri, 3261 ft above the Sea.

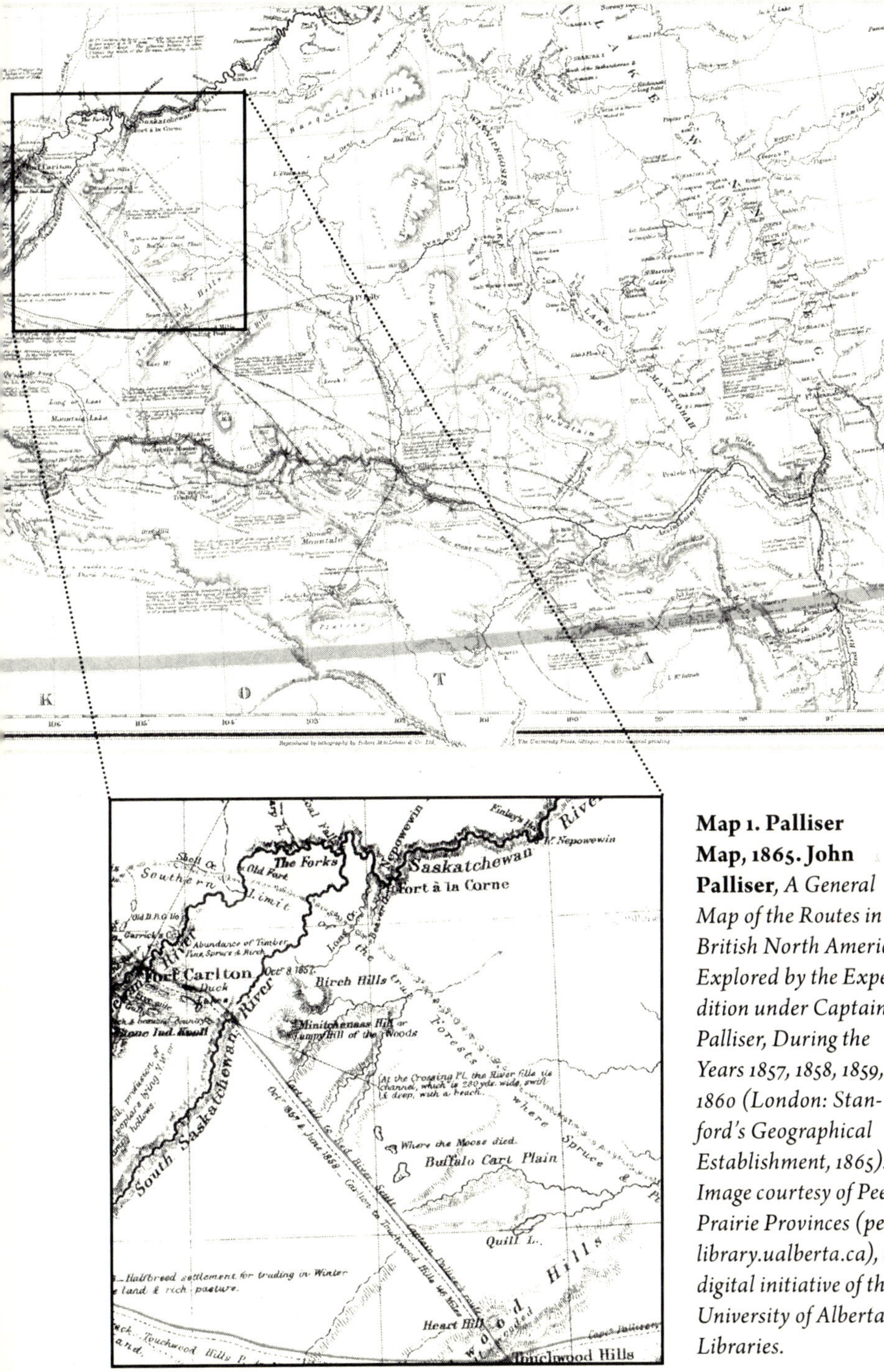

Map 1. Palliser Map, 1865. John Palliser, *A General Map of the Routes in British North America Explored by the Expedition under Captain Palliser, During the Years 1857, 1858, 1859, 1860 (London: Stanford's Geographical Establishment, 1865). Image courtesy of Peel's Prairie Provinces (peel.library.ualberta.ca), a digital initiative of the University of Alberta Libraries.*

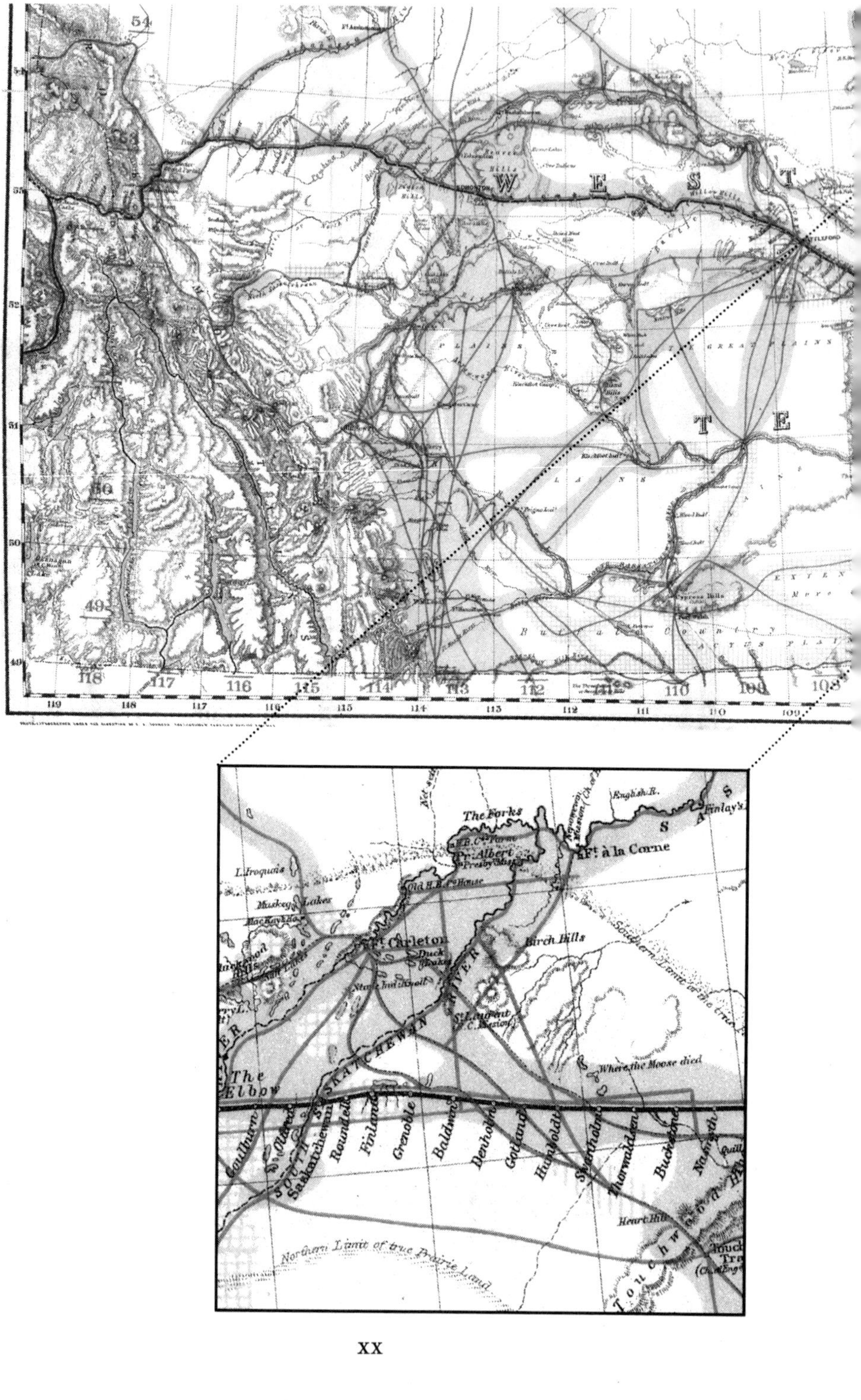
W
E
S
T
E
T
The Great Plains
Buffalo Country
The Forks
English R.
Ft. à la Corne
Pr. Albert
Muskeg Lakes
Ft. Carleton
Duck Lake
Birch Hills
The Elbow
Where the Moose died
Finland
Grenoble
Denholm
Humboldt
Thorwaldsen
Northern Limit of true Prairie Land

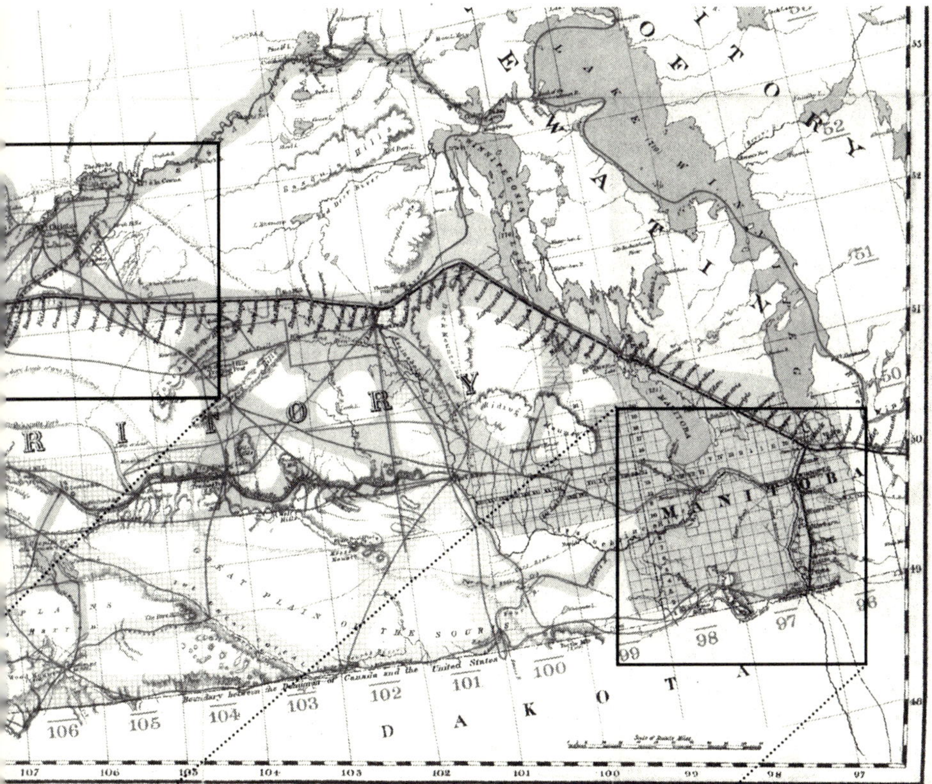

Map 2. Fleming Map, 1879. *Sandford Fleming,* Report in Reference to the Canadian Pacific Railway *(Ottawa: MacLean, Roger & Co., 1879). Image courtesy of Peel's Prairie Provinces (peel.library.ualberta.ca), a digital initiative of the University of Alberta Libraries.*

It is true that pioneer settler life was difficult in this agricultural revolution, as grasslands came under the plough. One is never far from nature on the prairies. Rainfall is not reliable. The drier sections are areas of agricultural hazard, and many adaptations were necessary to adjust to drier years. Yet, once the transcontinental railway was complete and branch lines were added around the turn of the century, the region was rapidly settled. Canada's greatest period of migration is immediately before World War I, when many immigrants, mostly from Europe, came to this region. In the three years of 1911 to 1913, before the war halted immigration, 1.1 million people emigrated to Canada, 401,000 in 1913 alone, a number that has never been exceeded. To put this in perspective, Canada's population in 1911 had been only 7.6 million. In 1901, Manitoba, Saskatchewan, and Alberta combined had only 420,000 people—by 1911 they had 1.3 million, and by 1921 they had just under 2 million.

This new agricultural society, based on small-scale agriculture using horse power on the farm, was barely in place by the 1920s when it was brought to its knees in the decade following by natural and economic forces. In the 1930s, the prairies were hard hit by years of drought and worldwide economic depression, especially severe on a wheat economy reliant on foreign markets. Eli Mandel describes the impact: "And the country itself, drought for many years, the / cattle dying, and the food rotten fish and decayed / eastern apples."[4] Mechanization brought further change as gasoline-powered machinery replaced horses. Farmers cultivated larger acreages, farm size steadily increased in the years following World War II, and migration from rural districts to cities grew.

This land is changing still. Machine power continues to grow. Farms continue to expand, forcing more farmers off the land. Farmsteads are abandoned and disappear, and the spaces between those left are larger and larger. Small villages are affected, and some disappear, too. Dennis Cooley notes: "train drains the prairie / dries each town each day into a cracker barrel."[5] Railway tracks, not a century old, are lifted. Slow, un-

4 Eli Mandel, "Mary Midnight," in *The Other Harmony: The Collected Poetry of Eli Mandel*, 2 vols., eds. Andrew Stubbs and Judy Chapman (Regina: Canadian Plains Research Center, 2000), Vol. 1, 312. All references to Mandel's work are from this two-volume collection.

5 Dennis Cooley, "in the garden," in *Country Music: New Poems* (Vernon: Kalamalka, 2004), 124.

obtrusive but potent demographic forces are at work on the landscape as it continues to be subtly altered. You can sense that space has opened up, but the land is no longer a commons.

During the twentieth century, new mineral resources, especially oil and gas, brought about profound changes in economic well-being and in time also raised serious concerns about environmental protection. Oil, first produced in the 1910s near Calgary, then from great reserves found in the 1940s near Edmonton, transformed the economy and propelled the growth of major urban centres. In the 1960s, exploitation of bitumen began in northern Alberta, north of the grasslands but closely associated with western prairie cities. Local environmental degradation and the effect of bitumen processing on climate change, now causes great local, national, and international concern. Di Brandt writes in furious dismay:

> Who shall be fisher king
> over this poisoned country,
> whose borders have become
> a mockery,
> blowing the world to bits.[6]

Despite all these changes, nature's presence on the prairies is undiminished. As in pre-contact times, one is always aware that life on the land is governed by unpredictable natural conditions. One summer morning many years ago, while filling up on gasoline at a Regina service station, I overheard two local men from the city earnestly discuss the *tenths of inches* of rain that had fallen the previous night. Their city's livelihood depended on such critical amounts. Lorna Crozier explains: "In the long dry heat everything awaits / the gazelle-footed touch of the rain."[7] Bonds with the land remain close, and in this precarious land, people remain careful observers of nature.

It is into this recently created and still visibly changing world that the poets discussed in this volume were born, and it is about this world that they write. Carl Tracie, too, is of this region, and he has studied it, thought about it, and written about it as a geographer.

For many years, geographers have made use of landscape paintings, novels, and music to help them understand and teach the geography of a

---

6 Di Brandt, "Zone: <le Détroit>," in *Now You Care* (Toronto: Coach House, 2003), 13.

7 Lorna Crozier, "Angel of Tigers," in *Inventing the Hawk* (Toronto: McClelland & Stewart, 1992), 53.

region. Creative arts assist such educational endeavours by providing a more profound sense of a region and the life of the people who live in it. In *Imagining Toronto,* for example, Amy Lavender Harris portrays that city through its literature, mainly making use of novels but including some poetry.[8] Tracie takes the bold step of devoting an entire book to delving into what poets from the prairie region can tell us through their poetry about where they live, or at least spent their formative years.

To write this book, Tracie has read prairie poetry comprehensively and deeply, and has thought about how prairie landscapes have affected the poets' imaginations and what insights we can gain from their poems about the prairie region and about life in this land. Where possible, he has corresponded with the poets to gain further insight into their work.

Tracie makes a distinction between popular and literary poetry. This study is mainly based on literary poetry, in which poets have a universal interest in ideas, in which they think and feel deeply, and in which they strive for memorable expression. Tracie does, however, devote one chapter to popular verse, and I cannot resist referring to one important attempt at that kind of writing, even though it was not meant for the general public.

The first written description of the Canadian prairies dates from 1690, composed in rhymed verse by the fur trader Henry Kelsey in a report on his observations to his superiors in the Hudson's Bay Company. His verse is important for geographical and historical reasons, but the quotation below also helps us understand why Tracie distinguishes carefully between popular and literary poetry. Kelsey travelled from York Factory on Hudson Bay to the prairies as the sole European with a group of First Nations people as they returned to their home area after trading at the Hudson's Bay Company trading post. It is here that he reports his first sight of that landscape, likely in present-day eastern Saskatchewan, south of the Saskatchewan River. Kelsey contrasts woodland and plain, mentions wildlife, especially the bison and the grizzly bear, and notes the First Nations' veneration for the latter. This is the land shown almost two centuries later on Palliser's map.

So far I have spoken concerning of the spoil
And now will accot. of that same Country soile

8 Amy Lavender Harris, *Imagining Toronto* (Toronto: Mansfield Press, 2010).

Which hither part is very thick of wood
Affords small nuts wth little cherryes very good
Thus it continues till you leave ye woods behind
And then you have beast of severall kind
The one is a black a Buffillo great
Another is an outgrown Bear wch is good meat
His skin to gett I have used all ye ways I can
He is mans food & he makes food of man
His hide they would not me it preserve
But said it was a god & they should Starve
This plain affords nothing but Beast &grass
And over it in three days time we past
getting unto ye woods on the other side
It being about forty sixe miles wide
This wood is poplo ridges with small ponds of water
there is beavour in abundance but no Otter
with plains & ridges in the Country throughout.[9]

Kelsey was clearly a fur trader, not a poet.

Tracie, as a geographer seeking the insight of poets, centres his work on the relationships between the specifically poetic imagination and the prairie landscape. His analysis is organized by six major themes: reflections on natural elements of the prairies, factors that affect poetic responses, conflicting reactions to the region, inherent spirit of the land, literary and popular poetry and their influence, and poetic and geographical imaginations in the prairie region. He selects the work of nine poets for particular analysis, though he discusses many more whenever appropriate. He brings together the voices of many poets on their feelings within the prairie landscape, the relationship that Indigenous peoples have to the land as expressed by both Indigenous and non-Indigenous poets, the vulnerability of rural and urban life in a difficult land undergoing profound change, and the damage done to the landscape. Some of the emotions expressed by the poets are distinctive to the prairies, although they are not exclusive to that region, such as responses to openness and the limitless sense of space and the feeling of vulnerability in a hazardous climate for an agrarian society. Theme by theme, Tracie carefully elucidates how the poetry gives us a fuller perspective of the region. In these chapters, we as readers are given the essence of

9 Henry Kelsey, *The Kelsey Papers* (Regina: Canadian Plains Research Center, 1994), 2.

many poets' rich understanding of the prairie landscape, transformed imaginatively into words.

Tracie is cautious about the influence of poetry on the public's general perception of the prairies, mostly because of poetry's limited circulation. He does note that there may be an indirect influence through education. Certainly, teachers in the humanities and social sciences, along with others, will be grateful to have this sensitive and insightful study of how some of Canada's most perceptive poets have reflected on the prairies. It is a landscape, in Tracie's words, that is still shaping.

John Warkentin
York University

CHAPTER 1

Between Two Worlds: Premises and Promises

The relationship between humans and the environment has long been an important theme for poets. The same is true for the geographer. In an exhaustive study of the development of geographic thought, Clarence Glacken identified three central questions that have focused geographic investigation since the Classical period. Two of them deal with the effect of the environment on humans and the effect of humans on the environment, questions that continue to engage geographers as they seek to understand spatial patterns of land and life in various areas.[1]

In pursuing these ends in the prairies, as well as in other regions, geographers have wrestled with combining science and art in their analyses. Some put more emphasis on physical factors or economic forces that could be quantified. Some used the prairies' plain-ness as the basis for revealing regular patterns of economic decisions implemented by rational people. Of course, many went beyond these quantifiable concerns to incorporate qualitative elements in their research. For them, and for cultural geographers in general, the "imaginative turn" in geography, with its emphasis on the qualitative resources of imagination

1 The third question—Is the earth a purposefully made creation?—has little import for this study. Clarence Glacken, *Traces on the Rhodian Shore: Nature and Culture in Western Thought from Ancient Times to the End of the Eighteenth Century* (Berkeley: University of California Press, 1967).

and emotion, signaled an increased opportunity to examine the work of artists of all sorts—painters, playwrights, novelists—to help illuminate the rich texture of a region that lies beyond or beneath the lineaments of the land.

In a seminal article from 35 years ago, the geographer Yi-Fu Tuan addressed this tension between the two approaches by adapting Dorothy Walsh's symbolic representation of the goals of scientists—a line representing "conclusion"—and artists—a circle representing "completeness"—into a garden-and-path analogy.[2] Scientific inquiry, like a path, is bounded, constrained if you will, by well-defined and well-understood criteria. A garden, however, is an expansive richness of experience and imagination. The path cannot contain the garden, but the garden can contain the path, and by choosing the latter, more inclusive, approach, the geographer can develop the kind of vision that recognizes the importance of both approaches.

Accordingly, geographers now stand with a foot in each of the two worlds of scientific tradition, which provides some basic measures of reality and understanding, and artistic tradition, which seeks realities beyond that which can be quantified. One perspective adds rigour, the other imaginative richness and depth. We seek to incorporate both in a regional analysis that presents the region as a complete entity; a fully realized whole. In our presentations, we want, as poet Lorna Crozier wants, the words we use to be both tame and wild; domesticated by scientific precision but wild with artistic imagination and emotion.[3] To do so, we must first learn "the secrets of seeing double,"[4] to echo Di Brandt's words; we must have "binary dreams"[5] if we are to have the "luxury of comparing landscapes."[6]

Although originally used to help produce an "enhanced geographical understanding and description of landscape" by employing artists'

---

2 Yi-Fu Tuan, "Literature and Geography: Implications for Geographical Research," in *Humanistic Geography: Prospects and Problems*, ed. David Ley and Marwyn Samuels (Chicago: Maaroufa Press, 1978), 194–206.

3 Lorna Crozier, "If a Poem Could Walk," in *Angels of Flesh, Angels of Silence* (Toronto: McClelland & Stewart, 1988), 41.

4 Di Brandt, "Heart," in *Now You Care* (Toronto: Coach House, 2003), 88.

5 Andrew Suknaski uses the term "binary dream" in his long poem *Silk Trail* (Toronto: Nightwood Editions, 1985), in which he twins East and West and the building of two trails: the silk road and the CPR.

6 Brandt, "Heart," in *Now You Care*, 88.

skills in creating "simplified and clarified landscapes,"[7] literature is now examined by geographers for the multi-faceted, multi-voiced expression of the experience of place. This is an important shift in the discipline from a focus on description and simplification to an appreciation of meaning and diversity; it is a critical shift from mimesis to metaphor, which brings into the study of geography "a web of social processes and intersubjective meanings," as James Duncan and David Ley observed.[8]

Geographer Paul Chamberlain, in noting several reasons to use literature in geography, quotes Tuan to say that literature "mediates among the contradictions and polarities of human experience," adding that "writers ... have proven to be exceptionally adept at articulating the ambiguities inherent in the human condition."[9] Poets have a particular facility in this regard, for, as Crozier says, poetry is the art form of paradox.[10] As they confront the paradoxes of prairie landscape and life, poets can suggest to geographers ways of dealing with enigmas, ambiguities, and ambivalences. They can underline for the geographer the need to search for the "between-ness" of truth about a region, to recognize that there is always a tension between knowing and not knowing.[11]

In seeking to understand place, then, geographers have found themselves influenced by the two worlds of environment and culture. Throughout the history of geography, different levels of significance have been attached to one or the other, fluctuating between the two extremes of environmental determinism and cultural determinism. The first emphasized the deterministic role of the physical environment in explaining patterns of economy and life; the second came as a brief reaction to this extreme view, and emphasized culture as the determin-

---

7 C. L. Salter and W. J. Lloyd, *Landscape in Literature,* Resource Papers for College Geography, no. 76–3 (Washington, DC: Association of American Geographers, 1977), 3.

8 James Duncan and David Ley, eds., *Place/Culture/Representation* (New York: Routledge, 1993), 11.

9 Paul Chamberlain, "Work in Progress on the Dasein of the Shakespearean Landscape," *Western Geography* 3 (1993): 87. Tuan himself takes up this challenge in his recent book, *Romantic Geography: In Search of the Sublime Landscape* (Madison: University of Wisconsin Press, 2013), in which he deals with the polarized values of the sublime experience with landscape.

10 Lorna Crozier, "Seeing Distance: Lorna Crozier's Art of Paradox," (interview by Elizabeth Philips) in *Where the Words Come From: Canadian Poets in Conversation,* ed. Tim Bowling (Roberts Creek: Nightwood, 2002), 152.

11 Patrick Friesen, "Gathering Bones," *Poetry Canada Review* 14, no. 4 (1994): 14–15.

ing factor. Today, most geographers see the physical environment as an important, rather than a determining, factor in understanding culture's inscriptions on the land.

Literary critics themselves acknowledge the "between-ness" of the two worlds. As critic and poet Arthur Adamson points out, "we live not in one world, but in at least two—the world as rational construct and the world as imagination. Reason makes one world, art inhabits both simultaneously. Meaning does not consist in the isolation of 'truth' but in the tension between two worlds."[12] Like the cultural geographer, writers also find themselves grappling with the tension between environment and culture, as perhaps best expressed by Eli Mandel: "What isn't clear is whether the prairies themselves are a form that imposes itself on the resistant self or whether it goes the other way around: we possess these stories, not even our own, and try to put their shapes on a world which resists fiercely."[13] The title for this study, borrowed from Louis Dudek's poem "At Lac en Coeur," seems to me to encapsulate that tension.[14] There is the natural landscape— a "world already made"— on which cultural elements work, "shaping [it] . . . to a form that I require."[15] Literary critics have also fluctuated between the extremes of environmental determinism—what was called "environmentalism"—and a form of cultural determinism that undervalued the influence of the natural landscape on literature.

And like the cultural geographer, literary critics, too, have for the most part arrived at an understanding of place as being comprised of both natural and human interactions. For instance, in *Land Sliding*, William New opines: "Landscape is a place, but it is also a body of attitudes in time, couched in the manner of speech and asking to be read in its own terms."[16] Elliott West, in a collection of essays on Wallace Stegner, notes, "a 'place' involves the meanings that humans have taken from an area and from what has happened there, the perceptions and emotions of individuals re-

---

12 Arthur Adamson, "Notes from a Dark Cellar: Ruminations on the Nature of Regionalism and Metaphor in Mid-Western Canadian Poetry," in *RePlacing*, ed. Dennis Cooley (Downsview: ECW Press, 1980), 238.

13 Eli Mandel, "Writing West: On the Road to Wood Mountain," in *Essays on Saskatchewan Writing*, ed. E. F. Dyck (Regina: Saskatchewan Writer's Guild, 1986), 153.

14 Although his phrase is fitting for my study, Dudek is not a poet from the prairies.

15 Louis Dudek, "At Lac en Coeur," in *Canadian Poetry: The Modern Era*, ed. John Newlove (Toronto: McClelland & Stewart, 1977), 79.

16 William New, *Land Sliding: Imagining Space, Presence, and Power in Canadian Writing* (Toronto: University of Toronto Press, 1997), 130.

sponding to their surroundings and to events."[17] In the same collection, William Kittredge says, "There is no such thing as a landscape; there are only the processes of nature, and those of location, which in humans derive so largely from our incessant storytelling."[18] Lawrence Durrell concludes, "Now, however, I am beginning to believe that the [human] wish is inherited from the site; that man depends for the furniture of the will upon his location in place, tenant of fruitful acres or a perverted wood."[19]

As a geographer, my own attempt to make meaningful observations about the interconnected themes of poetry, landscape, perception, paradox, and mystery on the prairies of the Canadian West reflects an attachment to this region's geography *and* its literature spanning the past five decades. My overriding feeling is one of respect: respect in the face of a land without bounds and a sky without end; respect for the multitude of artists who by their attachment, passion, and art have given voice to the enduring elements of this region, as well as to the unique relationships that people have to the prairie land. The interaction between poet and landscape is complicated, involving many paradoxes and tensions, and the relationship between the two raises questions that probe the roles of both geography and literature in understanding this region. Poets do not shy away from these complexities, and with their art they accommodate, if not resolve, these tensions. Some paradoxes, however, remain in that realm of mystery beyond words—a situation that frustrates, but does not still, the poetic voice. An attempt to illuminate both the commonalities within and the rich diversity of this prairie region by studying its poets and its poetry is a challenging and exciting task.

Overall, this study is guided by two central questions: First, how do the elements of the prairie landscape—land, sky, creatures, and cover—affect prairie poets and their poetry? Second, what potential

---

17 Elliott West, "Stegner, Storytelling, and Western Identity," in *Wallace Stegner, Man and Writer*, ed. Charles E. Rankin (Albuquerque: University of New Mexico Press, 1996), 64.

18 William Kittredge, "The Good Rain: Stegner and the Wild," in *Wallace Stegner, Man and Writer*, ed. Charles E. Rankin (Albuquerque: University of New Mexico Press, 1996), 39.

19 Lawrence Durrell, *Justine*, from an epigraph in John Lent, *Frieze* (Saskatoon: Thistledown, 1984).

influence does their poetry and the way they re-present this landscape have on the way residents and outsiders see the prairies?[20] In exploring these concerns, I have been continually tempted by a reductionist desire, to simplify what I increasingly found impossible to simplify; I was engaged, in Robert Kroetsch's phrase, with "effing the ineffable." However, I soon abandoned the idea of somehow distilling the essence of the region from its poetry (a task for which poets and novelists have been credited with special expertise)[21] and accepted the need to accommodate the vast complexities and intricacies of the artistic perspective. I want to honour the "enduring elements" that have characterized the prairie region and that have continued to serve as grist for the poet's imaginative mill while also honouring the rich and detailed elements of, and human reactions to, the variegated landscape of the prairies. I find myself confronting the same paradox that poets face: a desire for both individualism and universalism.[22]

There are other concerns that I need to address as well at the outset of this study: What is the prairie region? What do I mean by prairie landscape? Why use poetry? Who is a prairie poet? Which prairie poets should I include? Let me summarize my approach to each of these questions.

As a cultural geographer, I am concerned with region (the space within which the interaction between poet and landscape takes place) and influence. The concept of region assumes that spaces on the surface of the earth, both large and small, have some sort of coherence that makes the region hold together in ways that are recognizable to a wide variety of people and familiar to its inhabitants. A region may cohere as a result of common features, such as a similar terrain or ecology, or as a result of interconnected economic or political functions. People living in the region may have a common mindset, a similar way of viewing its physical and cultural components.

And yet, as Antje Schlottmann has articulated, one of the problems of attempting to define a region is that one is always involved in the

---

20 Probably the most exhaustive examination of aspects of these questions is New's *Land Sliding*.

21 "Whatever their ultimate use of landscape, authors tend to bring an artistic sensitivity to their work which encourages them to sense and communicate the essentials of landscape and space." Salter and Lloyd, *Landscape in Literature*, 3.

22 Louis Dudek, *The First Person in Literature: Six Talks for CBC Radio* (Toronto: CBC Publications, 1967), 57.

construction of the region while researching it.[23] This becomes, as Ulf Strohmayer notes, a circular task—the categories chosen for defining a region are often treated as self-evident and thus end up as self-fulfilling in any analysis.[24] I have nonetheless limited the prairie region I reference to the grasslands of the largely forested, and hence inappropriately named, *prairie* provinces of Manitoba, Saskatchewan, and Alberta, keeping in mind that the significant components of the prairie landscape—grassland, with its constituent inhabitants; awareness of space and distance; and big sky—diminish in intensity from the core of short-grass prairie to the parkland and forest on its perimeter. As a region of the mind, however, this area deemed *prairie* is much less well-defined and goes beyond the grassland core to include a portion of the parkland and bush in the contact zone between prairie and forest.

Although I have used grassland as the formal criterion for limiting the space I am considering, it is this last region of the mind that drives my examination of the ways in which poetry both expresses that coherence and contributes to it. Still, this region of the mind is most certainly rooted in the particularities and generalities of the prairie landscape.[25]

I use "prairie landscape" in the general sense of a field of view, the totality of physical elements that one sees and experiences when living on and moving about the prairies. The term encompasses not only the elements of the land itself (configuration, components, creatures, and cover) but also the elements of sky (appearance, weather, climate), the expansiveness of space and distance, and the physical changes to the landscape made by people living in the region. In geographic terms, I am interested in both physical and cultural landscapes, although my emphasis is on the physical. In the same way that the Ancient Greeks

---

23 "As I argue, the dilemma of being always involved in the construction of a region when researching 'it' (by naming it, referring to its boundaries, its inner homogeneity, etc.) can be solved by keeping the region in question a hypothesis ('region in suspenso')." Antje Schlottmann, "Limited Language/Linguistic Limitations: A Reply to the Reviews," *Acme* 4, no. 2 (2005): 272.

24 "The main point of this critique [from Antje Schlottmann, *RaumSprache*, 2005] is the taken-for-granted nature of the categories that are used to construct such regional forms of identity: the fact that they often are utterly circular in nature and thus end up becoming self-fulfilling prophecies even in academic writings, is, according to the author, a little-analysed and thus neglected phenomenon." Ulf Strohmayer, "On Not Taking Language for Granted," *Acme* 4, no. 2 (2005): 250.

25 See Adamson, "Notes from a Dark Cellar," 224.

came to understand the human body as an indivisible union of body and mind, a true understanding of the prairie as a region must involve seeing it as an indivisible union of the physical and the human. The landscape, in this sense, is not just "out there" but "in here," as Crozier's *Inside Is the Sky* intimates. I have considered and set aside other possible terms: environment (a term that comes easily to me as a geographer and that succinctly encompasses both physical and cultural elements, but which is freighted with an unhelpful connotation—environmental determinism—that suggests a particular emphasis that I do not intend), geography (a term that is much too general, as it encompasses both elements and approach), nature (also too general), and terrain (too limited).

And why poetry? As I have noted, geographers and others interested in the way art and landscape are intertwined have most often used the novel as a source of information and illumination.[26] Chamberlain points out several potential benefits of the novel: it may provide factual information, it gives a perspective on how people experience the world, and it may help to improve the literary quality of geographic writing.[27] Novelist Rudy Wiebe is more forceful, claiming that poetry cannot encompass the epic nature of prairie stories.[28] Whatever the truth of this claim or the challenge of assessing the poet's imaginative use of the prairie landscape, poetry, I believe, is well suited to exploring the variety of human interactions with the prairie. Poems are concise; the poet's observations and insights are compressed and distilled by way of image and metaphor. Poetic images evoke vivid representations of elements or experiences of a region, while poetic metaphors imaginatively and ambiguously, accommodate polarities.[29] Poetry has a unique ability

26 Marc Brosseau, in his comprehensive analysis of "geography's literature" notes: "I will concentrate my discussion on geographical research on fiction and more precisely on the novel, as most geographers have focused on this type of literature." Marc Brosseau, "Geography's Literature," *Progress in Human Geography* 18, no. 3 (1994): 335. This is largely true 20 years later.

27 Chamberlain, "Work in Progress," 85–108; Yi-Fu Tuan, "Literature, Experience, and Environmental Knowing," in *Environmental Knowing: Theories, Research, and Methods*, ed. G. T. Moore and R. G. Golledge. (Stroudsburg: Dowden, Hutchinson & Ross, 1976), 260–71.

28 "To touch this land with words requires an architectural structure . . . [a] poem, a lyric, will not do." Rudy Wiebe, "Passage by Land," in *Personal Fictions*, ed. Michael Ondaatje (Toronto: Oxford, 1977), 227.

29 "through metaphor to reconcile / the people and the stones." William Carlos Williams, "A Sort of a Song," *Selected Poems* (New York: New Directions, 1985), 145.

to startle the senses.[30] Poetry, for all its brevity, invites us into the real world—a world informed and transformed by imagination, a world of emotion, conflict, and paradox. Poetry enriches our understanding of what makes space place, and gives us a sense of region defined by resonances rather than by simplified similarities.

There are several challenges, however. I am foremost a reader and a fan—not so much a critic—of poetry.[31] Yet if this complicated interaction between poet and landscape is to be assessed, a certain degree of critical attention is needed. This involves determining not so much what is "good" poetry or "representative" prairie poetry, but how the content, cadence, and vocabulary of the poetry reflect the prairie experience.

There is, of course, another dimension to this interaction—that of time. In the introductory essay to their edited volume, *History, Literature and the Writing of the Canadian Prairies*, Alison Calder and Robert Wardhaugh point out that "on the plains, geography, history, and culture are inextricably linked, and that only by considering all these facets at once can we begin to understand the diverse cultural landscapes of the place."[32] In the intersection of environment, culture, and time (or as they call it, "history"), it is important to remember that "time" in this trilogy is expressed as memory. Poetry emerges from past observations, events, and emotions that have been not only re-imagined by the poet but modified by time and intervening experience. Hence, memory complicates the exchange between poetry and the prairie landscape. Given that all poetry is, in fact, memory, one must determine in what way the poet's memory of their observations reflects the "truth" about the prairie (or indeed, what kind of truth is being reflected), as well as what criteria to use in assessing this relationship. As one author put it, "mem-

---

30 Clarise Foster, "Consider Yourself Warned." A review of Di Brandt's *Now You Care.* (*Globe and Mail*, Saturday, April 17 2004). Online.

31 I take some comfort in George Woodcock's comment on readers: "We as readers should be prepared with our own understanding of a poet's work, however tenuous that understanding may be, before we listen to the critics. First understanding, and even first misunderstanding, are vital to an eventual comprehension of a poet's work." George Woodcock, "Introduction," *Canadian Writers and Their Works*, Poetry Series, vol. 11, ed. Robert Lecker, Jack David, and Ellen Quigley (Toronto: ECW Press, 1995), 12.

32 Alison Calder and Robert Wardhaugh, "When Is the Prairie?" in *History, Literature, and the Writing of the Canadian Prairies*, ed. Alison Calder and Robert Wardhaugh (Winnipeg: University of Manitoba Press, 2005), 4.

ory is a complicated thing . . . a relative to truth, but not its twin."[33] The relationship is fraternal, not identical.

Then there is the next challenge: Just who is a prairie poet? And is the term "prairie poet" a legitimate description and not subtly pejorative?[34] Should a prairie poet be defined by residence (present or past), content (references to prairie elements), style (anecdotal), or voice (vernacular)?[35] Residency, as Dennis Cooley points out, is an uncertain criterion, as one may be resident in the prairies but write as if one were somewhere else entirely.[36] His ultimate criterion for choosing the poets for his anthology *Inscriptions* is one that resonates with me: "The writing in some way or other had to show signs that it came out of the prairies or that it engaged with the place."[37] Laurence Ricou, Lorna Crozier, and Gary Hyland went a bit further in their selection of poets to include in their anthologies, requiring in their choice of poetry a sense of the prairies as home and as central to the writer's life.[38] I agree with this choice as well. Without a visceral involvement with the prairie and its elements, a poet can only write *about* the prairie, rather than *from* the prairie. Both perspectives accommodate poets such as Crozier, Patrick Friesen, Tim Lilburn, and Jan Zwicky who have moved from the prairies but continue to engage with that landscape. For these poets, home soil is portable. Friesen, for instance, claims his original home environment as the base layer, or basic "grid," which is absorbed into his life and affects his poetic process consciously or unconsciously; other layers or grids are built in

33 Barbara Kingsolver, *Animal Dreams* (New York: HarperCollins Perennial, 1990), 48.

34 The term "prairie poet" is seen by some as suggesting a limitation in the reach of their poetry—a regional restraint rather than a universal application of their work.

35 Frank Davey, "A Young Boy's Eden: Notes on Recent 'Prairie' Poetry," *Reading Canadian Reading* (Winnipeg: Turnstone, 1988), 213–29.

36 Dennis Cooley, ed., *Inscriptions: A Prairie Poetry Anthology* (Winnipeg: Turnstone, 1992), xv.

37 Ibid.

38 "I looked for poems that would show the quality and variety of prairie poetry, and especially for poems that both create and depend upon a sense of the locale and history of the Canadian prairies, however unscientifically that region is defined by the poems as a group. . . . the fertile questions are how the poet has created the region through language, and what details of the region he has used to reveal the universal. . . . In each case, though, the prairie is a prominent, and often persistent, focus of the poet's work." Laurence Ricou, *Twelve Prairie Poets* (Ottawa: Oberon, 1976), 6–7; "The extra-ordinariness of this place doesn't come from its topography—its relative flatness, its huge sky—but from its central position in the writer's life." Lorna Crozier, "Introduction," *A Sudden Radiance*, ed. Lorna Crozier and Gary Hyland (Regina: Coteau, 1987), xvii.

new environments.[39] Although I am not sure I subscribe to Northrop Frye's higher standard of only recognizing poets who have been raised in this region as prairie poets (others are "imaginative foreigners" in his estimation), the poets I have chosen do satisfy this requirement as well.[40]

Having decided—for my purposes at least—who is a prairie poet, the next task, considering the sheer volume of prairie poetry, is to narrow the field. First, should I use literary poetry or what is deemed "popular" poetry? Literary poetry is more likely to contain imaginative representations of prairie elements and prairie experiences, but may be less accessible and therefore less likely to influence the perception of most residents. Popular poetry may be more accessible to the general reader, but may not employ the imaginative reconstructions that are likely to effect shifts in the way this region is perceived. Popular poetry is perhaps more likely to confirm the comfortable (or uncomfortable) stereotypical views of the prairie, which may account for its continued popularity. Keeping these considerations in mind, I decided to focus most of my study on literary poetry, but with some consideration of popular poetry, too.

Within these limitations, I have chosen nine poets for special analysis: Di Brandt, Dennis Cooley, Lorna Crozier, Patrick Friesen, Tim Lilburn, Eli Mandel, John Newlove, Andrew Suknaski, and Jan Zwicky. Each has a substantial body of work and a long attachment to the prairie region.

To pose the question "how has the prairie landscape influenced prairie poetry?" is to assume that the prairie landscape does indeed have an influence on the poetry written in and about it, that poets writing out of a certain landscape are influenced by their physical context. [41] Writers themselves have said as much, voicing the opinion that their "primal

---

39 Patrick Friesen, e-mail message to author, April 12, 2003; February 16, 2004.

40 Northrop Frye, preface to *The Bush Garden: Essays on the Canadian Imagination* (Toronto: Anansi, 1971), ii.

41 Pamela Banting also posits these two questions as central to her work, although the anthology of literature she has chosen in which to deal with these questions is more broadly inclusive both in regional scope and literary genre. Her aim is to bring together a body of literature "which explored the ways in which we both imprint and are imprinted by geography." She uses the term "geography" in a more restricted sense than would suit most geographers. Pamela Banting, *Fresh Tracks: Writing the Western Landscape* (Victoria: Polestar, 1998), 10.

landscapes"[42] have influenced their art.[43] Many literary critics have affirmed this assumption with explicit statements. For example, Laurie Ricou observes: "The landscape, and man's relation to it, is the concrete situation with which the prairie artist initiates his re-creation of the human experience. Even those writers who do not use this image explicitly can be seen to be utilizing it tangentially."[44] Others insist that the poet/land interaction is a crucial element in understanding a regional literature.[45]

There are dissenting voices, however. Perhaps the most compelling is Eli Mandel, who throughout his career remained skeptical of the environment as a single determinant of Western writing, and argued for

---

42 This is a phrase Don Gayton attributes to a poet friend, and it refers generally to the special bond between children and their childhood environments. See Don Gayton, *Landscapes of the Interior: Re-Explorations of Nature and the Human Spirit* (Gabriola Island: New Society Publishers, 1996), 71.

43 "Surely one of the intentions of literature is just this: to acquaint us with the dangers of and to coax us into intimacies with the landscapes we wear." Robert Kroetsch, *A Likely Story: The Writing Life* (Red Deer: Red Deer College Press, 1995), 81; "The idea of landscape is incredibly complicated emotionally. It's no accident that a lot of poets work out of that notion." Kroetsch, "Uncovering Our Dream World: An Interview with Robert Kroetsch" (interview by Robert Enright and Dennis Cooley) in Cooley, *RePlacing*, 31; "[T]he landscape is part of [my] thinking, not an 'object.'" Patrick Friesen, e-mail to the author, April 12, 2003; and "[T]he landscape I return to in my mind, most of the time, is the landscape of my childhood—the short-grass, big-sky country of SW Sask." Lorna Crozier, e-mail to the author, February 9, 2004. Crozier's suite of poems in her chapbook *man from elsewhere* (Saskatoon: Jack Pine Press, 2013) bears out the impress of landscape on individuals.

44 Laurence Ricou, *Vertical Man/Horizontal World: Man and Landscape in Canadian Prairie Fiction* (Vancouver: University of British Columbia Press, 1973), xi; "The Canadian imagination thus far is mainly a function of a landscape and a climate, and only secondarily of a society." Desmond Pacey, "The Canadian Imagination," in *Essays in Canadian Criticism, 1938–1968*, ed. Desmond Pacey (Toronto: Ryerson, 1969), 234; "Any discussion of the literature of the west must of necessity begin with the impact of the landscape upon the mind." Henry Kreisel, "The Prairie: A State of Mind," in *Contexts of Canadian Criticism*, ed. Eli Mandel (Chicago: University of Chicago Press), 1971, 257; "[T]he regional voice *is* the landscape. Without it there is no art." Adamson, "Notes From a Dark Cellar," 224.

45 See Northrop Frye, *The Bush Garden* and *Divisions on a Ground: Essays on Canadian Culture* (Toronto: Anansi, 1982); D. G. Jones, *Butterfly on Rock* (Toronto: University of Toronto Press, 1970); Tom Marshall, *Harsh and Lovely Land: The Major Canadian Poets and the Making of a Canadian Tradition* (Vancouver: University of British Columbia Press, 1979); Ricou, *Vertical Man/Horizontal World* and *Twelve Prairie Poets*; Susan Glickman, *The Picturesque and the Sublime: A Poetics of the Canadian Landscape* (Montreal: McGill-Queens University Press, 1998); and Diana Relke, *Greenwor(l)ds: Ecocritical Readings of Canadian Women's Poetry* (Calgary: University of Calgary Press, 1999), among others.

a pluralistic approach.[46] He stated clearly that "literary and physical frontiers do not coincide,"[47] and that among the many problems to be resolved by those who focus on the environment is the limitation it places on the influence of such poetry. If prairie poetry, for example, arises from and is defined by the landscape of the prairies, can it ever be considered to be anything other than "regional?" Could universal themes ever emerge from poetry constrained by regional landscape images and metaphors? A. M. Klein re-enforces Mandel's critical view:

> To make writing rotate about geography, rather than admit geography as one of the many aspects of the creative process—is to pervert the purpose of our craft.... Love of one's environment, I admit, is a laudable and highly convenient virtue; but about it, one builds, at best, only minor literature.... [It] must inevitably end up by being parochial.[48]

However, even allowing a more modest role for environmental influence, the nature of the relationship between landscape and the writer, and the ways it is expressed, are not always clear. Deborah Keahey affirms Mandel's perspective, and rejects the constraining view of an environmentalism that demands that landscape is seen as the single defining element in prairie poetry. She suggests that rather than rejecting "place" and replacing it with "culture," place needs to be "reimagined as a creation of the social, psychological, and cultural relationships that people have to particular landscapes or physical spaces."[49] This view ac-

46 "Of course, regional literature, say Western Canadian fiction, is especially susceptible to an environmental approach, possibly because we tend to equate regions with particular space. But the land tells us little about genuine folkloristic elements; the western as outlaw story, the rogue figure of tall tales, ballads telling of domestic and border violence and terror." Eli Mandel, "Romance and Realism in Western Canadian Fiction," in *Prairie Perspectives* 2, ed. A. W. Rasporich and H. C. Klassen (Toronto: Holt, Rinehart and Winston, 1973), 203.

47 Mandel, "Romance and Realism," 199.

48 A. M. Klein, "Writing in Canada," in *Literary Essays and Reviews*, ed. Usher Caplan and M. W. Steinberg (Toronto: University of Toronto Press, 1987), 218–19. Klein, like many non-geographers, uses the term "geography" to refer to the physical environment.

49 Deborah Keahey, *Making it Home: Place in Canadian Prairie Literature* (Winnipeg: University of Manitoba Press, 1998), 7.

knowledges the complexity of writer–landscape interaction, suggesting a range of intervening elements that rules out simplistic relationships.

Even Mandel acknowledges that "the curious fact about attempts to define or characterize a tradition of Canadian writing is the inevitable, obsessive concern with physical landscape."[50] He also muses:

> Wonder how I belong here—a false claim? Later, as I drive to Fort Qu'appelle and Fort San I think, it's a physiological thing, the prairies. We fit spaces as our brain fits the world, the language mediates. It's not a question of whether one is horizontal man or vertical man but of the way your mind fits. You can feel it. For some reason these colours, these abstractions, these fields mean "home" to me and I can feel it in a gathering sense of words.[51]

Two additional factors complicate these matters further: local variations in the poet's "primal" landscape, and personal variations in the perception of that landscape. The basic elements of land, sky, and space are common elements across the prairies, but these, especially the first, vary markedly from area to area. Do local variations find expression in the work of individual poets? A further complication is the poet's perception. In defining landscape in art, Malcolm Andrews states that every artist carries a "framed representation of a section of the natural world, a cropped view, selected and reduced so that it can be a portable memento."[52] Pierre Dansereau suggests that this "portable memento" is in fact a landscape, shaped, or reshaped, by the artist's "inscape."[53] These interior mental images are shaped by a host of individual factors: personality, temporary mood, training, and experience. W. L. Morton

---

50 Eli Mandel, "Introduction," *Contexts of Canadian Criticism* (Chicago: University of Chicago Press, 1971), 23.

51 Eli Mandel, "Journal: Fort San: Beginnings, 1977," in *The Other Harmony: The Collected Poetry of Eli Mandel*, ed. Andrew Stubbs and Judy Chapman (Regina: Canadian Plains Research Center, 2000), Vol. 1, 415.

52 Malcolm Andrews, *Landscape and Western Art* (Oxford: Oxford University Press, 1999), 201.

53 "The pathway of sensorial impression to material interference is strewn with an imagery that makes the inscape a template for the reshaping of the landscape." Pierre Dansereau, "Introduction," *Inscape and Landscape* (Toronto: CBC, 1973), np.

suggests that for a new country to create its own literature and history, it must reconcile the "actual and the mind's landscape."[54]

What I would like to highlight here are differences that relate to the background story of different groups of poets. For those whose histories begin with settler ancestors, this story might involve memories of Europe brought forward to a new landscape through unique settlement patterns and architectural forms. The story would be full of early pioneering hardship, the challenges of unpredictable weather—especially during the 1930s—and overcoming these obstacles. In other words, the physical landscape would represent both new opportunities and harsh challenges; the story would revolve around making the prairies home. The background story for those of Aboriginal ancestry is much different. The story begins, rather than ends, with home. The story is one of already being at home in their environment, then of adapting to the first European advances into their homelands through the fur trade. Their story therefore also involves loss of land, loss of livelihood, and, especially in the era of the residential schools, loss of language and culture. For Aboriginal peoples, the question is not *how do you grow a poet*[55] in a new land, but *how do you grow a poet* in an occupied homeland, with a new language and the resonance of decades of abuse, oppression, and misunderstanding ringing in your ears? It would be reasonable to expect that the differing background stories, in addition to the personal differences of each poet, would result in differing perspectives on the landscape and different ways of expressing it in their poetry. Thus, the prairie poet observes and reacts to a landscape already shaped by a variety of factors, but also brings in other, more general, factors of race, gender, and location.[56]

Then there is the complication of memory. The poet is not only attending to the "real" landscape viewed through various personal and societal filters, but is relying on the memory of observation, itself subject

---

54 W. L. Morton, "Seeing an Unliterary Landscape," *Mosaic* (special issue: Manitoba in Literature) 3, no. 3 (Spring 1970), 9.

55 Robert Kroetsch famously asked this question in "Seed Catalogue," *Completed Field Notes: The Long Poems of Robert Kroetsch* (Edmonton: University of Alberta Press, 2000), 29–46.

56 A significant theme in the geographical literature of landscape and regions is the analysis of perception in regional image making.

to distortion, for the poetic expression of that remembrance.[57] The landscape might, in the words of American poet Charles Wright, remain in a person like a bee's sting,[58] but it is a *remembered* landscape, flawed and flexible.[59] If one were using prairie poetry as mimesis, as an attempt to fill in details of the prairie landscape, this would be a problem. However, if poetry is used to reflect imagination and emotion, this may be beneficial. In an early interview, Robert Kroetsch pointed out that it is the memory of landscape, rather than its reality, that allows it to be viewed as "as a metaphor, as a story, as a myth"; as such, it becomes a source for poetry.[60] This is precisely the basis of the rich variety of perception that allows us to break free from the stereotypical images of the prairies. It is the mythic reimagining by the poet's purpose, vision, and skill that gives rise to the possibility of seeing the prairie landscape from a more fully realized perspective.

In an attempt, then, to see the landscape of the prairies through the lens of poetry so as to arrive at a more fully realized vision of it, this study will begin with the stable elements of the prairie landscape—land and sky—and read for their potential influence on the poetry of the poets examined in the next chapter, "Poets of the Prairie: Enduring Elements of Prairie Landscape in Prairie Poetry." I will inquire into how best to determine the potential impact of the physical elements of the prairie landscape on poetry. In the following chapter, "Parallax: Race, Gender, and Location," I will examine some of the differing contexts out of which prairie poets write. For example, do female and male poets respond differently to the elements of the prairie landscape? Are there emotional and imaginative differences between Aboriginal and non-Aboriginal perspectives? Are "rural" poets more likely to be influenced by land-

57 For an interesting analysis of progressive distortion of regional images, see G. Malcolm Lewis, "The Recognition and Delimitation of the Northern Interior Grasslands during the Eighteenth Century," in *Images of the Plains: The Role of Human Nature in Settlement*, ed. Brian Blouet and Merlin Lawson (Lincoln: University of Nebraska Press, 1975), 23–44.

58 Charles Wright, "All Landscape Is Abstract, and Tends to Repeat Itself," in *Appalachia* (New York: Farrar, Straus and Giroux, 1999), 19.

59 Both of the terms "flawed" and "unreliable" presuppose a real or objective landscape that is viewed. In a sense, this kind of reality exists only in the quantitative measurements of the physical scientist.

60 Kroetsch, "Uncovering Our Dream World," 29, 31.

scape than "urban" poets? I have used the term "parallax" to convey the sense that not only can the same landscape be viewed from two different perspectives, but also that by combining those differing perspectives we can add depth to our images of the prairies.[61]

Next I will move from parallax to paradox, in "Paradox: Ambivalence and Ambiguity in Poet/Landscape Relationships." Here I explore the paradoxes inherent in the human experience of the prairie region and examine some of the ways which the selected poets deal with them. In "Beyond Paradox: Mystery and Silence" I examine the poetic response to those elements and experiences of the prairies that are beyond words—those mysteries for which the proper response is silence. Its main thrust is the way poets deal with the spiritual in the landscape, their attempts at "effing the ineffable."[62] In "Public Perception: The Influence of Literary and Popular Poetry" I return to the second of the central pair of questions by exploring the potential influence of the poets' re-visioning of the prairie landscape on the way that the prairie region is perceived. My focus here is on the relative impact of literary and popular poetry on how people, both residents and outsiders, "see" the prairies. Finally, in "'Shaping a World Already Made': Geography and Poetry" I bring together the observations of the previous chapters, evaluate the merits of prairie poetry as a source for regional understanding, and discuss the challenges of combining scientific and artistic approaches to regional geographical research.

We stand in two worlds seeking answers to two central questions about the nature of human/environment relations. The premises and the promises inherent in this study will help lead us from the path into the garden, and will help us to see the prairie richly and deeply, as shaping and shaped by its poets.

---

61 Dennis Cooley, in a different context, refers to Roman Jakobson's phrase "axis of combination," which conveys a similar meaning: it is not one view or the other that is privileged, but rather a combination of views that give the prairie perspective, or the perspective of the prairies, depth. Dennis Cooley, "The Vernacular Muse in Prairie Poetry," in *The Vernacular Muse* (Winnipeg: Turnstone, 1987), 214.

62 Robert Kroetsch, "Effing the Ineffable," in *Essays on Saskatchewan Writing*, ed. E. F. Dyck (Regina: Saskatchewan Writers Guild, 1986), 143–44.

CHAPTER 2

Poets of the Prairie: Enduring Elements of Prairie Landscape in Prairie Poetry

The most elemental and oft-mentioned physical elements of the southern grassland landscape are, in W. O. Mitchell's words, "the skeleton requirements ... of land and sky,"[1] or in the words of Wallace Stegner, "quiet earth, big sky."[2] The land, with its shape, texture, creatures, and cover, forms the stable ground of the prairie experience, and the sky, with its light, heat, wind, and precipitation, provides the variability. In addition to these, the scarcity of trees and the relatively level terrain give rise to a sense of space and of great, searching distances. If landscape does influence prairie poetry, these are the elements that one would expect to be imprinted most enduringly on the artistic mind.

In *small beneath the sky*, Lorna Crozier suggests a more detailed list of what she calls "first causes."[3] Several of these—light, rain, snow, sky, horizon, dust, wind, grass, insects—are characteristics of landscape that are common throughout the prairies, although only dust (mediated through elements of weather—drought and wind), grass, and insects are identified with the land itself. The rest reference the great dome of sky enfolding the land, which "change[s] and glow[s] and darken[s] under it."[4] The circle of horizon and the canopy of sky combine to create a pervasive sense of space

1 W. O. Mitchell, *Who Has Seen the Wind* (Toronto: Macmillan, 1947), 1.

2 Wallace Stegner, *Wolf Willow: A History, A Story, and A Memory of the Last Plains Frontier* (Toronto: Macmillan, 1967), 11.

3 Lorna Crozier, *small beneath the sky* (Vancouver: Greystone, 2009).

4 Stegner, *Wolf Willow*, 7.

and distance. One is always, like the castaway of Yann Martel's *Life of Pi*, at the centre of a circle, struggling with either boredom or terror.[5] This vastness also produces, as Wallace Stegner notes, a paradoxical awareness of both one's insignificance and one's position as a "challenging upright thing" in the midst of flatness.[6] Laurence Ricou emphasizes the sense of space or spaciousness in prairie poetry as a reflection of both isolation and the terrain, and its lack of trees.[7] A less-recognized characteristic of the rural prairies is stillness. This quietness at the heart of the natural sounds of the prairie speaks wordlessly to those who are quiet in themselves. It is tempting to relate this element to the laconic prairie person, and the idea that life lived away from the pervasive noise of urban places makes people relish silence, both in surroundings and in conversation.

Although these elements are common to the entire region, there are significant variations in landscape both regionally and locally. The terrain on the prairies ranges from the flatlands of the glacial Lake Agassiz in Manitoba—the flattest terrain in Canada—to the Cypress Hills, which straddle the southern border between Alberta and Saskatchewan—the highest point east of the Rockies. Between these extremes, the plains rise in westward steps to the Rockies, with local prominences such as Wood Mountain, Thunder Hill, and the Pembina Hills standing above them. The primary rivers and even their smallest tributaries etch deeply into the upland. These are skirted by trees, which, along with the trees associated with the major hills, make up the only forests in this otherwise treeless land. The variation in vegetation corresponds with a variation in rainfall, with the short grasses of the driest areas of the southern plains through to the tall grasses of the north and east as moisture increases. The tall grasses give way to bushy cover and forest toward the Canadian Shield and toward the parkland that marks the transition from grassland to forest on the northern and western rim of the prairies. The prairies can be seen as a palimpsest of level land and sky, but the etchings of physical forces, large and small, are everywhere.

5 Yann Martel, *Life of Pi* (Toronto: Knopf Canada, 2000), 214.

6 Stegner, "The Question Mark in the Circle," in *Wolf Willow*, 8.

7 Laurence Ricou, "Circumference of Absence: Land and Space in the Poetry of the Canadian Plains," in *Man and Nature on the Prairies*, ed. Richard Allen, Canadian Plains Studies 6 (Regina: Canadian Plains Research Center, 1976), 66–76.

What follows is a survey of a group of nine literary poets whose work arises from the physical elements of the prairie landscape, and an assessment of the influence of the prairie environment on their poetry. My interest lies in the way a close, focused observation of the prairie landscape by poets who claim an attachment to this region produces in the poet a vision of the region and its elements—in short, how the prairie leaves its impression on their art. I wish to identify how place or landscape fits "into the sounds and rhythms of a voice, images, definitions"[8] of those writing from and about the prairies. Place is a complicated thing,[9] made up of present observation coupled with remembered experience, and the poets I examine interact with the landscape in ways that transform the "objective" elements of landscape into a mythology critical to a full understanding of the prairie region.

All this to say that although the influence of the prairie landscape on prairie poetry can be complex, sometimes paradoxical, and even mystical ("much stranger than anything we yet know"[10]), the thesis on which this study rests is that the influence is indeed real. But what does this influence signify? Does the persistent engagement with the stereotypical elements of the prairies—land, sky, and space—merely signal a sentimental and unfruitful longing, a "report[ing] on the nostalgic and useless past?"[11] Or do the physical elements of the landscape comprise a significant and ongoing poetic reaction to this region? If so, what characteristics of prairie poetry point to this influence? What is the scale of the influence? Is it local, or general, or both?

The most obvious criterion for the influence of prairie landscape on prairie poetry, and the one I employ here, is the use of landscape images and descriptions. Poets writing from and about the prairie would be expected to include references to, or imagery of, the physical elements of the landscape they observe.

Two qualifications are necessary. My focus is limited to how poets and the landscape interact, which means that my assessment of their work does not engage the full range of their poetic sensibilities and concerns. Poets also

---

8 Mandel, "Writing West," 145.

9 Ibid., 155.

10 Mandel, "Romance and Realism," 211.

11 Diane Quantic, "Afloat on the Sea of Grass: Transforming the Myth," in *The Nature of the Place: A Study of Great Plains Fiction* (Lincoln: University of Nebraska Press, 1995), 127.

speak in a variety of voices and from a variety of perspectives; I attribute all such variety to the poets themselves, and so they are included in my analysis.

DI BRANDT

Di Brandt's primal landscape is the "flat chested earth" of southern Manitoba, which she wishes to see "feelingly."[12] Brandt's poetry explores several themes, three of which are of interest to prairie geographers: her love of the prairie illustrated by her use of vivid prairie images, her concern for the environment, and her empathy with the region's First Peoples, complicated by her family's participation in the loss of their land. The prairie's space and distance draws Brandt back home: "i want to go back to the prairies, / to emptiness, words circling around absence, the / straight horizon, home."[13] Although she expresses her passion for the prairie most directly in her essay "This land that I love, this wide, wide prairie,"[14] many of her poems resonate with her love for her primal landscape. In "Wake Up," Brandt expresses her deep attachment to the

> [w]ild scented meadow,
> grasshopper sung,
> sun drenched,
> holding us earthbound.
>
> In love with grass,
> and wonder.[15]

She praises elements of the rural countryside, recognizing the significance of life there:

> Transparencies, pink dawn
> above the trees,
> poetry of birds,
> symphonic,
> country matters . . .[16]

---

12 Di Brandt, "hear them whispering," in *Questions I Asked My Mother* (Winnipeg: Turnstone, 1987), 63.

13 Di Brandt, "waking up in Jerusalem," in *Jerusalem, beloved* (Winnipeg: Turnstone, 1995), 27.

14 In Brandt, *So this is the world & here I am in it* (Edmonton: NeWest, 2007), 1.

15 Brandt, "Wake up," in *Now You Care*, 45.

16 Ibid., 46.

Prairie people beyond Manitoba will resonate with her vivid rendering of

> that incredible Manitoba
> moment, brief wedge between winter & hot sun, snow
> & blasting heat, & by nightfall, every tree dripping
> with erotica, longing, & the sky, jealous as hell,
> unattached, throwing itself against every bare field,
> blasting the trees.[17]

Even away from the prairies, in the urban wilderness of Detroit, she is still

> sniffing around
> the railroad tracks
> in my usual quest for a bit of wildness,
> weeds, something untinkered with,
> goldenrod, purple aster, burdocks,
> defiant against creosote,
> my prairie blood surging
> in recognition and fellow feeling.[18]

Prairie metaphors appear in Brandt's most personal poems:

> i want the huge narrative
> of the river the curved cry of the land i want the
> straight blowing of birch leaves in strong wind
> the whistling of prairie grass your lit face in the
> distance coming to meet me your arms hot like
> August prairie sky all around me.[19]

Brandt's close attachment to the prairies reaches its culmination in her complete identification with the elements of the landscape, through imagery intimate in its detail:

> there is only this lake, these waves,
> these trees, this shade, this wind, & i, am growing tree
> roots, becoming gnarled, twisting among rocks,
> reaching for fire, am becoming water, rock, gravel,

---

17 Brandt, "little poet, how i found you again," in *Jerusalem, beloved,* 59.

18 Brandt, "Zone <le Détroit>" in *Now You Care,* 16.

19 Di Brandt, "prairie hymn," in *Agnes in the Sky* (Winnipeg: Turnstone, 1990), 61.

> melting into earth, my brown skin opening, sighing,
> trembling, licked by wind.[20]

In a paean of praise, filled with details of prairie land and life, Brandt exclaims,

> let me spend the rest of my life here, on the banks
> of the Saskatchewan, listening, to grass rustling,
> geese trumpeting their young, the smell of clover on
> the dry wind, last summer's leaves flaming in the
> October sun, the air sharp today, reminding of
> winter. . . .[21]

Elsewhere, she proclaims, "this earth is my home, my body, my mother, / unafraid & so, unutterably, beautiful."[22] Brandt's close identification with the prairie landscape surfaces in a phrase also used by both Eli Mandel in "Estevan, 1934" and Andrew Suknaski in "Pacific Western Flight North,"[23] indicating Aboriginal peoples' close ties with the earth: "I touch the earth, the earth touches me. / I feel the earth, the earth feels me."[24]

Brandt's love of the prairie, however, has its shadow side, as she often weaves together the positive images of the prairie landscape with the damaging impact of settler society on the land and on its ancient peoples. Brandt's concern with damage to the landscape and its care is especially evident in her collections *Now You Care* and *So this is the world & here I am in it*. I will examine this aspect of her poetry in the next chapter.

Brandt portrays not only a living landscape with vivid imagery and passion, but a diminished landscape as well, with its losses in beauty and variety. She relishes small victories—"Prairie happily reclaims / homestead"[25]—but realizes that the prairie's problems, and its solutions, are beyond individual action. Hers is not a call for a return to the good old days, but rather for a respectful and humble consideration of the prairie

---

20 Brandt, "there is only this lake, this wind," in *Jerusalem, beloved*, 67.

21 Brandt, "this is it! i've found it at last! nirvana, the Elysian fields, heaven," in *Jerusalem, beloved*, 43.

22 Brandt, "why do you keep doing it," in *Jerusalem, beloved*, 32.

23 Mandel, "Estevan, 1934," in *The Other Harmony*, Vol. 1, 159, and Andrew Suknaski, "Pacific Western Flight North," in *East of Myloona* (Saskatoon: Thistledown Press, 1979), 12–13.

24 Brandt, "Dog days in Maribor: Anti (electric) ghazals," in *Now You Care*, 39.

25 Brandt, "Exhibition Notes," in *Now You Care*, 80.

landscape and its ancient peoples. It is also "a call for a more passionate and embodied erotic relationship with the earth . . . the poet's ecology is a sexy, joyful appreciative ecology."[26]

DENNIS COOLEY

Dennis Cooley was born in Estevan, Saskatchewan, and grew up on a nearby farm. He is, by his own admission, "tethered to the prairies like a mule."[27] Although he has lived in Winnipeg for several decades, his memories and the images of his poetry reflect his home landscape of the southern Saskatchewan prairies, dominated by light and sky. Cooley's prairie is not a tranquil place, however. It is a place of epic encounters with space and the elements:

> settlers . . . on the Canadian prairie
> moved into a huge silence wavered
> on air there like birds in a desert
> & emptiness not to be believed
>   tumbled past.[28]

Cooley imagines, through the eyes of a persona, Steve, what the sense of space would have been like for the First Peoples, as well as the cultural landscape within this immensity:

> where they made their camps
> must have thought it would never go away
>
> what this must have been once a vast
> grass a fox came through and forever
> huge world so impossibly large
> buffalo in mosquitoes stampeded into never
>
> so silent you must have felt god
> hold his breath when you stand
> the suns steady pressure the wind
> imagine mile after mile sun and sun
> sun & wind grass this tall &
>   the tall yellow

---

26 Di Brandt, e-mail to the author, June 29, 2015.

27 Dennis Cooley, in *Passwords: Transmigrations between Canada and Europe*, ed. Hans Braun, Wolfgang Klooss and Markus Müller (Kiel: l&f Verlag, 1996), 96.

28 Cooley, "this only world," in *this only home*, 130.

flowers in that wind the stars
shining with tipi rings medicine
wheels turtle effigies rubbing stones
flies & dung & sweat
bluestems right up to the horses bellies
poetry roaring gently in their dreams.[29]

His poems are also alive with vivid images of winter's cold and summer's heat and storms, as well as their impact on prairie people. In winter,

the silenced house
snaps and gives
in the tightening cold
exhales its stale
warm breath
draws my body's heat
into the snowhard
wind pumping
black/white
outside
the empty window;[30]

thats when air hardens
to whale bone wraps us up
in girdles and the sky rings
our lives in pewter & silver
plate irons our days smooth as Dresden;[31]

winter
& the sky
so huge so creaky
sun & snow
bright where you walk
coyotes talk to themselves
close their eyes against the light.[32]

---

29 Dennis Cooley, *the bentleys* (Edmonton: University of Alberta Press, 2006), 70. This is a volume of poetry from the perspective of the fictional Bentley family in Sinclair Ross's novel *As For Me and My House*.

30 Dennis Cooley, "Jan/us," in *Leaving* (Winnipeg: Turnstone, 1980), 4–5.

31 Dennis Cooley, "winter is when snakes," in *Perishable Light* (Moose Jaw: Coteau, 1988), 68.

32 Cooley, *Country Music*, 26.

"[T]he sudden singe of summers"[33] brings its own extremes. "[I]nside the prairie at 100° / bugs drowning / we wait in pockets of heat;"[34] "outside / the land / lasered with light / fine green hairs / the long slow wind."[35]

One can feel the heated landscape inhabited by the Bentleys:

wwrrhhk
wrrhhk
walk thru weeds & stubble
scatter of
grasshoppers
paper rubbing
against sun

heat stumbles/
fields behind drifting
long tongues of dust
licking their neck & arms
storms of gasses
fenders so hot
they cant touch
& all the while some
one on a one-way
is pulling
the field
a black skirt
shut behind
the blotchy skin
disappearing.[36]

Summer's heat brings on evening storms with

shattered skies
clouds rattle in
loud screams of rain
sound of trains trying to stop

---

33 Dennis Cooley, "III," in *Fielding* (Saskatoon: Thistledown, 1983), unpaginated.

34 Cooley, *Country Music*, 5.

35 Dennis Cooley, "swept/," in *sunfall: New and Selected Poems, 1980–1996* (Concord: Anansi, 1996), 178.

36 Cooley, *the bentleys*, 117.

. . . .

long cranes hurl swiftly
the long careen of their calls
spot the gray canvas
are struck into day
like nails.[37]

What is needed, rather, is

the small rain down doth rain
. . . .
needles of a sewing
machine and it will raise
braille on the fields.[38]

Other seasons are more moderate:

in spring
trees jet green & their fingers
thin as tin in winter
speak minerals

life pumps dumbly
their fingers (in silence) touch
air we breathe
shape it but we dont
listen we shake in cold
they hold their breath

& when sun puts an arm around
they let out
their breath/
breathe
easy so you can see

their puffs of green in spring
trees blowing
on their hands to keep them warm.[39]

Fall, too, is a time of gathering and fulfillment:

---

37 Cooley, *the bentleys*, 126.

38 Cooley, *Country Music*, 14.

39 Cooley, "in spring trees," in *Perishable Light*, 73.

how we forever climb
(when we auger
august) out of granaries
                    teeming with wheat
    eyes & nostrils clogged
        coughing into the sudden
                        (eyes hurt)   relief
                of air & light

& how our hearts are canaries
that bend & pick the golden seeds

how then we sit
    & we sing

eyes bright as gasoline.[40]

Although Cooley's poems are full of prairie light, in both summer and winter, in "night prairie" he depicts the intense darkness and isolation of a prairie night:

an immensity i saw once
  :   night on the prairies

an enormous sky far as you can see
the earth lets go in yeast
a shrill sun filled
        with insects   & wind

  :   all of it — scooped out
a huge excavation of light
            so that darkness pours

                seas of it
            at night fills the land.[41]

That enormous sky, "so open it has only bottom," also has "only room to be at home in."[42]

Cooley sketches the landscape on which people and the elements play out their epic encounters with deep feeling and evocative detail:

40 Cooley, "auguries of innocence," in *Perishable Light*, 16.

41 Cooley, "night prairie," in *this only home*, 10.

42 Dennis Cooley, *Irene* (Winnipeg: Turnstone, 2000), 30.

Yellow Grass where the Souris River once began

what was it like

curled on the verge of

a long white absence

the prairie that rustles silently

around us

sundogs

sprung open low on the sky

sun a sunken period hung in their parentheses

(gone now on a second take)

leaks its chilled light

bleakly

even now hauling its way

back to life. . .[43]

telephone posts trail

/like pencils/

on the other side

virgules that measure

our passing

sinking to periods

out of sight

their brittle braille

43 Cooley, "III," *Fielding*, unpaginated.

stipples the prairie
wires that hum &
sigh in the heat &
the cold
& loudly shed the wind in storm.[44]

These extremes leave their mark on prairie people:

in spring our thoughts like the roads
are barely passable

& then in no time the heat
whap whap
beats dust out of the roads
sky hangs out
its worn & dirty carpet
. . . .
impossible to conceive
to explain such weather, such grunts

except we are born to it
a patient people
durable as rocks in the northeast
obdurate & implausible in waiting
in love as unyielding.[45]

In a wonderfully appropriate analogy, Cooley sees the prairie as a parchment on which farmers and townspeople inscribe their lives:

each spring they ruled the land
like foolscap those farmers
laconic as typewriters
scraped its face free
from the fat of winter
from the water marks
spring left in its pressing.[46]

---

44 Cooley, "IV," *Fielding*, unpaginated.

45 Cooley, *the bentleys*, 56.

46 Cooley, "prairie vernacular," in *Perishable Light*, 8.

Small towns changed as

> train drains the prairie
> dries each town each day into a cracker barrel
> wind a gray squirrel in the streets
> track a spinal column
> spavined over ties
> . . . .
> across the enormous parchment
> we scribble shabby stores ram-shackle sheds
> where they have drifted up on the shores of eternity
> our scrawl over the prairie i think
> is at times barely literate
> a gouging of gerund
> a debris of noun. . . .[47]

Cooley imagines his father's springtime seeding as an intimate correspondence with the earth, because "seeds brought out the author in him." After greeting spring, barley, and wheat, his father

> wrote rapeseed once but it didn't
> write back a lot of his correspondents
> never replied some years
> he hardly heard a thing
> he'd drag those pencils across the fields
> & wait & wait
> & wait
> he wanted to keep in touch.[48]

The prairie is also a place of the remembered pleasures and events of ordinary life: clearing the garden in the fall,[49] country fairs,[50] baseball,[51] and getting stuck in prairie gumbo.[52] The smaller prairie residents also inhabit his poems:

---

47 Cooley, *Country Music*, 124, 128.

48 Cooley, "every year my dad drew lines," in *sunfall*, 145.

49 Cooley, "Clearing the Garden," in *Leaving*, 28–29.

50 Dennis Cooley, "estevan fair," in *Dedications* (Saskatoon: Thistledown, 1988), 20–23.

51 Cooley, "Fielding," *Leaving*, 15–17; "georgian chant," in *Dedications*, 33–35.

52 Cooley, "a real prairie poem," in *Dedications*, 24.

birds work edges of water
expectant as nurses
robins black birds grackles circle
the sprinkler shh sshh shH
they hop and wade
pants to their knees and baby
jays drink but do not douse
their stubby blue flames
new robins with measles
wash their small feet

bird-silent they
/ dip into mouths

pull their irridescence
in sweaters over their heads
later they will show
their young the small
voltage under their wings.[53]

It is Cooley's grounded attachment to the prairie that allows his words, like a kite, to soar and swoop and snap:

this is our country
it is here we tap in
put our eager ear
          to the ground
. . . .
this is our country
          it is here we fall
                    into place
in it we
                    let loose
   rain down in wind.[54]

53 Cooley, "littoral, june" in *sunfall*, 166.

54 Cooley, "on the way to estevan (thanksgiving saturday /85)," in *Perishable Light*, 3.

LORNA CROZIER

From her first volume of poetry, *Inside Is the Sky,* published in 1976, to *Small Mechanics*, published in 2011, the landscape of the southern prairies has had a permanent place in Lorna Crozier's poetry.[55] Although her work is not constrained by landscape, it is nonetheless a constant imaginative source for her poetry, which, in the words of Nathalie Cooke, "is grounded in the dailiness of life ... yet it gestures to a world of magic that lies both within and beyond that everyday world."[56] Crozier's primal landscape is the short-grass prairie of southern Saskatchewan. It leaves its imprint on her poetry, as seen in her vivid evocations of the effect of light, space, sky, wind, and weather on the prairie experience; in her identification with nature; in her celebration of wildness over human control; and in her imaginative and transformational cameos of prairie plants and creatures. These subjects are intertwined artfully and powerfully in many of her poems.

Space, distance, and sky combine to create one of the prairie's most enduring and moving images. Crozier's prairie sky is "an eye that never blinks," with "no end / to it here," and that "gives you / all the room you need / to grow small."[57] It is like God's yawn,[58] and is "twin to the ocean: / the same restlessness, the blue unfolding."[59] It creates a feeling of spaciousness so large the poet doubts whether even Jesus could find her here.[60]

---

55 Crozier herself often refers to the influence of the landscape on her writing: "On the prairies we live in a great nothing that is something, and we arrive at meaning through absence rather than through presence. I'm not sure I know what that implies, but I know it's essential to my writing.... I don't see how anyone can write about anything else other than the place that shapes them even though imagination also shapes that place into more than the literal." Crozier, "Seeing Distance," 149; "But the landscape I return to in my mind, most of the time, is the landscape of my childhood—the short-grass, big-sky country of SW Sask." Lorna Crozier, e-mail to the author, February 9, 2004.

56 Nathalie Cooke, "Lorna Crozier and Her Works," in *Canadian Writers and Their Works*, Poetry Series, vol. 11, ed. Robert Lecker, Jack David, and Ellen Quigley (Toronto: ECW Press, 1995), 98.

57 Lorna Crozier, "All the Room You Need," in *A Saving Grace: The Collected Poems of Mrs. Bentley* (Toronto: McClelland & Stewart, 1996), 22. Crozier adopts the persona of the fictional Mrs. Bentley from Sinclair Ross's novel *As For Me and My House.*

58 Lorna Crozier, "God's Mouth," in *Apocrypha of Light* (Toronto: McClelland & Stewart, 2002), 54.

59 Lorna Crozier, *Bones in Their Wings: Ghazals* (Regina: Hagios, 2003), 5.

60 Lorna Crozier, "This Sky Demands a Certain Patience," in *Whetstone* (Toronto: McClelland & Stewart, 2003), 2.

In "Wilderness," Mrs. Bentley's reaction to prairie space conveys a sense of awe and fear:

> but where there is no bush,
> the wilderness is different.
>
> It's really space that rushes at you
> in spite of fences, the grid roads
> laid in graphs across the earth.
>
> A space not as empty as
> you might imagine, it's a thing itself
> minus details you can't separate
> the whole into any parts.
> The worst is
>
> it doesn't need you.
> It goes on and on whether the land
> is broken or not, whether a town makes
> its small exclamation mark or flattens out.
>
> What's most like the prairie
> is the mind of God, the huge way
> he must have of looking at the world.
> That's why I feel small and scared
> inside myself, and yet at times
> full of wonder.[61]

A similar sentiment appears in section 8 of the poem "Time to Praise," after a man posts a sign reading, "Someone is Watching You":

> His simple desperate act
> to protect what little was left,
> the boards he or his father
> sawed and nailed,
> enclosing in four walls
> an empty space
> within the emptiest space anyone can imagine
> outside of the desert or the sea,
> stretching so far it makes you think
> of eternity.[62]

---

61 Crozier, "Wilderness," in *A Saving Grace*, 77–78.

62 Crozier, "Time to Praise," in *Inventing the Hawk*, 97.

A closely related element, which figures everywhere in Crozier's poetry, is the pervasiveness and intensity of prairie light. The title of Crozier's 1995 collection, *Everything Arrives at the Light*, could well summarize her love affair with light, and it is not surprising that of the first causes she names in her prairie memoir, the first is light.[63] In her poem "On the Seventh Day," for example, she depicts God absentmindedly creating light and then more light until "[t]he light / was so blinding, so dazzling / God had to stretch and stretch the sky to hold it."[64] The light is

Shattered

starshine, mica, glass—
light throwing punches

oracular and quick
from every corner. It bruises

the eye, beauty
too small a word for what's

so radiant and fast.[65]

She also writes of the intensity and violence of light: "I walk / into light's brass fist, its knuckles / gleaming,"[66] and in a description of Drumheller's badlands, she writes: "Sunfist pounds / the backs of buttes / stretched taut as skin."[67] These images contrast with the delicacy of aspen, which "signs whole alphabets of light."[68]

Darkness is not the antithesis of light,[69] but somehow rather its companion—a binary, a not-yet-light:

Like these they move
with ease through any kind of dark

63 Crozier, "first cause: light," in *small beneath the sky*, 1.

64 Crozier, "On the Seventh Day," in *Inventing the Hawk*, 10.

65 Crozier, "As the line moves. The leap! Thrashing there," in *Apocrypha of Light*, 79.

66 Lorna Crozier, "The Older Sister: Everything Yearns," in *What the Living Won't Let Go* (Toronto: McClelland & Stewart, 1999), 65.

67 Lorna Uher [Crozier], "Drumheller," in *Crow's Black Joy* (Edmonton: NeWest, 1978), 64.

68 Crozier, *Bones in Their Wings*, 39.

69 Crozier sets light and dust as opposites, rather than light and darkness. See "first cause: dust," in *small beneath the sky*, 2.

for after all, they'll tell you,
it's just the light
falling so far into itself
it hasn't reached the bottom yet.[70]

In "Garden in Winter" she expresses this same thought:

The shadows are white,
that is to say, there are no shadows
just light
like nothing ever seen before.

Imagined light
                    pure and crystal
emptied of everything
but itself.[71]

In "Rebuttal to the Higher Power" she combines this binary with imagery of prairie grass:

Beneath you grass stretches its roots
      farther than an arm and hand
can reach into water. They douse for darkness,
draw it up to meet the light, or is it light

the dark becomes on this other side
      where footsteps fall?
Through hollow stems, grass siphons
the can't-be-seen

      and sends it out ignited.
It's what gives the shine to everything
      that roots, inclines, or rises only inches.[72]

In "Genesis" she continues this paradoxical binary, suggesting that even darkness has its own light:

But light
at the bottom, under

---

70 Lorna Crozier, "Night," in *Everything Arrives at the Light* (Toronto: McClelland & Stewart, 1995), 25.

71 Lorna Crozier, "Garden in Winter," in *The Garden Going On Without Us* (Toronto: McClelland & Stewart, 1985), 119.

72 Crozier, "Rebuttal to the Higher Power," in *Whetstone*, 40.

stone, under each
tread of the bear's wide paw,

earth-light under earth,
light of the burnt-out,
light under the eyelid,
under-tongued,
the fierce

unsaid, un-
redeemable light.[73]

Indeed, as Crozier suggests: "Travelling at the speed of darkness / everything arrives at the light."[74]

Although sky, space, and light are in themselves compelling components of the prairie landscape and of Crozier's poetry, it is weather that is most directly felt. Beginning in the late 1920s, the land turned alien—a decade of dust darkening the skies and obliterating the hopes of farmers across the southern prairies.

Crozier says that not only did the drought and the depression mark the generation that lived through it but "the dark shadow ... cast its grit and darkness" over the generation that followed, too,[75] making it a prominent event in prairie history and a recurring theme in her poetry. Three of her poems are entitled "Drought,"[76] and the Great Depression and its effects on farming families are detailed in many poems. These include "Journey,"[77] a poem about a trip to bring a rain stone to the parched prairie; "Riding the Borders of the Land,"[78] about the impact of the drought on a prairie wife; "The Whistling Swans Are Gone,"[79] in which a droughty prairie longs for anything green; and "Berry Picking,"[80] a dark poem about what drought and failure can do to a man. In "Burial, Partridge Hill," Crozier speaks forcefully of drought through the persona of Mrs. Bentley:

---

73 Lorna Crozier, *Small Mechanics* (McClelland & Stewart, 2011), 13.

74 Crozier, "The Sea at the End of the World," in *Everything Arrives*, 80.

75 Lorna Crozier, e-mail to the author, January 21, 2007.

76 See Lorna Uher [Crozier], *Inside Is the Sky* (Saskatoon: Thistledown, 1976), 11; Lorna Crozier, *The Weather* (Regina: Coteau, 1983), 34; and *Whetstone*, 20.

77 Uher [Crozier], "Journey," in *Crow's Black Joy*, 44–45.

78 In Crozier, *The Weather*, 30.

79 In Crozier, *The Weather*, 43.

80 In Uher [Crozier], *Crow's Black Joy*, 55–56.

> I've never seen the dust
> this bad. The world
> turns upside down, the sky's
> the earth. Among the graves
> badgers dig their way to heaven.
> . . . .
> Five years of being burnt out,
> blown out, hailed out,
> and now they plant
> their only son.[81]

Several references to this desperate time appear in Crozier's long poem, "Time to Praise." A legless man "walks his combine / in long sure rows . . . following / the same straight path across the field / as the land blows away," and an "isolate woman . . . carries water / from the well to her garden that will never grow" and waits for her child "for the first time in her life / to hear the sound of rain. Of *rain*." The poet asks:

> Who will come back to the fields
> scraped to the bone, the houses
> stripped of paint? The broken
> machines, the wells gone dry,
> the earth itself giving up,
> clouds passing over like the dispossessed,
> moving to nowhere
>   we can name
> but moving away.[82]

"The Photograph I Keep of Them" is a succinct and poignant portrait of drought's effect on a farming family:

> Behind them the prairie
> tells its spare story of drought.
>
> They tell no stories.
> Not how they feel
> about one another
> or the strange landscape
> that makes them small.

81 Crozier, "Burial, Partridge Hill," in *A Saving Grace*, 34.

82 Crozier, "Time to Praise," in *Inventing the Hawk*, 89, 90, 96.

I can write down only this
for sure:
        they have left the farm,
        they are going somewhere.[83]

Crozier's acute observation[84] and expressive imagery imprint ordinary elements of weather on the reader's mind. After a snowstorm,

[t]he countryside's been seeded

by an albino farmer
and his team of tundra swans.[85]

"Winter Day" captures the feeling of prairie winter:

                    In winter you are closer
to heaven though you may not know it
....
Stand still: you'll hear the hands of the wind
working, without commission,
freeing from the nothingness of snow

the forms it finds along the fenceline,
the ribs of drifts climbing up the ditches,
hollows where deer have rested for the night.[86]

Crozier's passion for the prairie landscape is perhaps most evident in the poems in which she identifies with the prairie's natural elements, a theme that threads through her entire body of work. In some poems, she expresses this as being enveloped in nature, such as in "Fortress,"[87] while in others *she* envelopes nature, such as in "Inner Space," in which the poet ends: "inside / is the sky."[88] In other poems she expresses this identification as transformation—becoming one with nature, either in desire or in death. She ends the poem "Consummation" with: "Her eyes

83 Crozier, "The Photograph I Keep of Them," in *The Garden Going On*, 27.

84 Crozier describes her approach in "To See Clearly": "The task: to see clearly / so that even the ear becomes a kind of eye / taking you beyond the small circle / of your sight—even the mouth— / magpie, magpie over the southern hill." Crozier, *Whetstone*, 18.

85 Crozier, "There is no road without you," in *Apocrypha of Light*, 71.

86 Crozier, "Winter Day," in *Whetstone*, 49.

87 In Uher [Crozier], *Crow's Black Joy*, 21.

88 Uher [Crozier], "Inner Space," in *Inside Is the Sky*, 42.

were sky and water. / No longer cold no longer quiet / she was motion she was prairie."[89] In "All the Dancing Girls Lie Down," death brings union with nature and freedom: "Look, the wind / is a woman / and she dances."[90] The poet yearns for transformation in "Midsummer Morning Run," ready to be fox or wild cat, dissatisfied with the human condition: "I am tired of this heaviness, sick of sorrow, / the sounds we make to give the world / a human shape." The poem ends:

> O, to lean in one direction
> to know the sky the way a tree knows it,
> halfway to heaven, inarticulate,
> the dead among the green wheat
> holding their tongues.[91]

In "Too Much Brightness" she suggests, "[s]oon I'll be / all running light and water,"[92] while in "Change of Life," a woman is transformed into a horse:

> Drenched with sweat, she tosses
> back her hair, thick and golden,
> her own warm light
> falling all around her.[93]

In "Shadow," the poet wishes

> [t]o be doppelganger,
> the soft underside of wings,
> the part of cumulus that slides
> thin promises of rain across the wheat.
>
> To disappear. To be blue
> simply because snow has fallen
> and it's the blue hour of the day.[94]

---

89 Uher [Crozier], "Consummation," in *Crow's Black Joy*, 59.

90 Lorna Uher [Crozier], "All the Dancing Girls Lie Down," in *Humans and Other Beasts* (Winnipeg: Turnstone, 1980), 78.

91 Crozier, "Midsummer Morning Run," in *Everything Arrives*, 5.

92 Crozier, "Too Much Brightness," in *Everything Arrives*, 41.

93 Crozier, "Change of Life," in *Everything Arrives*, 122.

94 Crozier, "Shadow," in *Whetstone*, 22.

When she is not expressing her identification with nature through transformation, Crozier is expressing empathy for the creaturely world, such as in "Game Farm,"[95] "Pariah,"[96] "Skunks,"[97] "Sturgeon,"[98] and "Fear of Snakes."[99]

Crozier celebrates wildness as desirable and freeing, and portrays human domination of the wild in all its forms as a perversion of the natural order. In this way she reverses an aspect of the garrison/wilderness antinomy; I will examine this aspect of Crozier's poetry in the chapter "Beyond Paradox: Mystery and Silence."

She makes other renderings memorable through striking imagery. Spiders are "little death stars, / little abattoirs."[100]

> Bees without
> picks and pit lamps
> crawl backwards
> from the perfumed
> shafts, their miners'
> faces dusted gold.[101]

A line of ants "is time / tracking itself. It is one / vast mind moving forward."[102] Snakes are as "still / as the green / on the underside of ice, / ... // their yellow eyes / old as amber."[103] Sometimes only the traces of animals are left to remind us of their presence:

> Here you always know
> what went before
> you
>   the circling of a coyote's paws
>   at the base of a chokecherry tree
>
>   the oriental graphics of
>   cricket trackings

95 In Uher [Crozier], *Humans and Other Beasts*, 19–21.
96 In Crozier, *The Weather*, 72–73.
97 In Crozier, *Inventing the Hawk*, 109–10.
98 In Crozier, *Inventing the Hawk*, 111–12.
99 Crozier, *Angels of Flesh*, 13.
100 Crozier, "Summer Small Talk," in *Whetstone*, 56.
101 Crozier, "Karl Marx Observes the Flowers," in *Whetstone*, 57.
102 Crozier, "Lines for the Earth," in *Angels of Flesh*, 136.
103 Crozier, "Sleeping with Snakes," in *Inventing the Hawk*, 29.

the faint brush of a hawk's wing
by a rabbit trail
suddenly stopped.[104]

In several of her poems, Crozier describes with elegiac feeling, landscapes and prairie experiences that have either been lost or changed beyond recognition—remembrances that are charged with desire and longing, and that, for her older readers, recall in vivid detail, familiar prairie scenes, experiences, and emotions. The countryside and dying prairie towns are seen through a father's eyes;[105] and we read about the hardscrabble life of a prairie settler whose obdurance mirrors the land on which he struggled to raise a family in "Time to Praise."

Crozier brings to stereotypical landscapes imagery that presents them alive and fresh to our minds:

Swaths of wheat cross the fields
in currents so thick they cannot move.
Summer run-off. How much ripeness
they must carry, how much light
caught in stalk and seed head.
I want to float down their clotted water,
my body's sails catching the heart's
held breath. It takes me nowhere,
this slow flux, the rows stopped
in mid-motion, the day's long lethargy.
Wind minnows flicker in streams of wheat,
in the lingering of an eye, golden
like the goat's at the edge of the field
where the grass isn't cut. His horizontal pupils
slant the light, making everything lie down.[106]

How does the prairie landscape influence Crozier's poetry? Her poetry absorbs the prairie landscape and reflects it back to us, familiar yet changed and charged with light, as full of promise as the fragrance of the first drops of rain striking dusty soil.

---

104 Uher [Crozier], "Sand Hills," in *Crow's Black Joy*, 49.
105 Crozier, "The Father: A Thin Poor Music," in *What the Living*, 51–52.
106 Crozier, "Summer's End, Saskatchewan," in *What the Living*, 78.

PATRICK FRIESEN

Patrick Friesen's primal landscape is the bushy edge of the southern prairies in Manitoba. The level terrain of the bed of glacial Lake Agassiz is broken only by the broad rivers meandering toward Hudson Bay. The sky here is as big as on Lorna Crozier's prairie, but the sense of space and distance is diminished by the cover of bushes and small trees. Friesen views this terrain[107] as the first layer in a series of landscapes that make up his personal archeology, and that he carries about with him. As he puts it, "the body is a memory of landscapes."[108] This perspective is most clear in a series of poetic fragments in his collection *A Broken Bowl*.[109] His childhood landscape is the ground from which his poetry springs,[110] and he returns to it throughout his career. Friesen, like Gwendolyn, "never left / though she moved away."[111] Memory, therefore, is a critical component of his poetry, and is rooted in the landscape and experiences of his Manitoba childhood: "a red-winged blackbird swaying on a reed in the ditch isn't very much / ... / but it's something a splash of blood a clear song a dream a memory / ... / this echo of northern lights and marsh /... entering your eyes and ears and skin an invisible tattoo / a braille you feel and read but nothing revealed."[112] These serve as touchstones with which to contrast the pervading uncertainty and yearning of his later life.

On a more philosophical level, Friesen is a poet continually caught in, and attempting to grasp or explain, the "between-ness" of life's experiences: between father and son (explored most searchingly in his "pa poems"), between flesh or touch and "ghost,"[113] between "smoke"

---

107 Friesen prefers this term, explaining that "landscape" is both clichéd and suggests a "framing" that puts the observer outside what is viewed, a spectator rather than a participant. "Terrain," on the other hand, situates the person within the elements of land and sky, a stance that is essential to his work. Sky, even in the bushy landscape of Steinbach, Manitoba, is expansive and significant, yet as intimate as the air we breathe. Patrick Friesen, e-mails to the author, April 12, 2003; February 13, 2004; September 7, 2004; and September 9, 2004.

108 Patrick Friesen, "ellice avenue," in *st. mary at main* (Winnipeg: The Muses, 1998), 76–77.

109 Patrick Friesen, *A Broken Bowl* (London: Brick Books, 1997). See in particular pages 90, 93 and 95.

110 See Clarise Foster, "An Interview with Patrick Friesen," *CV2*, 24, no. 3 (Winter 2002): 14.

111 Friesen, "umbilical city," in *st. mary at main*, 23. Gwendolyn of the poem is poet Gwendolyn MacEwan.

112 Friesen, *Broken Bowl*, 19.

113 Patrick Friesen, "bluebottle" and "without ghost," in *bluebottle* (Winnipeg: Turnstone, 1978), 9; 43.

and "stone,"[114] between yearning and fulfillment; between words and silence, and between presence and absence. Although many of the poems arising out of this ambiguity are essentially philosophical, they also could be seen as embodying the paradoxical quality of life on the prairies—the attempt to balance fulfillment and failure, a theme I will develop in more detail in the chapter entitled "Paradox: Ambivalence and Ambiguity in Poet/Landscape Relationships." It would be easy to characterize Friesen's poetry as dark and depressing were it not for his honesty. Like John Newlove, Friesen sees the world as it is, with its darkness and terror and impermanence, but he also sees that which is luminous, transcendent, and permanent. The longing for some explanation of these contradictory elements, some understanding of the connection between the mutability of the material and the transcendence of the spiritual, energizes much of his poetry. Yet even these poems are grounded in and illuminated by images of the landscape of southern Manitoba, and are alive with its sights, sounds, plants, and animals.

Friesen's poetry is shot through with prairie light. The sky, "billowing / like a parachute overhead,"[115] is less prominent.[116] "[O]ur light" he explains,

> is clear
> thorkkelson glass[117]
> with blue clouds shimmering inside
> and bare branches scratching the horizon
> with their calligraphy
> our light is not human
> not shaped nor interpreted
> this is a cool light
> a blue silk umbrella
> arching over the city
> as light as whispers
> in the tent of the world.[118]

114 Patrick Friesen, "anna first dance," in *You Don't Get to Be a Saint* (Winnipeg: Turnstone, 1992), 7.

115 Friesen, "big dave meets stephane grappelli," in *st. mary at main*, 88.

116 Friesen suggests that the bushy nature of the landscape, compared to the open spaces of the grasslands, accounts for this shift.

117 A reference to the work of Manitoba glassmaker Ione Thorkelsson.

118 Friesen, "thorkkelson glass," in *st. mary at main*, 68.

It can be

> light bursting from seedlings the field's dark soil lit one morning in
> pale green fire who would have thought
> where there was nothing there is light and light is nothing you can
> hold
> . . . the world nothing but light
> behind shadows.[119]

He speaks of "living in prairie light like pale blue fire,"[120] and being "bombed by the sun."[121] He remembers his boyhood, during which there was "only wonder and a / simple faith in light," and "each thing lit from inside because it is because it is a small sun each thing for a moment blessing the world." It was a time when he was "lost in light" and "living in light."[122] Friesen sees an interplay between light and wind: "wind plays with light among the aspen leaves;"[123] and "the music teacher / listens to the wind / with perfect pitch // we are parts / of the weather / light sifting through."[124] His tribute to Winnipeg is filled with light—noting that at times there is so much that it erases the need for memory: "light pouring through / like the first day"[125] and "you forget everything / nothing being born / but the light."[126]

In addition to light, rivers, wind, and bush are the most important elements in Friesen's primal landscape. The rivers that speak most clearly are the small streams, the Manitoba wind has its own peculiar voice, and the bush is all around.[127] Rivers weave through Friesen's poetry with symbolic significance: "what I love is the drift of day the way clouds accumulate . . . / I love night with rain at the window . . . / divining clear water the first river beneath the willow everything / turning

119 Patrick Friesen, "light in june," in *the breath you take from the lord* (Madeira Park: Harbour, 2002), 57–58.

120 Friesen, "corydon avenue coffee," in *st. mary at main*, 20.

121 Patrick Friesen, "bombed by the sun," in *jumping in the asylum* (Toronto: Quattro, 2011), 18–19.

122 Patrick Friesen, "poem for a dog," in *carrying the shadow* (Vancouver: Beach Holme, 1999), 44.

123 Friesen, "solace," in *jumping in the asylum*, 22.

124 Friesen, "fingerprint," in *carrying the shadow*, 58.

125 Friesen, "god's stench," in *st. mary at main*, 51.

126 Friesen, "the moon in the streets," in *st. mary at main*, 91.

127 Patrick Friesen, e-mail to the author, December 2006.

on the sound of rain."[128] Rivers connect widely different places—"Alexandria Seville or Winnipeg all flowing rivers of / passage and light in those narrow streets"[129]—and symbolize memory—"waking back into the deepest sleep of rivers and all / you've forgotten carried in that current."[130] The edge of the river is a place of remembrance and musing.[131]

The "blue prairie wind"[132] is a constant:

> on the prairies you walk through
> god's breath most of your life
> if that's how you think of it
> and the redtail soars
> and long grasses sway
> and you're never any further
> down the road.[133]

The wind has different personalities. It can be a "meister eckhart wind" or a "jackfish wind" or "the river's still wind."[134] Sometimes it is

> a song
> from voice to voice
> the song
> wind in the wheat
> on the cemetery grass.[135]

In Winnipeg, the wind is like light, "flooding through my car / with the smell of the prairie."[136] Memory is like the prairie wind, Friesen says, "but memory like the wind wears away at the world and though wind / remains memory does not."[137]

---

128 Friesen, "first river," in *the breath you take*, 77–78.
129 Friesen, "son," in *jumping in the asylum*, 21.
130 Friesen, "koestler's window," in *jumping in the asylum*, 37.
131 Friesen, "fragment," in *Broken Bowl*, 117–18.
132 Friesen, "son," in *jumping in the asylum*, 21.
133 Patrick Friesen, "wind," in *Earth's Crude Gravities* (Madeira Park: Harbour, 2007), 30–31.
134 Friesen, "mongolian radio ray price fiddles hank locklin and spruce tree sighs," in *jumping in the asylum*, 51–52.
135 Friesen, "fragment 19," in *Broken Bowl*, 103.
136 Friesen, "holland and treherne," in *st. mary at main*, 13.
137 Friesen, "give me flesh and give me wine," in *the breath you take*, 75–76.

Although death is ever-present, Friesen's poetry is also alive with details of the landscape he grew up in. It "is daubed with ashen easters, / with blue-eyed grass and goldenrod . . . the birdsfoot violet in the churchyard,"[138] and contains spear grass, gooseberries, thistles, snakeroot, and "yellow fields and crows."[139] A hawk "scours the earth with its ravenous gaze a consuming fire"[140] and a rabbit is "drawn / into the landscape / or / down the hole / to hades."[141] At dawn, a bird is "dreaming its music toward morning . . . the song like a struck match."[142] The icon of the prairie marsh, the red-winged blackbird, is ever-present: a "red patch fluttering on a reed,"[143] a "bloody bird bowing the cattail,"[144] a "red-winged blackbird at pentecost hovering above the marsh."[145] Cattails that "burn with blackbirds / their smoke rising / into dusk" stimulate memories and remembrance. The poem "columbine" describes birds and the landscape, and hints at the union of flesh and spirit:

> the black bird
> red-chevroned with a
> slash of yellow
> spitting out small notes
> before its throaty trill
> from the roadside marsh
> with flies buzzing by and
> heat shimmering in the wheat
> with a breath of air
> in the leaves of the willow
> and earth and water and
> the old story of angel
> finally happy in the wings
> of matter.[146]

---

138 Patrick Friesen, "terrain," in *the lands i am* (Winnipeg: Turnstone, 1976), 13.
139 Friesen, "lions and blasphemy," in *You Don't Get*, 37.
140 Friesen, "give me flesh and give me wine," in *the breath you take*, 76.
141 Friesen, "rabbit," in *st. mary at main*, 67.
142 Friesen, "give me flesh and give me wine," in *the breath you take*, 75.
143 Friesen, "lucifer," in *jumping in the asylum*, 56.
144 Friesen, "clearing poem 6," in *the breath you take*, 22.
145 Friesen, "bombed by the sun," in *jumping in the asylum*, 18–19.
146 Friesen, "columbine," in *Earth's Crude Gravities*, 96.

The sense of space here is somewhat limited by bushes, but this is nonetheless a place where "thunder's rolling in prairie's rolling in horizon rolling in,"[147] and where there is

> all that room
> where the buffalo roamed
> horizon at your feet
> the sky billowing
> like a parachute overhead
> . . . .
> the stubble field is silent
> with crickets
> the city's horizon piling up.[148]

And yet "there's nothing but cloudless sky / the blue that gathers birds / so lightly they disappear / what's left behind is song / which I remember from the marsh."[149] In that wide sky "a prairie storm [is] boiling grey and blue torn by lightning and the volcanic cauldron of the hidden sun,"[150] and on a summer's day in a small town, "the mid-afternoon is silent / and still as a photograph / in the unearthly heat."[151]

If, as Friesen suggests, the bush cover is an intermediary between land and sky— "a reaching," as he calls it[152]—then clearings are significant as places where land and sky meet. Although the clearing is a mark of human activity—"this is not nature this scrub and thistle this clearing this is human this is broken land"[153]—it is also a place of semi-openness and light, of discovery, memory, and desire. It is a place where "you can say anything . . . a place you can't go wrong."[154] Friesen stresses that in his "clearing poems," the landscape is not intended as metaphor or symbol; rather it is a "part of my thinking, not an 'object' that I write about, or try to interpret. It is physical detail put into words. Reference points. The words a map of the life lived there."[155] Landscape, therefore, enters a poet's life and influences his work.

---

147 Friesen, "leaving town," in *carrying the shadow*, 38.
148 Friesen, "big dave meets stephane grappelli," in *st. mary at main*, 88.
149 Friesen, "summer dream," in *Earth's Crude Gravities*, 73–74.
150 Friesen, "light in june," in *the breath you take*, 58.
151 Friesen, "small town," in *carrying the shadow*, 53.
152 Patrick Friesen, e-mail to the author, September 7, 2004.
153 Friesen, "clearing poem 6," in *the breath you take*, 21.
154 Friesen, "clearing poem 18," in *the breath you take*, 38.
155 Patrick Friesen, e-mail to the author, April 12, 2003.

TIM LILBURN

Tim Lilburn's poetry is influenced by his childhood spent in Regina at the edge of open prairie,[156] the summers he spent at his uncle's farm south of Windthorst in southeastern Saskatchewan,[157] and, later in his life, the prairie and parkland near Saskatoon. The landscapes he encountered in his childhood introduced him to the land, and he later entered them with a deep desire to participate in their essential character. For Lilburn, these are landscapes where "[e]verything is odoured with infinity; / snow moves through high grass; everything is infinite."[158] Lilburn suggests that people can only feel at home in the landscape by entering it with desire and longing, rather than by having a relationship with the land based on control and manipulation. To translate his experiences into poetic expression, Lilburn uses a vocabulary that is rich, unusual, and evocative, and maintains a perspective that privileges his identification with the animate and that breathes life into the inanimate.

The rural landscape is literally brought to life, and to death. In "Spirit of Agriculture, 1986," he imagines a barn in the morning light as it "climbs up unto itself... free, weightless." But at the same time, "farms are dying." They

> scuff in their nervous straw, throwing links of their machinery, laneways
> ....
> There is a rumour among the farms
> there is a place in the West
> they must go to die,
> where all the Indians have gone, land of dreaming
> ....
>
> I have seen them moving
> to that place like hills
> moving.
> ....
> Now the land turns in its chemical sleep, corn
> floating on lakes of nitrogen, and the almost-awake banker dreams in town
> of a sistine, jet-fuel-bright sky, money's salmon run
> ....

---

156 Tim Lilburn, "Afterword: Walking Out of Silence," in *Desire Never Leaves: The Poetry of Tim Lilburn*, ed. Alison Calder (Waterloo: Wilfrid Laurier Press, 2007), 43.

157 Tim Lilburn, e-mail to the author, July 16, 2014.

158 Tim Lilburn, "Paradise of the Cells," in *Moosewood Sandhills* (Toronto: McClelland & Stewart, 1994), 47.

> He sharks out in the gliding skin of his sleep
> . . . .
> He cleans the highway of farms hit crossing in the night.[159]

When Lilburn emphasizes the natural process of growth rather than human manipulation and destruction, his images are more positive:

> Antlered wheat; like eros
> it travels between the unknowable darkness
> of sky and the unknowable darkness of earth.
> The world is wide.
> The wheat is trustworthy, sky thinking into soil.
> In evening, thin pale flames over the fields, you see
> this through aspens, the grain's ejaculatory flutter
> under the aurora borealis.[160]

Although the small-farm rural landscape of the prairies is marked by change and death, enduring life can be found in its creatures, and Lilburn's poetry is full of details of their lives. The groundhog—"jittered earth chunk," "loam rat," "earth pig"—"pops like cracked wheat from a toaster, unholed," a "woolly verb motioned / like glee, its spurt scatting / benzedrine hype in my blood's gummy / adagio," "lumbering into the adjacent instant / where possible life flexes," an animal of "unsiloed muscle."[161] "[A]uto-body blue" dragonflies, "are / eye-sewn to a stick poking from the water, Islamic shadows on the water."[162] Coyotes, whose "bad bearing wobble of . . . voices just as night begins,"[163]

> slouch-jog out of the moth-coloured trees down to the river
> after supper, jive-dekes, weightless as Amway sales talk,
> a garage sale of moves.
>
> This is the life of light in matter.
> This is the flesh.[164]

159 Tim Lilburn, "Spirit of Agriculture, 1986," in *Tourist to Ecstasy* (Toronto: Exile Editions, 1989), 50–52.

160 Lilburn, "Discipline of Secrecy," in *Moosewood Sandhills*, 42.

161 Tim Lilburn, "Grim Invocations IV," in *Names of God* (Lantzville: Oolichan, 1986), 75.

162 Tim Lilburn, "The Book that Changes Everything," in *Kill-site* (Toronto: McLelland & Stewart, 2003), 37.

163 Lilburn, "Sleeping Four Nights in a Tree," in *Kill-site*, 18.

164 Lilburn, "Solo on Orthodoxy," in *Moosewood Sandhills*, 32.

Such poetry goes beyond memorable description to suggest a mystical union of flesh and spirit: "this wedding of vagabond light / and beaconed matter, spirit and muscle."[165] It is a union that Lilburn strives for in nature.

In *Moosewood Sandhills,* Lilburn offers a more extensive and prolonged treatment of the relationship between the living landscape and humans, and in so doing he provides detailed description of a segment of the prairie landscape. "Restoration" sums up his desire to truly see as a deer and to be at one with it, and when he does he wanders with it in a landscape of "high bush cranberry," of "Moon Lake, the diamond willows / old ox-bow lake, reeds round it," and of "the shadows of the frost-burnt roses / and the shade of the smell of water in which reeds and elms are rotting."[166] This kind of attentive observation, he says, will change your perspective—it "will set up a small / homestead of thinking in you."[167]

Lilburn's poetry is illuminated by a vast humility that should attend the observation and understanding of natural things, landscape included. To fully engage with it, one must recognize one's poverty in relation to the living landscape. Lilburn tells the reader that when they "walk into the thicket of the book [of nature]," they will realize that, in comparison to that denseness, they are "poor."[168]

The larger elements of distance and wind are here, too: "Distance thrums, it's full of nerves / —over the flats, / the roll of it south over the big grass."[169] He writes:

> The wind here, in dusk, in vetch light, loam
> of light, wind full of black flecks, wind from it could be
> anywhere, north most likely, a little
> west, full of bruises, wind full of the metallic
> taste of never arriving home.[170]

And of course there is light:

---

165 Lilburn, "Grim Invocations, V," in *Names of God*, 76.
166 Lilburn, "Restoration," in *Moosewood Sandhills*, 65–66.
167 Lilburn, "Night," in *Kill-site*, 54.
168 Tim Lilburn, "Slow World," in *To the River* (Toronto: McClelland & Stewart,1999), 7.
169 Lilburn, "You Sleep Your Way There," in *To the River*, 53.
170 Lilburn, "Marriage and Agriculture," in *To the River*, 63.

A big light lifts from the naked wheat:
            if we take off our clothes emptiness starts
            to polish our skin from the inside, the pitch of this
                        light building until the knife-edge
                        of it is held to our throats.
A light bucks in the wheat and lifts above it.[171]

"Sleeping Four Nights in a Tree" contains echoes of the double world that Mandel envisioned, although here the other world is one of renewal, or at least the possibility of renewal: "Turn over this world and there is another world," writes Lilburn. "Beside this world is another world."[172]

Lilburn gives us a sense of the intimate connections that are possible between the landscape and its creatures, and he improvises a language to express this.

ELI MANDEL

Eli Mandel was born and raised near Estevan, Saskatchewan, and spent his early adult life in Regina. Although perhaps the most common image of Mandel is that of a displaced, disillusioned wanderer, out of place wherever he finds himself, and despite the suggestion that he had "no long-term experience of the life and culture of the region,"[173] his body of poetry bears the impress of his boyhood prairie landscape. He admitted as much himself: "I think of myself now as a prairie poet, a writer whose being was formed by the experience of living on the prairies as a boy. I think the first six to ten years are absolutely essential. There's no way of escaping that."[174] This, together with a later statement, seems to indicate an almost mystical sense of belonging: "For some reason these colours, these abstractions, these fields mean 'home' to me and I can feel it in a gathering sense of words."[175] Mandel refers to being marked for life by a mouse his mother saw while pregnant with him, twinning his mother's

171 Lilburn, "Poverty," in *To the River*, 44.

172 Lilburn, "Sleeping Four Nights in a Tree," in *Kill-site*, 18.

173 R. Alexander Kizuk, "Desert Words: Eli Mandel's Poetry," book review of *The Other Harmony*, *Canadian Poetry* 49 (2001): 113. A rather easy dismissal of Mandel's three decades of boyhood and manhood on the prairies.

174 Quoted in Dennis Cooley, "Eli Mandel and His Works," *Canadian Writers and Their Works*, Poetry Series, Vol. 10 (Toronto: ECW Press, 1992), 193.

175 Eli Mandel, "Journal: Fort San: Beginnings, 1977" in *The Other Harmony*, Vol. 1, 415.

superstitious belief with a prominent element of the local landscape that left an impression on him—the Souris River.[176]

It is impossible to read Mandel's poetry and criticism without a sense of the profound thoughtfulness he brought to both. He found no easy answers, nor did he engage in knee-jerk responses to either his nurturing landscape or to those who wrote about it. For Mandel, the unbounded spaciousness of the prairie itself appears to have prevented any easy boundaries from also encircling the range of emotion it generated. Like John Newlove, he found the prairie both compelling and disquieting, and his poetry expresses this ambivalence.

Although Mandel's poetry progressed from being dense and often obscure to writing that Cooley suggests turned "towards . . . the edges of vernacular,"[177] his whole body of work is peppered with references to prairie landscape and life. Taken as a whole, it reveals new ways of perceiving familiar landscapes. Also, perhaps more than many of the poets considered here, he engages the local landscape of his childhood through references to the river valleys (the Souris, the North Saskatchewan, and the Qu'Appelle Valley) near his homes, along with the more general themes of weather, light and plains.

Mandel describes in vivid language the natural processes that moulded the prairie landscape. He recognizes the glaciations and ice melt that shaped the plains:

> The land goes out like sea at Frenchman's creek,
> Dipped from Dakota where the ice-head lolled
> And nodded in the sun; here too is sea-wrack
> In the land a thousand miles from sea, rolled
>
> Out of God knows where and beached against these shoals,
> The ridge of Mary's valley. A gull screams
> Looking for water over these bones and shells.[178]

He notes differences between past and present landscapes:

> But north from here the indivisible line
> Divides two lands like the actual river,
> A finger of God pushing hills into plains

176 Mandel, "Birthmark," in *The Other Harmony*, Vol. 1, 244.

177 Cooley, "Eli Mandel," 199.

178 Mandel, "Val Marie, IV," in *The Other Harmony*, Vol. 1, 17.

Like clothes through a wringer, pressing
The past into its present form before
Us, and assumed by the frayed and folded land.[179]

In striking language, he describes the westward circulation of marine air:

As air is spirit so it shapes
The light cyclone of the weather,
Points, circular, the whirling vane,
The mild twisting cock, gathers
The moist sea in a dove-blue bosom
And parades its dragons, camels,
Castles in the sky.[180]

Many of Mandel's landscape images are of winter. From Montreal he muses, "my country is not a country / but winter / rivers of ice."[181] This assessment is bolstered by comments about prairie winters in other poems:

There are nights cold enough to kill. They remind me of my boyhood,
how much I loved the winter on the prairies, never
believing it was deadly
. . . .
The truth is in the long dead winters where we live.[182]

This is where the "blue men / of Saskatchewan" with voices that "squeak / like heels on ice"[183] live, where the "clean pure northern snow" is like "dandruff, dead skin, / sluff of a dead god / in whose hair / like fleas / we are white entangled knots."[184] This is a prairie winter, which is ominous and dangerous: "Here in the Regina library / . . . / I hear an endless drone. . . . / The prairie night / grows deadlier in its cold. I listen to the dark / come on."[185]

Summer is equally dangerous: "the reeling plains look southward / and the heat gathers like a beast."[186] Mandel recalls:

179 Mandel, "Fair in Town," in *The Other Harmony*, Vol. 1, 18.
180 Mandel, "Poems and Chorus from The Four Winds, II," in *The Other Harmony*, Vol. 2, 709.
181 Mandel, "Envoi," in *The Other Harmony*, Vol. 1, 233.
182 Mandel, "*Grandfather's Painting*: David Thauberger," in *The Other Harmony*, Vol. 1, 336.
183 Mandel, "Ice Palace," in *The Other Harmony*, Vol. 1, 24.
184 Mandel, "Blizzard," in *The Other Harmony*, Vol. 1, 46.
185 Mandel, "Beach at Miraflores," in *The Other Harmony*, Vol. 2, 659.
186 Mandel, "Orpheus in the Underworld," in *The Other Harmony*, Vol. 1, 85.

in the estevan summer
hazardous as desert hear
gopher squeaks momentary hawks
lean in the pushing and shoving
wind   the sun breathing
heat
    and the impossibility of death[187]

He observes the sun, "his arms flailing / wheat and skin."[188] And in a metaphor appropriate to Estevan's resource base, he uses the image of "furnace, and wind / over the coals, over the hot coal sun."[189]

Prairie light figures less overtly in Mandel's poetry than in that of most other prairie poets, but the prairie light still illuminates his poetry, giving it a "Magic Realist" character.[190] When light appears in a poem, it is often muted. On the surface of Lake Wabamun there is "no sun / only / light / hurting / in its / endless / dance,"[191] and light that is changed by "thunder / and sky / towel / wet sand / in yellow light."[192] Elsewhere there is the "last light wheeling / over the land."[193]

Wind is also an ever-present force, both literally and imaginatively. There is "the sea // Of wind pouring over the face of north,"[194] and "you can see / the wind here the grass / always bending the stone unmoved."[195] Mandel observes that "today the sky is torn by wind: / a field after a long battle / strewn with corpses of cloud,"[196] and "[i]n the unknowable space between this room / and the running mane of the horizon / where dimmer than thunder the clouds / shudder and toss under the wind's whip / I have been dreaming of horses."[197] Mandel imagines another prairie behind the one that exists, with wind connecting the two: "Nothing on either prairie changes though the winds blow / across immensities your

187 Mandel, "returning from war," in *The Other Harmony*, Vol. 1, 258.
188 Mandel, "petroglyphs at st victor," in *The Other Harmony*, Vol. 1, 260.
189 Mandel, "Science Fiction," in *The Other Harmony*, Vol. 2, 723.
190 David Arnason, Dennis Cooley, and Robert Enright, "Interview with Eli Mandel, March 16/78," in *Essays in Canadian Writing*, 18/19 (Summer/Fall 1980): 70–90.
191 Mandel, "Wabamun," in *The Other Harmony*, Vol. 1, 161.
192 Ibid., 160.
193 Mandel, "petroglyphs at st victor," in *The Other Harmony*, Vol. 1, 261.
194 Mandel, "Val Marie, III," in *The Other Harmony*, Vol. 1, 17.
195 Mandel, "near Hirsch a Jewish cemetery," in *The Other Harmony*, Vol. 1, 248.
196 Mandel, "From the North Saskatchewan," in *The Other Harmony*, Vol. 1, 143.
197 Mandel, "Hippolytus," in *The Other Harmony*, Vol. 1, 87.

heart would shrivel to imagine / knowing they pass between the worlds and can be heard to do / so on the road to Wood Mountain."[198]

Mandel's perception of the landscape of the prairies reflects his general ambivalence about life itself. Some images are positive: "This goodly frame, the earth, each of its sons, / With nature as a text, and common theme,"[199] and some are even nostalgic: "late alone I remembered / it was not Spain but Estevan, / that home, I meant."[200] Other images suggest that the prairie is an innate part of his persona: "I carry the souris / on my brow / the river / in my head / the valley / of my dreams / still echoes / with her cry."[201] This same *souris*, or "the mouse // . . . // runs through the province of poetry."[202]

However, other images urge us to understand that "this / simplicity / this land is / treacherous."[203] The surveyor, trying to order this vast landscape, stands "at a correction line / he reads the wind's grammar // rhetoric falls from trees // in a simple sentence of land / a disappointed syntax."[204] Amid the details of a prairie landscape, the human drama ends in disappointment, with only the land continuing on:

> the point is
> the story
>   that
> one no one
>   told
>
> and yet
>   cattle
> on lean flanked
> land leaning
> toward plain
>
> and yet
>   shacks
> coal fire
> despair

198 Mandel, "the double world," in *The Other Harmony*, Vol. 1, 279.
199 Mandel, "Estevan Saskatchewan," in *The Other Harmony*, Vol. 1, 15.
200 Mandel, "Locality," in *The Other Harmony*, Vol. 1, 194.
201 Mandel, "birthmark," in *The Other Harmony*, Vol. 1, 244.
202 Mandel, "souris river," in *The Other Harmony*, Vol. 1, 245.
203 Mandel, "badlands," in *The Other Harmony*, Vol. 1, 246.
204 Mandel, "Saskatchewan Surveyor," in *The Other Harmony*, Vol. 1, 188.

the
barbed wire
wolf willow
river ice

but never
a third act
plotting

end or
even

beginning

land
and long
land
and
land.[205]

The details that Mandel gives of his landscape imply failure: "improbable as a blue kidney, the lake, its alkali spume / hung on the rim, the hub a sunk sun, gave up the white / wreckage of trees, black flies."[206] Preacher's words "rattle in my ears / like dried kernels / like grain shaking in dry fields // fields burn and are not burned."[207] Then, paradoxically, the image turns beautiful with the "smell of clover / like sweet stars in a green sky."[208]

Perhaps no single poem captures this ambivalence as clearly as Mandel's "Ancestral Voices Prophesying War," in which he speaks in three Aboriginal voices: that of an old man, a young man, and a woman. The male speakers give voice to different perspectives on the prairie landscape. The old man speaks of a lush land, a land "rich with the bones of bison," where "wheat shoots shine / In the green sun, gulleys gush / Water," and where "There are gods / In the land." The young man sees things quite differently:

It is a dray-horse
Of a land, all tendon and the froth

205 Mandel, "Narrative Poem," in *The Other Harmony*, Vol. 1, 196.
206 Mandel, "The Dialogue of Last Mountain Lake," in *The Other Harmony*, Vol. 1, 42.
207 Mandel, "Canto," in *The Other Harmony*, Vol. 1, 188.
208 Mandel, "Wabamun," in *The Other Harmony*, Vol. 1, 162.

Of bitten steel upon its mouth.
See on its flanks the hard blue scars
Of time, the whip, and welts of dusty green.
See where the river sinks into the land.[209]

The built landscape of settlement fares little better: "A small town bears the mark of Cain / . . . / Lies on the land, squat, producing / Love's queer offspring only,"[210] while another town is "far in the past / despicable, squat / a huddle of shacks / like mourning women."[211]

While Mandel has a fine sense of the landscape and the processes that shaped it, he also shows an acute sensitivity to the ways people attempt to control it, evident in their inscriptions of ambition and power:

Under David Thauberger's painting
showing his grandfather's house
and that giant horse standing above it,
the town of Holdfast, wheat fields,
church, elevators, and prairie grass
. . . .
You wouldn't believe how large the horse is
in Thauberger's painting above the TV set
and yet it only portrays a symbol of how his grandfather
ruled the land, the power by which the little town
was run, the motor of the little town called Holdfast
. . . .
We stand over the land, fathers,
and over our homes and over each other.
We have terrible forces inside us.[212]

In so many cases, the end result is a landscape of disappointment and failure: "the wind-break / on the farm that Barak plowed to dust / makes images would ruin public poetry,"[213] and "clapboard buildings on a ridge / pastel fields tree stumps / an overturned quebec heater / iron bedstead rusting / useless springs / . . . / and in a concrete vault its floor

209 Mandel, "Ancestral Voices Prophesying War," in *The Other Harmony*, Vol. 2, 649.
210 Mandel, "Estevan Saskatchewan," in *The Other Harmony*, Vol. 1, 15.
211 Mandel, "Orpheus in the Underworld," in *The Other Harmony*, Vol. 1, 85.
212 Mandel, "*Grandfather's Painting*: David Thauberger," in *The Other Harmony*, Vol. 1, 335, 336.
213 Mandel, "Pictures in an Institution," in *The Other Harmony*, Vol. 1, 125.

/ littered with prairie I find / scripture a farmer's exodus."[214] Mandel's character Fuseli gives a bitter description of failure and social unrest in the "Dirty Thirties":

> And the country itself, drought for many years, the
> cattle dying, and the food rotten fish and decayed
> eastern apples, my house leaning crazily over the
> hill looking toward the valley where the dun-coloured,
> dusky hills browsed like bulls, and the bone-grey
> houses stared from their empty sockets at the
> bone-grey houses staring from empty sockets; the
> miners sullen, and the blood-red police streaming
> through the cemeteries vowing death.[215]

Mandel brings the prairie landscape to us in striking images, but there is an underlying feeling that he does so from a divided centre. On the one hand, his poetry has the familiarity and force of someone writing "out of place," and more specifically out of that "home place," where Mandel spent more than three decades and which he so eagerly sought to regain. On the other hand, his depictions of the landscape also have the distance of a poet who remains "out of place." When Mandel says of the Aboriginal women, "they touched stone / they touched / earth,"[216] the phrases are tinged with a longing for the same rooted connection to the land. He is left, however, with an unfinished sense of belonging, of one still writing himself back into the land. He says, "our history is in motion curved / like straight correction lines / earth-measured on a western grid / place known through time time / measuring place,"[217] with "windows / facing inward / 'an ideal / inserted into the plane / we call reality' words / warning this is the place / you reach / to name / remember and recite."[218] Despite, or perhaps because of, his conflicted perspective, Mandel's is a rewarding reinterpretation of the prairie landscape.

214 Mandel, "the hoffer colony," in *The Other Harmony*, Vol. 1, 266.

215 Mandel, "Mary Midnight," in *The Other Harmony*, Vol. 1, 312.

216 Mandel, "Estevan, 1934," in *The Other Harmony*, Vol. 1, 159.

217 Mandel, "doors of perception," in *The Other Harmony*, Vol. 1, 242.

218 Mandel, "the return," in *The Other Harmony*, Vol. 1, 241.

JOHN NEWLOVE

John Newlove was raised in the semi-forested area of Kamsack, Saskatchewan. Although his poetry is influenced by this treed environment, as well as by his later encounters with the mountains and coasts of British Columbia, his poetry also reaches to the "green plains" of the prairies adjacent to his home. "Give me back the green fat / fields of the place where I learned / to be human,"[219] he writes. Newlove's peripatetic wanderings were anchored "on the prairies / I always come back to," although the influence of this environment is mixed: "there is the wind / and the numbing snow five months long / at best, blowing endurance / and stupidity into the people."[220]

Despite his emotional attachment to the prairies, his home place could not hold him. He describes Kamsack as a

> [p]lump eastern saskatchewan river town,
> where even in depression it's said the wheat
> went thirty bushels and was full-bodied,
> the river laying good black dirt each year:
> but I found it arid, as young men will.[221]

Even the sense of space seemed to draw him away:

> Never knowing how we got there
> one day we woke and saw the sky,
> limitless, serene, capable
> of black cloud and lightning,
> the land limitless, yellow
> with grain in summertime,
> light green in spring, stretching
> to the edge of the world
> but never ending; and it made us
> want to go.[222]

There are details of the small-town life that he left: the casual shooting of wild dogs in town, the snowplow that was "simply / some alternate of a golden summer's / wheat-threshing machine," swimming in Dead

219 John Newlove, "Vancouver," in *Moving in Alone* (Toronto: Contact Press, 1965), 49.
220 Newlove, "Seeing Me Dazed," in *Moving in Alone*, 21.
221 Newlove, "Kamsack," in *Moving in Alone*, 49.
222 John Newlove, "The Sky," in *Lies* (Toronto: McClelland & Stewart, 1972), 13.

Horse Creek or in farmers' dugouts, jumping into snowdrifts from "Peter The Lordly Verigin's / palace on the edge of town," a drunken father, schoolyard fights,

> bruised knees, cut fingers,
> nails in feet, far walks
> to watch a horse's corpse
> turn slowly and sweetly to bone."

All of this added up to "a 9-year-old's year-long / night and day in tiny / magnificent prairie Verigin."[223] Another poem adds unflattering detail:

> Saturday night
> kamsack is
> something
> to lie about,
>
> the streets full
> of indians and
> doukobours,
> raw men and
>
> fat women.[224]

As well as recording the intimate details of his primal landscape, Newlove also responds to the sense of space and distance in the prairies:

> To listen to the high-pitched wind
> in winter removes the idea of hills,
> makes clear the real geometry
> of the land: east from the mountains
> and east to the giant lakes and the river
> no single distinction to ruin
> the total wholeness of sweep
> of the earth, untouched by the lights
> of the cold and isolate cities.[225]

---

223 Newlove, "Verigin, Moving in Alone," in *Moving in Alone*, 82, 83.

224 John Newlove, "Indian Women," in *Black Night Window* (Toronto: McClelland & Stewart, 1968), 40.

225 Newlove, "East from the Mountains," in *Moving in Alone*, 50.

And:

One long look down the undulating line of prairie
leads to the horizon; no mountains stop the vision;
the gold fields sway easily.

If you would walk through them,
black clattering birds rising up,
the stiff grain rasping as you pass,

if you would walk,
your body floating like a ghost,
the smallest swirl behind it,

if you would walk that undulation,
seeking the horizon, you would never find it,
even for one long look.[226]

What is the effect of this space and distance on people? Newlove writes that "[e]veryone is so / lonely in this / country that / it's necessary / to be fantastic."[227] The droughty depression also left its mark:

Ride off any horizon
and let the measure fall
where it may—

among the piles of bones
that dot the prairie

in vision and history
(the buffalo and deer,

dead indians, dead settlers,
the frames of lost houses

left behind in the dust
of the depression,

dry and profound, that
will come again in the land

and in the spirit, the land
shifting and the minds

---

226 Newlove, "If You Would Walk," in *Lies*, 50.

227 Newlove, "Everyone," in *Black Night Window*, 20.

blown dry and empty—
I have not seen it! except

in pictures and talk—
but there is the fence

covered with dust, laden,
the wrecked house stupidly empty)—

here is a picture for your wallet,
of the beaten farmer and his wife
leaning toward each other—

sadly smiling, and emptied of desire.[228]

These are words that stand for a thousand pictures.

As for the influence of different landscapes, Newlove suggests that they vary so much as to prevent sensible communication between their inhabitants:

So you live of the sea;
and I am the dry acrid land.

You have the sweet fish swimming
and dull mannerly grain grows in me.

Your blood shines in curving darts;
I grow in calculated rows.

So I say I love you,
and you say Why do you hate me?

I speak in a foreign language;
you don't know what I say.[229]

He finds a similar division in himself: "Not to lose the feel of the mountains / while still retaining the prairies / is a difficult thing,[230] but concludes:

228 Newlove, "Ride Off Any Horizon," in *Black Night Window*, 34–35.

229 Newlove, "Why Do You Hate Me?" in *Lies*, 80.

230 Newlove, "The Double-Headed Snake," in *Black Night Window*, 42.

> As one beauty
> cancels another, remembrance
> is a foolish act, a double-headed snake
> striking in both directions, but I
> remember plains and mountains, places
> I come from, places I adhere and live in.[231]

The push and pull of the prairies, along with both his own experiences and those of other prairie people, lead Newlove to admit that "[t]here is always so much more to be said than can be said."[232] He writes:

> One compiles, piles, piles
> these masses of words, verbs,
> massifs, mastiffs barking meaning,
> dried chips
> of buffalo dung, excreta from beasts
>
> the prairie fed, foddered,
> food for generations: men roaming
> as beasts seen through dips
> in history, fostered by legend,
> invented remembrance. Scenes shake,
>
> the words do not suffice.[233]

Even his memories of the prairies are not to be trusted: "Memories drift past; / they cannot be grasped. // To remember without lying is difficult."[234] Newlove seems to want to love the prairie unreservedly, but he sees "that we all make the world what we want. / Our disappointment lies in the world as it is."[235]

If there is a solution to the varied experience of the prairies, it may lie in Newlove's cry at the end of "Resources, Certain Earths": "Let me swallow it whole and be strong, /. . . . // Let me know it well / and be strong and complete and be saved."[236]

---

231 Ibid., 43.

232 Newlove, "When I Heard of the Friend's Death," in *Black Night Window*, 63.

233 John Newlove, "The Prairie," in *The Cave* (Toronto: McClelland & Stewart, 1970), 35.

234 Newlove, "Company," in *Lies*, 23.

235 Newlove, "Remembering Christopher Smart," in *The Cave*, 57.

236 Newlove, "Resources, Certain Earths," in *Moving in Alone*, 74.

ANDREW SUKNASKI

Andrew Suknaski's primal landscape was the forested slopes of Wood Mountain in eastern Saskatchewan. Suknaski states his manifesto in *Wood Mountain Poems*:

> this great centre ring and something
> holding me around my heart the way
> a wired stone anchors
> the cornerpost of the nearby fence running north
> and west to the village
> where i grew up—i claim these things
> and this ancestral space to move through and beyond
> stapled to the four cardinal directions
> this my right
> to chronicle the meaning of these vast plains
> in a geography of blood
> and failure
> making them live.[237]

With this, Suknaski, like Eli Mandel, writes himself back home on the prairies.

There is surprisingly little direct landscape description in Suknaski's poetry, but there is a vivid sense of what the landscape means to people. Homesteading is hard; suicide and despair are all too common.[238] There is the bitter humour of men driven to harvesting and thrashing thistles—"*must be going 40 bushels to an acre*"—as the only crop on droughty land.[239] Other poems honour the perseverance of the early homesteaders:

> remembering
> the sacrifice
> it took
> to turn horizon
> and forest
> into something
> of remembered
> steppes.[240]

237 Andrew Suknaski, "Indian Site on the Edge of Tonita Pasture," in *Wood Mountain Poems* (Toronto: Macmillan, 1976), 78.

238 Andrew Suknaski, *Phillip Well* (Prince George: Caledonia Writing Series, 1973).

239 Suknaski, "Jim Lovenzanna," in *Wood Mountain*, 31.

240 Andrew Suknaski, "Tulova/1979," in *In the Name of Narid* (Erin: The Porcupine's Quill,

For Suknaski, however, this remembering is inhabited by people other than his own:

. . . there was
another people
with their own DREAM
spanning these vast plains
and parkland
. . . touching earth
they yearned for country
and HOME
                    . . . denied
by those who could not
touch earth.[241]

These people not only touched earth, but also recognized its spiritual significance:

manitou
        'the great spirit'
as the santees
of these southern prairie hills knew
the sioux word
                also meaning
                'the prairie'

spirit and prairie
one.[242]

The tension between the Aboriginal peoples' and the settlers' claims to the same land produces tension in Suknaski himself, and is reflected in his poetry. His manifesto, stated above, argues for his "inalienable right to honor both the Aboriginal peoples and white ethnic peoples who were mutually victimized by the white supremacist."[243] The landscape he describes, then, is a storied place for both its Aboriginal peoples and its white occupants, both of whom deserve to be honoured—although in his attempt to do so he cannot escape "a divided guilt." He writes:

1981), 45.

241 Suknaski, "Pacific Western Flight North," in *East of Myloona*, 12.

242 Andrew Suknaski, "Manitou," in *Octomi* (Saskatoon: Thistledown, 1976), 7.

243 Frances C. Locher, ed., "Andrew Suknaski," in *Contemporary Authors*, vol. 101 (Detroit: Gale Research, 1981), 492.

"The obvious price of this art, built on the sentient wish to never fully empathize with a single people, is a guilt anchored in a deep sense of betrayal."[244]

Suknaski's clearest attempt to honour both Aboriginal peoples and white settlers is his *Wood Mountain Poems*. He combines Aboriginal and pioneering settler photographs, and uses Dakota, accented English, and regular English in his poems to make this desire concrete. The poems touch on familiar scenes of village life on the prairies: the Chinese café where people gathered to gossip and socialize, the slow death of local businesses as larger towns sap trade, the implement-sponsored "show" in the town hall, the excitement of the steam locomotive, farm auctions, and ball games. Most significantly, the poems bring to life the people and their foibles. These recent immigrants live out old connections to the natural world:

> men joke about the old times
> and their quaint ways remaining
> as a living almanac
>
> a myth grows:
> the full moon—
> the ideal time to seed
> slaughter
> and procreate.[245]

And always, no matter where Suknaski is, the prairie and its life is always on his mind. He "become[s] lonely / when the rooster cries / on the far side of the gate the way / he did back on a farm / in the canadian prairies."[246] In an oblique reference to Mandel's two worlds, and a more direct reference to Robert Kroetsch, he writes that the Chinese pheasant

> *searching for pebbles*
> *along*
> *li po's*
> *long*

244 Ibid.
245 Suknaski, "Wood Mountain Almanac," in *Wood Mountain*, 27.
246 Andrew Suknaski, "On First Looking Over Iraklion," in *Leaving* (Seven Persons: Repository, 1974), 69.

narrow
mountain road
north
is the same
pheasant
that flies
from all those
prairie roads
between
wood mountain
and
heisler. . . .[247]

Suknaski is, however, a poet on the move:

there is still the nuzzling question of earth
you stand on claim
but you know you must move on
shouldering into strong wind at night;[248]

searching for
the meaning of country
or something to call
home;[249]

listening to what
the dry grass murmurs
in vernacular of wind
attuned
to memory;[250]

and looking for "*tulova* / that final peace / with spirit / and earth."[251]

JAN ZWICKY

Jan Zwicky comes from the northern edge of the prairie where it meets parkland, an area somewhat peripheral to a focus on the prairies. Although her poetry is influenced by her childhood here, some of her most evocative landscape images are of the prairies. Zwicky feels "the five-

247 Andrew Suknaski, "Narayan," in *The Land They Gave Away* (Edmonton: NeWest, 1982), 157.

248 Suknaski, "Now It All Begins Like This," in *In the Name of Narid*, 97.

249 Andrew Suknaski, "VII," in *Montage for an Interstellar Cry* (Winnipeg: Turnstone, 1982), 40.

250 Suknaski, "IV," in *Montage*, 33.

251 Suknaski, "Tulova/1979," in *In the Name of Narid*, 45.

mile sky billowing over us,"[252] "the luminous sky / big as an outflung arm,"[253] and the sky that is "a single / perfect sound, an open / throat, the *now* / that's everywhere and all there is / of time."[254] She expresses wonder at the commonplace components of a summer day:

> sitting in the dirt,
> the clumps of shorn alfalfa,
> the crack in the dust,
> hay down your collar, a wasp, the aspens
> luminous.[255]

Zwicky combines details of the prairie landscape with its sense of space and distance:

> The air is hazy with evaporating ice, still
> you can see for thirty miles:
> sheds, dugouts, the gridlock
> of stubble and summerfallow, windbreaks
> paralleling the section lines, and the road
> like some edict of connection,
> empty.[256]

Like other prairie writers, her poems breathe light:

> and you are almost blind
> with light: on either side of you
> it floats across the fields, young barley
> picking up the gold, oats white,
> the cloudy bruise of alfalfa
> along the fencelines, the air itself
> tawny with haydust, and the shadows of the willows
> in the draw miles long, oh it is lovely
> as a myth.[257]

---

252 Zwicky, "Poppies," in *Songs for Relinquishing the Earth*, 56.

253 Zwicky, "Beethoven: Op. 95," in *Songs for Relinquishing the Earth*, 65.

254 Jan Zwicky, "Small Song: Blue," in *Thirty-seven Small Songs and Thirteen Silences* (Kentville: Gaspereau, 2005), 16.

255 Zwicky, "Beethoven: Op. 95," in *Songs for Relinquishing the Earth*, 65.

256 Zwicky, "Highway 879," in *Songs for Relinquishing the Earth*, 75.

257 Zwicky, "Driving Northwest," in *Songs for Relinquishing the Earth*, 80.

How many kinds of light are there? Zwicky lists them for us:

> Wood light, meadow light,
> the fencepost silver
> in the afternoon's long stare;
> beast light, the satin flash
> of horserump or the brown hand
> in the saskatoons;
> cloud light and willow light,
> the dead light of the salt marsh
> and the hammered brilliance
> of the dugout under wind;
> even the rain in its night singing,
> the night rain in its forgetting,
> is a kind of light.[258]

Zwicky's musical analogies are rich with rural landscapes:

> A-flat: cream's richness,
> like a good field in April, a blackness
> you wanted to eat,
>
> or in August, the string's breath thick
> with heat and dust, like
> being able to breathe weight,
>
> stooking, to have felt the chest thicken with brightness,
> as though light were substance, as though it
> carried the dark field inside itself, gleaming
> to have breathed that brightness, have become
>
> weight, that roll of hills
> their brocade of wheat and barley.
> To have lifted to the horizon
>
> like earth, fallen
> like a rib-cage, stillness,
>
> a long bright sigh of dust.[259]

---

258 Zwicky, "Small Song: Prairie," in *Thirty-seven Small Songs*, 25.

259 Zwicky, "Beethoven: Op. 127, Adagio," in *Songs for Relinquishing the Earth*, 68–69.

Her study of an August landscape captures the intense stillness of a summer day emptied of activity, leaving only its traces:

> Above the fenceline,
> drifts of crows, the sky a blue breath
> on the glass pane of the afternoon.
> In the distance, house and barn,
> the bronze bell of their silence:
> no one in the yard.
>
> Swather blades,
> the windrows and the stubble,
> the loose combs of the ditch grass,
> red-gold, glittering: everything
> an echo, everything
> alight with emptiness.[260]

Zwicky's acute analysis of how we (should) see landscapes hones our ability to make sense out of the variety that is the prairie landscape. Her aim is similar to other prairie poets who search for "the perfect word," and, if they could find it, they would "nail / mind to the world."[261] Zwicky's work is the product of informed observation, artistic skill, and a love of the prairies.

According to D. M. R. Bentley, "Poems may be a part of a verbal universe but not one that is independent of the physical world."[262] The physical elements of the prairies not only have provided a base for the fine elegiac poetry examined here, but they continue to provide an imaginative base for contemporary prairie poetry as well. Indeed, the continuing literary importance of the physical elements of the prairies is confirmed by the rise of ecopoetics and the emergence of Aboriginal peoples' poetic voices. This poetry, however, contrasts with the popular and more sentimental poetry of an earlier era.[263] It recognizes the paradox of hard realities coupled with a deep love of the prairie—a paradox that revolves

260 Zwicky, "Study: August Fields," in *Thirty-seven Small Songs*, 53.

261 Zwicky, "The Geology of Norway," in *Songs for Relinquishing the Earth*, 35.

262 D. M. R. Bentley, as quoted in Relke, *Greenwor(l)ds*, 26.

263 The differences between these types of poetry are discussed in more detail in chapter 6—Public Perception: The Influence of Literary and Popular Poetry.

around the physical facts of land, sky, and space. It is about people and by people "who loved this country in spite of itself."[264] As Crozier has said, "It's a landscape of paradoxes, a winter country that is both terrible and beautiful. It isn't mellow and it doesn't produce mellow people or mellow poems."[265]

The durable essence of the prairie region is in its physical components, and their continuing influence has produced a continuity of concern in these prairie poets. Many of them continue to focus on the same physical landscape of the prairies that informed the work of earlier poets, such as Mandel and Newlove.

What makes an emphasis on the elements of the prairie landscape an enduring theme? I would suggest several reasons. First, it is hard to escape the region's stereotypical elements of land, sky, and space. Even in the cities, a countryside that is "rolling on into infinity"[266] is only minutes away, and is even, from taller buildings at least, readily visible. Urbanites experience the same extremes of weather as farmers or ranchers, even though the economic welfare of the latter is more immediately tied to them. Although the small farm is increasingly anachronistic in the current rural landscape, and although we may regret "that something [has] been removed that went to the heart of the province's temper and being,"[267] the mega-farms of the current agribusiness landscape are not immune to the same vagaries of wind, rain, hail, and temperature, and must deal with same variations in soil, slope, and drainage. In other words, they, too, must interact with the same landscape.

It may also be that human modification of the land is less evident here than in other parts of settled Canada. Just as poets imaginatively shape the prairie landscape, several generations of people have shaped it physically. But unlike the shaping of forested regions, which has replaced a wild, natural landscape with a visibly different landscape dominated by human inscription and artifact, the settling of the prairies

---

264 Marilyn Dumont, poetry reading, "The Last Best West or Just Like the Rest: Interrogating Western Canadian Identities" Conference, Kamloops, British Columbia, September 13, 2007.

265 Lorna Crozier, "The Real Truth, The Poetic Truth: An Interview with Lorna Crozier," by Doris Hillis, *Prairie Fire* 6, no. 3 (Summer 1985): 4–15.

266 Lorna Crozier, e-mail to the author, January 21, 2007.

267 This comment was used by Rex Murphy in describing the Maritimes in his *Points of View* (Toronto: McClelland & Stewart, 2003), 21.

resulted in few significant changes to the terrain. Despite attempts by the first settlers to control the "new and naked land"[268]—the bare, black soil of fallow that highlights cultivated versus uncultivated land, the emphasis on rectangularity and the pride in the straight lines of cultivation—the land remained essentially naked, if no longer new. It is true that there has been diminishment and replacement. Plant and animal species have been eliminated or curtailed. Crops have replaced grass. But the shape of the land has largely been unchanged. The fields offer only a thin veneer of stability and control over the enduring land, and, as has happened in the past, they can revert to grassland in the face of prolonged drought. Townscapes and cityscapes are spatially inconsequential to the vastness of the prairie expanse and suggest only localized domination of the environment—and even these places of total human transformation cannot control the vagaries of weather. W. J. Keith notes that a literary transition paralleled the gradual transformation of the Ontario landscape by clearing, reflecting the physical changes.[269] It is no surprise, then, that a lack of significant changes in the prairie landscape would result in a prairie literature that continues to focus on the durable, "skeleton requirements, simply of land and sky."[270]

Further, it is the rural perspective of poets who focus on the natural landscape that has been more conducive to memorializing the earlier history of the First Nations people, whose stories are now becoming a significant part of the literature of the prairies. This recognition of the "haunting" of prairie landscapes[271] is clearly evident in Newlove's poem "The Pride":

> not this handful
> of fragments, as the indians
> are not composed of
> the romantic stories
> about them, or of the stories
> they tell only, but
> still ride the soil

268 Ron Rees, *New and Naked Land: Making the Prairies Home* (Saskatoon: Western Producer Prairie Books, 1988).

269 W. J. Keith, *Literary Images of Ontario* (Toronto: University of Toronto Press, 1992).

270 Mitchell, *Who Has Seen the Wind*, 1.

271 James Kneale, "The Poem That Responds to London: Writing Landscape" (unpublished paper presented atWriting Landscape Symposium, March 2007).

> in us, dry bones a part
> of the dust in our eyes,
> needed and troubling
> in the glare, in
> our breath, in our
> ears, in our mouths,
> in our bodies entire, in our minds, until at
> last we become them.[272]

The work of Crozier, Brandt, Cooley,[273] and Suknaski contain similar acknowledgements of the pre-European occupation of the prairies, and in Mandel's poems there is a longing for a rooted connection to the land, such as that held by Aboriginal peoples.

Perhaps another reason for the enduring emphasis on the physical environment is the increasing attention paid to environmental concerns, and the devastating impact of progress on the land. This concern can be found in Di Brandt's poetry and essays (especially in *Now You Care* and *So this is the world & here I am in it*), and in the writings of Cooley, Crozier, and Newlove, and it is reinforced by recent critical work in ecopoetics, such as Diana Relke's *Greenwor(l)ds*. This emphasis on identifying with the land, accepting the land on its own terms, and cooperating with the land counters the traditional emphasis on domination. The emphasis on these themes link these poets to Métis poets like Emma LaRocque, Gregory Scofield, and Marilyn Dumont, for whom the celebration of, and concern for, the physical environment are important themes.

Poets re-present the stereotypical prairie elements in ways that re-fashion their commonly held associations. Put another way, the poets' perceptions and emotions flesh out the "objective reality" of the landscape, which is "loved / for its poetry of form, color, textures, / not as a scientist loves it." For poets, landscape lies "in the net or nest of perception, / seen then re-seen, recognized, wrought in myth."[274] According to Lorna Crozier:

272 Newlove, "The Pride," in *Black Night Window*, 111.

273 See, for example, Dennis Cooley's "the heft of rocks," in *correction line* (Saskatoon: Thistledown, 2008), 74–77.

274 Denise Levertov, "The Faithful Lover," in *Evening Train* (New York: New Directions, 1992), 20–21.

> The place I return to imaginatively is a lost place. Not even the same people inhabit it any more. Yet when I return, the wind says the same things to me, the sky continues to promise that something of note is about to happen, the wild grass grows from roots established long in the past, the Swift Current creek seeks the S. Sask. River at the same place. There's difference, but there's also a long going-on, which is the "truth" that poets try to get at. The what-remains when the ephemeral has passed.[275]

This returning to place is what Mandel argued for when he suggested that what set Western (prairie) writers apart was not place but attitude—an attitude pointing toward a return to place, to the West.[276]

Both Dorothy Livesay's early pronouncement that "[w]ild raspberries and grass / Are here to stay"[277] and Jan Zwicky's later sentiment that "all comes to naught, / . . . but the earth, sweet stillness, / remains, will remain"[278] attest to the permanency of landscape and its continuing influence on the poetry of the prairies. Prairie poets remind us of the constancy of the physical environment, the ambiguity of its constituent elements, and the paradoxes inherent in living in this "harsh and lovely land."[279] For regional geographers who are also searching for "the perfect word," for ways to bring together the "real" world and what the mind makes of it, prairie poets offer an imaginative perspective, an inventive language, and a passionate engagement with the prairie landscape.

---

275 Lorna Crozier, e-mail to the author, February 9, 2004.

276 Mandel, "Writing West," 145–158.

277 Dorothy Livesay, "'Haunted House,'" in *Collected Poems: The Two Seasons* (Toronto: McGraw-Hill Ryerson, 1972), 36.

278 Zwicky, "Beethoven Op. 95," in *Songs for Relinquishing the Earth*, 63.

279 Marshall, *Harsh and Lovely Land*.

CHAPTER 3

Parallax: Race, Gender, and Location

Technically, parallax is the angular difference of displacement along two lines of sight. In literature, however, the term is used as an analogy for different points of view. It is this second use that I have in mind here, although my assertion is that the differing points of view enhance depth of vision. Like binocular vision, which gives depth to our sight, parallax gives perceptual depth to our vision of the prairie region. The trick is to keep both eyes open.[1] Doing so brings together perspectives that on their own resist a nuanced view of the prairies.

In this chapter, I move beyond the work of poets as individuals to consider them as members of larger and more inclusive groups. Comparisons within and between these groups reveal further perspectives on the prairie landscape and its influence. Although the act of observing and writing is singular, there are elements characteristic to the observations and writing of these larger groups that would otherwise go unrecognized in a consideration of the work of single poets. Perspectives common to these larger groups emerge. For example, if we assessed education as a category, we might hypothesize that the landscape depicted

1 "How to live more than one life at once. / How to see, to become, at once, more than one thing." J. Michael Yates, *Parallax: Poems* (Surrey: Sono Nis, 1971), np. Or George Bowering of Rilke: "[he] was lucky enough to see the visible and the invisible at once." George Bowering, preface to *Changing on the Fly: The Best Lyric Poems of George Bowering* (Vancouver: Raincoast, 2004), 8.

by self-educated Al Purdy or Milton Acorn would differ from that depicted by academically oriented Dennis Cooley or Jan Zwicky. Keeping our eyes open to these differences should produce a more complete analysis of poets' expressions of prairie landscape.

From a wide range of possible comparisons, I have chosen three that seem to hold promise for revealing these differences: Aboriginal/non-Aboriginal, male/female, and rural/urban. These are not necessarily discrete groupings; combining elements from the three groups—rural Aboriginal women, or non-Aboriginal urban men, for example—could create a dizzying number of variations. I have, therefore, made only the most general observations on more complex combinations. Nonetheless, it seems reasonable to expect that within the broad purview of literary poetry, differences of race, gender, and location would influence content and perhaps style. If this is so, it should be possible to find differences in the poets' relationships to their environments, and in the influence of their poetry on the general perception of prairie landscape. Clearly, choosing these three pairs of characteristics excludes any number of other personal characteristics among poets, but race, gender, and location seem significant enough to warrant further study.

I should point out that although these pairs are treated as polarities, my purpose is not to highlight differences, if they exist, but rather to clarify differing expressions of the prairie landscape and to bring to the fore views that otherwise may have been overlooked. As noted earlier, I also wish to emphasize the importance of keeping our eyes open to all perspectives on the prairie landscape. One further point: poets want their poems to be judged on their own merits rather than evaluated as some sort of special pleading because they belong to a particular group. No such evaluation is intended here.

ABORIGINAL PERSPECTIVES

From a general knowledge of the culture and history of Aboriginal peoples in the prairies, one would expect several themes to surface consistently in their poetry: a close connection with the land; the loss of land, culture, and self-determination through treaties and residential schools; discrimination, either by overt racism or more subtly through ignorance and disregard—the cloak of invisibility; and, with all of this as background, the difficulties of finding their place in contemporary society while preserving their heritage. Obviously the first of these—connection with the land—would influence the impact of landscape on Aboriginal poetry. However, an intimate connection to the land also makes the loss of that land more potent, not just because it was the source of their cultural and economic sustenance, but also because its loss resulted in lost dignity, status, and place.

I am well aware that my attempt to underscore what I feel to be Aboriginal perspectives on landscape could be perceived as arrogant. I have attempted, as much as possible, to let the poetry speak for itself without attributing any motivation or attitude. I need to make clear, too, that although I have identified some commonalities in perspective, no one view stands for all Aboriginal poets, any more than one view would stand for all non-Aboriginal poets. I am also aware that by identifying these perspectives, I might seem to be suggesting that there are certain characteristics innate to Aboriginal poetry, which make it Aboriginal. Both Emma LaRocque and Marilyn Dumont speak to this point in powerful terms, and I trust it will be clear from what follows that the reach and value of Aboriginal poetry is far greater than my concern with landscape.

Aboriginal peoples' connection to the land is both profound and difficult to explain. As Rosanna Deerchild remarked, "explaining this physical and spiritual connection to the land is like explaining why my eyes are brown or how it is I was born Cree. I don't know. It just is."[2]

Marilyn Dumont expresses similar feelings:

> this land is
> my tongue   my eyes   my mouth
>
> this headstrong grass and relenting willow
> these flat-footed fields and applauding leaves
> these frank winds and electric sky
>
> are my prayer
> they are my medicine
> and they become my song
>
> this land is not
> just a platform for my dance.[3]

---

2 Rosanna Deerchild, *Manitoba Scene,* CBC online, www.cbc.ca/manitoba/scene/books/2011/04/11/post/.

3 Marilyn Dumont, "not just a platform for my dance," in *A Really Good Brown Girl*

The actual depiction of landscapes in Aboriginal poetry is less frequent than one might expect, given this profound connection to the land, but where it does occur, it conveys a sense of comfort rather than a challenge to human control. In a poignant poem by Armand Ruffo, a mother embodies elements of landscape to caress and soothe her child:

> prairie grass flows
>
> I will be a sparrow
> perched on your body
> softness slowly rustling
>
> prairie grass flows
>
> I will be a wind
> washing past
> cooling you gently
> and in the morning
>
> prairie grass flows
>
> I will be a dew
> cleansing
> a rainbow arc
> revealing
> the many colours of our day
>
> prairie grass flows.[4]

For Connie Fife, the landscape is a place of dreams and remembrance, of refuge and renewal:

> where are you
> heart of my heart?
> what landscape cradles you
> within her arms?
> are you in the place of dreams
> where you are held
> by the bluest of blue
> whispered to by sheaves of wheat
> spoken to by stone
> soothed clean
> by these words?[5]

(London: Brick, 1996), 46.

4 Armand Ruffo, "Chant for Mother and Child," in *Opening in the Sky* (Penticton: Theytus, 1994), 69.

5 Connie Fife, "For Our Sons and Daughters," in *Poems for a New World* (Vancouver:

With solitude by my side
I recalled a room in my own past.
My life made up of wheat,
buffalo
and unexpected rains.[6]

In the midst of a west coast landscape, Dumont remembers her prairie home:

I miss the North Saskatchewan that runs through
those trees that shoot up black and grand
from its cool hips,

I miss those spruce that
defy the flatness,
gloat at the pressing palm sky, the
loaded rifle earth and
grow anyway.[7]

Even beyond memory, the landscape is indelibly imprinted on its people:

but no one does shake it   one can relocate   or live with it   eventually we do
accept it into our faith
        of this place we hold
                in the land
                        surely it is our mother
                                still in her body

we come to repeat ourselves   repeat the idea   of ourselves kept
in the long land and sky   kept in our joints that crack with the bite of frost
the overbite   it has over bitten its stay before   frost, yes
this climate, it resides in us.[8]

Aboriginal poets also use the landscape metaphorically to express less positive feelings. Dumont turns a depiction of snow into a striking analogy for white people's sense of superiority over ignorant Aboriginal peoples:

Ronsdale, 2001), 13.

6 Fife, "Mt. Douglas Beach," in *Poems for a New World*, 25.

7 Dumont, "Liquid Prairie," in *Really Good Brown Girl*, 65.

8 Marilyn Dumont, "We come to repeat ourselves," in *that tongued belonging* (Wiarton: Kegedonce, 2007), 45.

it's as if we lived in a nation that was eternally snow covered
that we never saw what lay beneath the fluffy stuff
that we didn't have enough shovels
that we were snowed-in,
a snow blower wasn't a luxury
that we lived in a constant *whiteout*
a snow job
where snow-blindness was endemic.[9]

Snow serves as a symbol for white culture, obscuring or obliterating Aboriginal culture, or at least threatening to do so. Bruce Chester writes of a more ominous sense of the searching distances of the prairies:

It is winter
the snows fly
in the wake of
passing cars
as I learn what
it is like
to be hungry
to be alone
in the vast emptiness
that stretch out
into unimaginable
distances from
both sides
of a Prairie road
taking its emptiness
into my soul
into my bones.[10]

Wind and light, staples of the depiction of the prairie landscape, add to this sense of loneliness:

The wind has pulled the remaining leaves away   the light is sharp   steeper than before   its shine sharpened by the rasp of cracked ice   and all the lonely afternoons look lonelier   because the natural light drains off.[11]

---

9 Marilyn Dumont, "On the surface," *Prairie Fire* 22, no. 3 (Autumn 2001): 193.

10 Bruce Chester, "The Hungry Moon," in *Gatherings: The En-owkin Journal of First North American Peoples*, Vol. 2 (1991): 47.

11 Dumont, "one season turns away," in *that tongued belonging*, 48.

The impact of the prairie on Aboriginal poetry also finds expression in the sense of wholeness in the relationship between people and the land. Elements of landscape are animated by this intimate interaction, celebrated as gifts rather than commodities, as well as for their abundance, variety, and provision. We see this, for example, in Beth Cuthand's description of buffalo:

> "They were our life the life
> of the prairies
> We loved them
> and they loved us.
> Sometimes they were so many
> they flowed like a river
> over the hills into the valleys.
>
> I saw them. I knew them.
> I helped my mother
> cut away their skin
> chop their bones
> and dry their meat
> Many times
> many times.
>
> Aye, but now they are gone
> ghosts all ghosts. . . ."[12]

We see it also in Louise Halfe's descriptions of how, while people gather "*blue and cranberries, pin and bunch berries, / mushrooms, rosehips, mint and muskeg,*" wild creatures observe their activity: "*Juncos, chickadees, nuthatches, and whiskey-jacks flew, scolding. / Squirrels hoarded pine cones and hazelnuts. In the thicket / bear, moose, elk and deer watched.*"[13] There is a sense of a community of plants, animals, and people living in harmony. In another poem, Halfe writes from the perspective of someone who has committed forty years of memories to paper, making permanent an intimate connection with the land:

---

12 Beth Cuthand, "Four Songs for the Fifth Generation," in *Voices in the Waterfall* (Vancouver: Lazara, 1989), 39.

13 Louise Halfe, "Listen: To the Story," in *The Crooked Good* (Regina: Coteau, 2007), 22.

The fruitful feast of forty:
cranberries and currents
hives in high branches
thorns catching jeans, scratches
of bears at anthills, calling
loons in blueberry flats
all caught on paper leaves.
She's flown with the best of them,
free in their knowing.[14]

Elements of the landscape are not merely observed and remembered; they are assimilated in a way that reveals spiritual and symbolic meaning. Elements are eaten, literally and figuratively, as an act of spiritual communion and complete union with the land. For Dumont, eating tripe becomes an act in which eater and eaten become one (as well as an act of resistance to the "white judges," waiting to judge the meal). The tripe is "welcome[d] . . . into our being," signifying something more than mere food for the belly:

[we] sink our teeth into its rubbery texture
chew and roll each wet and tentacled piece
swallow its gamey juices
until we had become it and it had become us.[15]

In other poems, the land is consumed figuratively, as when Halfe writes: "I tumbled that hillside / back into myself,"[16] and "I am inhaling mountains."[17] The sense here is that of complete identification with the land.

In some poems, natural components, both organic and inorganic, are claimed as part of the poet's own constitution. Halfe writes:

I'm meat and bones,
dust and straw,
caterpillars and ants
hummingbird and crow.

Of these I know
in the bones of the lodge.[18]

14 Louise Halfe, "Roots and Wings," in *Bear Bones & Feathers* (Regina: Coteau, 1994), 121.
15 Dumont, "The White Judges," in *Really Good Brown Girl*, 11.
16 Halfe, "*ê-kwêskît*, Turn-Around Woman," in *The Crooked Good*, 3.
17 Halfe, "Everyday is a Story," in *The Crooked Good*, 5.
18 Halfe, "Bone Lodge," in *Bear Bones & Feathers*, 3.

Elsewhere she writes:

> Today I opened a box.
> I wanted to know what I'm made of.
>
> Stones. Feathers. Bones. Skins.
> I don't understand this.
> I greet each one as they caress
> my face, my fingers, my eyes—
> lay them tenderly in order, size, family.
>
> Coyote, bear, deer, fox,
> mallard, raven, owl, chickadee,
> weasel, mouse, rabbit, squirrel.[19]

Sometimes the sense of union is expressed as a desire to become assimilated with the landscape, rather than assimilating it. Cuthand writes:

> I am a clear green stone
> gleaming polished
> piece of the Earth
>
> I am a clear blue pool
> washed by a waterfall
> dusted in mist
>
> I am the Emerald Mountain
> selfless
> unfettered
> free.[20]

In another poem, she imagines someone becoming a tree: "until you reach / for the earth to find: / a new face / a new voice / a new covering / for your name."[21] Dumont expresses a similar sentiment:

> you enter by breathing in deep
> and when you breathe out
> you're inside

19 Halfe, "*ê-kwêskît* Pandora," in *The Crooked Good*, 102.

20 Cuthand, "Horse Dance to Emerald Mountain," in *Voices in the Waterfall*, 30.

21 Cuthand, "He," in *Voices in the Waterfall*, 32.

a tree branching out
your palms running up
the inside of trunks
into limbs that reach
for spring air and hope.[22]

Sometimes the elements are given human qualities, such as in Halfe: "The wind has mouth. Water arms. / Rocks feet. / Sun face."[23] Dumont recalls

the lodge-
pole's slender sway stirring the sky bluer than suede the wind's mouth
warm and smelling of pine rehearsing summer imaging itself
the sound of swift water.[24]

Fife yearns for a future characterized by the unity of humans, both male and female, and landscape, in which

twinned heart
reminders of all life found in this
plush forest of self
woman within man
man inside woman
twinned spirit
a gathering in the hillsides of a country where woman
life
creation
are seen as one.[25]

The yearning becomes singing, as expressed in Ruffo's "Paleo Song":

as tongues
that have risen on fin
descended on wing
born of earth
and breath
as the song goes.[26]

---

22 Dumont, "recovery," in *Really Good Brown Girl*, 39.

23 Louise Halfe, *Blue Marrow* (Regina: Coteau, 2004), 78.

24 Dumont, "my life, a sweet berry," in *that tongued belonging*, 11.

25 Connie Fife, "Stains," in *An Anthology of Canadian Native Literature in English*, 2nd ed., ed. Daniel David Moses and Terry Goldie (Toronto: Oxford, 1998), 433.

26 Ruffo, "Paleo Song," in *Opening in the Sky*, 10.

These are tongues that speak the language of the creatures of the sea, air, and land. Ruffo reminds us that this must be more than just a romantic dream:

> There is no Hollywood sunset
> and no rider sinking into it
> There is no dial to touch
> We are here
>   Touch this spot
>   this Earth
>   We share.[27]

The plea to "touch this Earth" expresses the deep connection we must all share if we are to move beyond the dream of a "Hollywood sunset."[28]

Halfe mourns the loss of land, but more than this she mourns the loss of independence and dignity that attended it: "My memory snared / by my people, beggars in the land / that once filled their bellies.[29] One can hear the absolute sadness in her long poem *Blue Marrow*:

> *When that five dollar came,*
> *one for each Indian,*
> *we the Squaw brides*
> *stood along the sidelines,*
> *no longer the Mothers*
> *of this land.*[30]

Women had lost their place of significance in Aboriginal society as nurturers (the land was their mother), and were relegated to the sidelines in more ways than just at treaty payment time. Not only was land lost through treaty; many people also lost the sense of the rural landscape as they left the reserve for a life in the city. The poetry that deals with this shift expresses a sharp sense of a lost connection with rural landscapes and a sense of the overwhelming artificiality and strangeness of the urban landscape.

---

27 Ruffo, "Mandate," in *Opening in the Sky*, 14.

28 Suknaski uses this phrase and its opposite to contrast the Aboriginal and non-Aboriginal regard for the land; Mandel uses it to convey a yearning for the connection Aboriginal peoples have to the land.

29 Halfe, *Blue Marrow*, 32.

30 Halfe, *Blue Marrow*, 67.

LaRocque sees the grid-like rigidity of urban streets and the power-driven erections of urbanites as attempts to mask their fear of the earth:

> And the streets!
> Look at the streets
> All in parallels and perpendiculars
> Spawning concrete erectiles,
> Straight-ups, phallus-powers
> As if afraid of earth
> And her Kiva gentleness.[31]

The contrast here between Aboriginal peoples' inherent love of the earth and the non-Aboriginal masked fear of it is pronounced. A similar contrast is expressed by Kateri Damm:

> at night there are no voices
> singing me gently to sleep
> though i know they whisper
> outside these strange walls
>
> i look to the sky for sweet light
> of stars
> but night is never dark here
>
> i long to join the dance of the earth
> - i knew the movements once
>
> i dream of the wind
> the damp smell of the earth
> and the footsteps of animals dancing
> by moonlight
>
> my body is tired and aching
> blood rushes to my feet
> drains into the pavement
> is pulled through my scalp.

---

31 Emma LaRocque, "When I First Came to the City" in *Our Bit of Truth*, ed. Agnes Grant (Winnipeg: Pemmican Publications, 1990), 341. LaRocque identifies her work and much Aboriginal writing as resistance works, words in a "war of words" countering the colonizing texts. She notes also that, more recently, emphasis has shifted from resistance writing to "writing home." Emma LaRocque, e-mails to the author, March 22, 2014; May 13, 2014; and May 18, 2014. See also the introduction to LaRocque's *When the Other Is Me: Native Resistance Discourse, 1850–1990* (Winnipeg: University of Manitoba Press, 2010), 3–16.

The result for her is: "i lose track of the land."[32]

LaRocque points out the complex implications of losing the land. In her poem "'Progress'" she notes that "stealing earth" involved so much more than the loss of territory; it also involved "stealing sun dance"—the loss of cultural practices, and their associated spirituality, which are central to the Aboriginal way of life:

Earth poet
so busy
touching
        the land
scape
mad modern man
must make[33] me
look at
cold steel spires
stealing earth and sun
        dance.[34]

Elsewhere she writes:

In the city
one awakes to the sound
of man-made mobility:
        coughing motors,
        clanging truck boxes,
        wailing sirens,
        tire screeches

that leave "treadmarks on my soul."[35]

LaRocque and Rita Bouvier lament the futility of urban poets and artists trying to retain the rural way of life:

Where does it go
the log-cabins,

---

32 Kateri Damm [Akiwenzie-Damm], "i lose track of the land," in *Gatherings* 2 (1991): 29.

33 Corrected from "take" to "make." Emma LaRocque, e-mail to the author, March 22, 2014.

34 Emma LaRocque, "'Progress,'" in *Native Writers and Canadian Writing*, ed. William New (Vancouver: UBC Press, 1995), 137.

35 LaRocque, "The Geese Over the City," in *Our Bit of Truth*, 341.

woodstoves and rabbit soups
we know
in our eight year old hearts?

I tried to hold it
with my Minolta
As Sapp stills it
with paint and brush.

I ran out of film,
and Sapp out of brushes.[36]

[T]here is no place
that feels like home
anymore
the city has just become
another place
out of time
and the bush
is desperate
for yesterday.[37]

The profound connection to the land expressed in Aboriginal poetry is visceral, internalized, and assimilated. Although non-Aboriginal poets express concern for the environment and on occasion a desire to identify with it in more than superficial ways (see Crozier and Lilburn, for example), their connection to land is rarely if ever expressed with the same depth of feeling.

For non-Aboriginal poets, the love of the prairie landscape tends to have nostalgic undertones, a remembering of things that are permanent in a changing world.[38] For Aboriginal poets, the connection is a part of the poet's life and has deep spiritual significance.[39] Although

36 LaRocque, "Nostalgia," in *Native Writers*, 132.

37 Rita Bouvier, "*Epikwetamapiyan*," in *Blueberry Clouds* (Saskatoon: Thistledown, 1999), 52.

38 "The place I return to imaginatively is a lost place. . . . Yet when I return, the wind says the same things to me, the sky continues to promise that something of note is about to happen, the wild grass grows from roots established long in the past, the Swift Current Creek meets the S. Sask. River at the same place. There's difference, but there's also a long going-on. . . . The what remains when the ephemeral has passed." Lorna Crozier, e-mail to the author, February 9, 2004.

39 For a detailed examination of connections to the land see Kateri Akiwenzie-Damm, "We Belong to this Land: A View of 'Cultural Difference'" in *Literary Pluralities*, ed. Christl Verduyn (Peterborough: Broadview, 1998), 84–91.

much of the depiction of landscape in Aboriginal poetry is also nostalgic, the loss of land for Aboriginal peoples was not voluntary and was freighted with more repercussions—what Dumont calls the "loaded rifle earth."[40] Many non-Aboriginal farmers also lost their land, but it happened through impersonal forces: the perceptible vagaries of weather and the abstract forces of economic efficiency. The loss of land for Aboriginal peoples, on the other hand, was the result of forceful human action, driven by ignorance, misunderstanding, and greed, and accomplished through deceit.

In general terms, there is a vast difference in the experience of home between settler society and Aboriginal society. Settler society had to make the prairie home, while to Aboriginal society the prairie *was* home, and had been for time out of mind. Consequently, settlers engaged in activities designed to reshape the natural landscape, forcing it into forms that were familiar, domesticated, and productive. To transform what to them was wilderness into an agricultural landscape that would sustain a new society was the dream of both prairie settlers and eastern entrepreneurs. The end of this process was an industrialized rural landscape in which many farmers increasingly lost their rapport with the land, as well as a completely humanized urban landscape—both maintained in the face of a challenging environment by technological changes that promised ever-increasing production and comfort. Consequently, controlling or mastering the landscape, or at least adapting to a challenging environment of inconsistent weather and commodity markets, is still a part of what it means to be a prairie dweller, whether urban or rural (perhaps there even remains a remnant of the fear of the land at which LaRocque hinted). The home-making task has been made concrete in the cultural landscape with inscriptions that speak of conquest, control, and commerce, and that tend to be linear, rigid, and relatively durable.

Aboriginal society, on the other hand, has been at home in this "wilderness" for generations; it has sustained their hunting and gathering culture, and their way of life was one that did not deplete the land's resources. Adaptation, rather than control, was the order of the day. Randy Lundy suggests that what characterizes *aboriginality* (his term) is "a sense of belonging, a sense of being at home in a land that is much larger than the human homes we articulate in our specific languages and

40 Dumont, "Liquid Prairie," in *Really Good Brown Girl*, 65.

cultures."[41] The inscriptions of the Aboriginal cultural landscape are less durable; they tend to be circular and open, and speak of continuity, cooperation and completeness. The few remaining marks of traditional Aboriginal culture on the prairie landscape relate to spirituality (stone circles) or episodic habitation (tepee stones), although the present extent of prairie grassland owes much to their annual burning of grasses to enhance buffalo grazing.

The paradoxical love/hate relationship with the landscape that surfaces frequently in non-Aboriginal prairie poetry is absent in the Aboriginal poetry I have studied. Perhaps the emphasis on harmony rather than domination results in a greater acceptance of the uncertainty of the prairie environment. Regarding the prairie as home certainly would temper their perspective on the vagaries of the prairie landscape, especially considering the Aboriginal understanding of union with the natural environment. If indeed this particular paradox is absent, there are many others to replace it, for poetry, it seems, inevitably deals with paradox and ambiguity. If they exist, they might be expected to revolve around issues of belonging and identity, and of community values, and even these are exacerbated by the loss of land. Aboriginal peoples have been largely dispossessed of both land and the way of life that developed on it, leading to the loss of dignity and status. Many have been driven to alcohol and violence to compensate for this loss, resulting in a collapse of community and family values, values that formerly maintained personal and societal harmony. Aboriginal peoples are in the precarious position of attempting to fit into the larger Western culture while preserving (or reclaiming) their own way of life, and they face these challenges, in many cases, without a territory to serve as the ground for such a task.

Métis poets especially deal with the paradox of belonging and not belonging—this is a two-pronged challenge, or, as Cree poet Curtis "Shingoose" Johnie puts it, "I got both feet in two canoes."[42] Dumont's divided experience is not uncommon: at school she played with the Indian kids whose parents were friends with her parents, and after school she played with the neighbourhood kids who were white.[43] Gregory Scofield's poem "Divided" expresses the difficulty of fitting in with

41 Randy Lundy, "Poetry and the Prairie: Writing, *Aboriginality*, and the Land," in *Plain Speaking: Essays on Aboriginal Peoples and the Prairie*, eds. Patrick C. Douaud and Bruce W. Dawson (Regina: Canadian Plains Research Center, 2002), 82.

42 Curtis "Shingoose" Johnie, "Reservation Blues – A Song," in *Gatherings* 2 (1991): 55.

43 Dumont, "Memoirs of a Really Good Brown Girl," in *Really Good Brown Girl*, 15.

either group. In the eyes of the Aboriginal community, he is not "Red enough," but he also refuses to be their "white whipping-boy":

> Growing up in an all-white town
> I never forgot my red half   It counted big
> Especially if you looked not right white
> But wrong white   To white people that's off-white.[44]

Bouvier's response to the divide between Aboriginal and white culture was to try to blend in:

> I grew up on an island
> livelihood based
> on the land
> hunting, fishing
> and trapping
> I wanted to be a teacher
> like Sister Biseault
> when it happened
> I am not sure
> this feeling of separation
> the coming apart
> and I am a chameleon
> blending for safety
> changing
> to escape hostility
> a hierarchy
> based on the colour
> of one's skin.[45]

These Métis poets highlight the real need for the widespread acceptance and recognition of their distinctive Métis culture.[46]

American historian Frederick Turner has attempted to identify the core differences between Aboriginal and non-Aboriginal worldviews. He argues, for example, that the Aboriginal worldview is myth-based and cyclical, while the non-Aboriginal, western worldview is fact-based and linear, differences that affect both the way in which the world is per-

---

44 Gregory Scofield, "Divided," in *Kipocihkân: Poems New and Selected* (Madeira Park: Nightwood Editions, 2009), 27.

45 Bouvier, "A Conversation with Peter Gzowski," in *Blueberry Clouds*, 37.

46 Emma LaRocque, "Conversations on Metis Identity," *Prairie Fire* 7, no. 1 (Spring 1986): 19–24.

ceived and how it is given meaning.[47] In terms of landscape, a myth-based, cyclical worldview seems in keeping with the close connection that Aboriginal culture has to its natural environment, as well as the way this connectedness is reflected in Aboriginal poetry. Dumont points out a potential limitation of ascribing this analysis to all Aboriginal people: If certain recurring cultural elements are the key to defining Aboriginal poetry, does the absence of these elements make her work less Aboriginal? Does it make *her* less Aboriginal?

> There it is again, the circle, that goddamned circle, as if we thought in circles, judged things on the merit of their circularity, as if all we ate was bologna and bannock, drank Tetley tea, so many times 'we are' the circle, the medicine wheel, the moon, the womb, and sacred hoops, you'd think we were one big tribe, is there nothing more than the circle in the deep structure of native literature? Are my eyes circles yet? Yet I feel compelled to incorporate something circular into the text, plot, or narrative structure because if it's linear then that proves that I'm a ghost and that native culture really has vanished and what is all this fuss about appropriation anyway? Are my eyes round yet? There are times when I feel that if I don't have a circle or the number four or legend in my poetry, I am lost, just a fading urban Indian caught in all the trappings of Doc Martens, cappuccinos and foreign films but there it is again orbiting, lunar, hoops encompassing your thoughts and canonizing mine, there it is again, circle the wagons. . . .[48]

Using only a few and perhaps clichéd characteristics to define Aboriginal poetry could constrain the artistic freedom of Aboriginal poets. They, like non-Aboriginal poets, wish above all to be read for and evaluated on their poetic art and craft, not merely as poets of a particular group or race.[49]

One final challenge should be noted. Aboriginal writers, especially those who are deeply connected to their Aboriginal heritage and language, must contend with several shifts in expressing their art: whether

47 Frederick Turner, *Beyond Geography: The Western Spirit Against the Wilderness* (NY: Viking, 1980).

48 Dumont, "Circle the Wagons," in *Really Good Brown Girl*, 57. In fact, the whole section of this volume entitled "White Noise" deals with the tension of where Métis writers belong. The same concern is expressed in Scofield's poems, particularly "Divided," "Call Me Brother," and "Between Sides."

49 My thanks to Emma LaRocque for stressing this overarching concern. Emma LaRocque, e-mail to the author, March 22, 2014.

it be the transcription of oral forms into texts—song/poems in their original language that are meant to be sung—or the translation into English of poems written in their original language (as Bill Cohen writes: "We've so many people with wonder / in their voices—and yet // there are so few / gifted translators"[50]), or writing in a language that is not only foreign but freighted with associations of repression, oppression, discrimination, condescension, and hate.[51] Maria Campbell discusses these challenges in an interview with Doris Hillis:

> There are difficulties with trying to develop Native writers. First, our tradition is oral storytelling and, in a way, I feel we should hang on to that. But we don't have storytelling circles any more. So we need to write because times are changing. . . .
>
> Working with Native writers has helped me not to hate the English language so much.[52]

Robert Kroetsch suggests that a major challenge for writers is, *How do you write in a new country?*[53] For the Aboriginal writer, the question is, rather, *How do you write in an old country in a new language?* It is quite possible that the naming and storytelling associated with landscape features are so tied to the orality of Aboriginal cultures that expressing them in English, for poetry or otherwise, is viewed as a betrayal of their cultural values.

What might this shift from orality to text mean in the present context? The Jesuit literary critic Walter Ong noted a remarkable similarity between the bicameral mind that American psychologist Julian Jaynes found evidence of in ancient oral cultures (in which one hemisphere of the brain is open to uncontrollable "voices," attributable to the gods, and the other processes speech) and the psyche of today's oral cultures.

---

50 Bill Cohen, "Lonely Metaphors Are Story-less Figures," in *Gatherings* 10 (1999), 82.

51 Connie Fife, ed., introduction to *The Colour of Resistance: A Contemporary Collection of Writing by Aboriginal Women* (Toronto: Sister Vision Press, 1993).

52 Maria Campbell, "'You Have to Own Yourself:' An Interview with Maria Campbell," by Doris Hillis, *Prairie Fire* 9, no. 3 (Autumn, 1988): 52.

53 Robert Kroetsch, "On Being an Alberta Writer: Or, I Wanted to Tell Our Story," in *The New Provinces: Alberta and Saskatchewan, 1905–1980*, ed. Howard Palmer and Donald Smith (Vancouver: Tantalus, 1980), 221.

He also noted that the influence of the voices began to diminish after the development of the alphabet.[54] For past Aboriginal cultures, then, the voices might be seen as being the elders' voices, passing on their wisdom through stories. These stories would feature the repetition of formulaic elements, slightly altered to suit a particular audience, and often involving landscape components that were given importance by significant events. Elements of the landscape, then, would not be significant apart from their place in the story, and thus less likely to be described for their own sake. Since the shift to an alphabetical print medium is relatively recent in Aboriginal history, a residual orality that values story above all could explain the limited amount of landscape description in written Aboriginal poetry. Where communication is understood and celebrated *in community,* landscape description of the kind common in self-referential, non-Aboriginal poetry would be less important. Non-Aboriginal culture distances itself from landscape through observation and study, whereas Aboriginal culture embraces the land, making detailed landscape description of secondary importance, even unimportant.[55]

Further, in Aboriginal cultures, with their intimate connection to the land, landscape details would be common knowledge, which would make any description of them unimportant. The intimate connection to the land continues to be assumed, but what bears emphasizing and repeating in print, owing to the wrenching experience of losing land and a way of life is naming past grievances, and reclaiming and retaining past practices. In an oral culture, landscape represents time and space concurrently, and deals with story rather than history, while landscape to someone who is non-Aboriginal is merely space—a space that must be named and inhabited to become both story and history, and specifically a history canonized in text, not speech. This written history becomes "truth."[56]

Much Aboriginal poetry is message-oriented, with a deep-seated didactic purpose, sometimes directed at the non-Aboriginal community,

54 Walter Ong, *Orality and Literacy: The Technologizing of the Word* (New York: Routledge, 1982), 29–30.

55 "Human beings in primary oral cultures, those untouched by writing in any form, learn a great deal and possess and practice great wisdom, but they do not 'study.'" Ong, *Orality and Literacy,* 8.

56 Although note Eli Mandel: "our history is in motion curved / like straight correction

sometimes at the Aboriginal community itself, and often at both. These are messages of resistance to colonizing texts, attitudes, and policies; courage and persistence to the colonized; and hope for the future. These messages are so important that they overshadow the type of descriptive word-pictures that tend to be valued by more text-oriented cultures. Ruffo, for example, thinks of shouting Aboriginal concerns from the rooftops or lobbing "poetry-bombs" into society to draw attention or to stimulate a reaction.[57]

Societal perspectives on landscape are quite different for Aboriginal people and non-Aboriginal people. For Aboriginal cultures, landscape is a nurturing, mothering presence to be welcomed and respected. The recurring phrase "all my relations" encapsulates this connectedness to both living and non-living elements of the landscape. Although many non-Aboriginal people have respected the environment, enjoyed its beauty and variety, and worked to protect it, the underlying ethos of the settler society has been to view land as a commodity with primarily economic potential. The Aboriginal relationship to the land is, in general, built on cooperation and adaptation, whereas for non-Aboriginal culture it is built on domination and control. In the words of English nature writer Richard Jefferies, the landscape surrounded them but did not enter them.[58]

These cultural contrasts with respect to landscape are, of course, broad generalizations and are not always evident in their respective poetry, or at least are less striking than one might expect. Aboriginal poetry does express a more organic and holistic relationship with the land, but many of the non-Aboriginal poets I have considered also respect the land and deplore its abuse, often identifying the greed and control of their own culture as a source of this abuse. On the whole, they tend to treat Aboriginal themes with understanding and sympathy, and at least two feel somehow complicit in the loss of Aboriginal peoples' land because of their ancestry.

One surprising difference, however, is that non-Aboriginal poetry is replete with striking word-pictures of the prairie landscape; Aboriginal poetry has fewer, and where details occur they tend to be lists of plants

---

lines / earth-measured on a western grid / place known through time time / measuring place." Mandel, "Doors of Perception," in *The Other Harmony*, 242.

57 Armand Ruffo, "Drum Song," in *At Geronimo's Grave* (Regina: Coteau, 2001), 52–54.

58 Ronald Blythe on Richard Jefferies' view of humans and nature. Ronald Blythe, *Characters and their Landscapes* (New York: Harcourt, Brace and Jovanovich, 1984), 11.

and animals. As I've noted above, Aboriginal poetry assumes an awareness of, and intimacy with, the landscape—an intimacy that Lilburn reaches for in his dizzying depictions of prairie creatures.[59] Similarly, Crozier is quite aware of the implications of naming as a means to control nature,[60] but such concerns are absent from Aboriginal poetry. The lists of names in Halfe,[61] for example, have none of the sense of imposing control, but are rather a joyous celebration of the liberality and variety of nature. Animals are assumed to be natural in their wild state, and landscape features are named for the activities happening among them rather than as a way of imposing a culture onto them.[62]

In summary, Aboriginal poetry can give us new ways to envision the prairie landscape and remind us of the necessity of the old ways of caring for it. Together, these poets and their poetry enrich and enhance our understanding of the prairie region.

GENDERED PERSPECTIVES

One of the most pervasive and long-standing associations in literature is between women and landscape. Literary critic Annette Kolodny[63] traces the "woman is landscape" metaphor over more than 300 years of American writing, and concludes that the association produces two reactions: a yearning to return to the nurturing care of Mother Earth, and an incestuous violence toward the landscape—both with overtones of masculine energy. Cultural anthropologist Sherry Ortner examines the universality of male superiority and domination of females across cultures and concludes that men tend to be engaged in culture-enhancing tasks while women are relegated to species reproduction and related tasks, thus cre-

---

59 See, for example, "Grim Invocations, IV," in *Names of God*, 75.

60 Crozier, "Mother Tongue" in *Angels of Flesh*, 47–48; "Animals Created by Silence," in *Inventing the Hawk*, 134.

61 See Halfe, "Bone Lodge," in *Bear Bones & Feathers*, 3; "Listen: To the Story" and "ê-*kwêskît* Pandora," in *The Crooked Good*, 22, 102.

62 Keith Basso suggests that naming, or renaming for non-Aboriginal people, is a way of exerting control and dominance, while Aboriginal naming enriches the topography by associating places and features with significant events or religious experiences. Keith Basso, *Wisdom Sits in Places: Landscape and Language among the Western Apache* (Albuquerque: University of New Mexico Press, 1996), 120–121. See also New, "Naming Shapes Attitudes," in *Land Sliding*, 28.

63 Annette Kolodny, *The Lay of the Land: Metaphor as Experience and History in American Life and Letters* (Chapel Hill: University of North Carolina Press, 1975).

ating the superior/inferior and culture/nature dichotomies.[64] Diana Relke addresses the issue of male dominance over both nature and women in her ecopoetical critique of several female Canadian poets.[65]

A particularly persistent expression of the association between women and the land is the depiction of the landscape in terms of the female body: "Both [landscape and the feminine] are vessels for our conception of beauty. The wild graces and symmetries that originally defined beauty for us were first seen in women and then, in the next breath, transferred to natural landscapes. Legions of painters and photographers have honored this connection."[66] Walt Whitman explores this connection in his "I Sing the Body Electric":

> As I see my soul reflected in nature;
> As I see through a mist, one with inexpressible completeness and beauty,
> See the bent head, and arms folded over the breast—the female I see.[67]

Stephen Spender expresses the same sentiment in more general terms: "travellers... / ... across feminine land indulging its easy limbs / In miles of softness."[68] On the prairies, Eli Mandel makes use of the connection in "Two Dog Poems":

> sometimes I think hills
> upon the bare breast of Calgary
> excite those milk-white cowboys
> who
> milk this bursting sky.[69]

The female connection with nature is even more intimate in Mandel's "Animals, Gods, and Wise Men," in which women are those "who branch out like trees / ... / whose feet are roots."[70]

---

64 Sherry Ortner, *Making Gender: The Politics and Erotics of Culture* (Boston: Beacon, 1996), 21–42.

65 Relke, *Greenwor(l)ds.*

66 Gayton, *Landscapes of the Interior*, 75–76.

67 Walt Whitman, "I Sing the Body Electric," *Leaves of Grass*, quoted in Gayton, *Landscapes of the Interior*, 76.

68 Stephen Spender, "The Landscape Near an Aerodrome," in *Poetry of the Thirties*, ed. Robin Skelton (London: Penguin, 1964), 82.

69 Mandel, "Two Dog Poems," in *The Other Harmony*, Vol. 1, 168.

70 Mandel, "Animals, Gods and Wise Men," in *The Other Harmony*, Vol. 2, 650.

This association can lead to a belief that it is just as natural for men to dominate women as it is for them to dominate the land. In an analysis of landscape painting, British scholar Gillian Rose argues that the male gaze sees women, like landscape, as subjects to be dominated, controlled, and used.[71] If these associations continue to influence landscape poetry, and prairie landscape poetry specifically, what characteristics reflect this influence?

As potential subjects of male domination, one might expect female poets to express a heightened sensitivity to the domination of land and people, empathy with the objects of abuse and mastery, and outrage at outright abuse, such as environmental damage,[72] or at the many ways of exerting mastery, such as the domestication and mistreatment of animals. One might expect men, on the other hand, to be more likely to view environmental damage as the cost of productivity and progress, and less likely to be sensitive to domination. In landscape terms, women might be seen as more likely to express an intimate attachment to or identification with undomesticated nature and to decry limiting the wild through any form of control. As well, one might expect female prairie poetry to display a positive spiritual sensitivity to the landscape,[73] to be attuned to the sense of landscape's mystery and spirituality.[74] For example, Di Brandt notes that women artists have often shown a "spiritually inflected sensibility that focussed on survival and harmony with the non-human world, rather than championing further territorialization and conquest."[75]

If gender plays a role in the way poets view the prairie landscape, received wisdom would suggest that female poets would be more likely to react negatively to domination of the land and its creatures, to decry anything that smacks of control, and to express sympathy for the subjects of such domination.

---

71 Gillian Rose, "Looking at Landscape: The Uneasy Pleasure of Power," in *Reading Human Geography: The Poetics and Politics of Inquiry*, ed. Trevor Barnes and Derek Gregory (London: Arnold, 1997), 266–76.

72 Di Brandt, e-mail to the author, April 23, 2003.

73 Carol Fairbanks has argued this for prairie fiction. See *Prairie Women: Images in American and Canadian Fiction* (New Haven: Yale University Press, 1986), 252.

74 Gayton, *Landscapes of the Interior*, 75–76.

75 Di Brandt, "A New Genealogy of Canadian Literary Modernism," in *Wider Boundaries of Daring: The Modernist Impulse in Canadian Women's Poetry*, ed. Di Brandt and Barbara Godard (Waterloo: Wilfrid Laurier Press, 2009), 12.

Many of Lorna Crozier's poems illustrate these reactions. For her, naming as a form of control originated with Adam, who

> lined up all the animals
> and carved his cold hard alphabet
> beginning with the first
> letter
> of his own name.[76]

In "Animals Created by Silence," an absence of naming implies freedom and serenity:

> Now
> there is only the snow
>
> the snow and the silent animals
> free in the forest,
> the luminous meadows,
> with no one
> to call their names,
> no one to name them.[77]

In "The Fall of Eve," Crozier equates the artistic impulse with the freedom of the wild: "everything Adam couldn't name[78] / fell into poetry and silence."[79] And in "The Day of the Animals," she writes of an imagined day when the wild animals reclaim their skins, tusks, and feet, free themselves from soup and bag, and vanish:

> Only the animals
> man has tamed or broken
> remain, less
> beautiful than they once had been,
> for all that is wild
> has gone out of them, even
> the Appaloosa in the bluegrass meadow
> eats only the hay thrown over the fence
> and will not run.[80]

---

76 Crozier, "Mother Tongue," in *Angels of Flesh*, 48.

77 Crozier, "Animals Created by Silence," in *Inventing the Hawk*, 134.

78 That is, the aspects of creation that couldn't be controlled.

79 Crozier, "The Fall of Eve," in *Apocrypha of Light*, 22.

80 Crozier, "The Day of the Animals," in *Inventing the Hawk*, 7.

For Crozier, mastery, in the form of domestication, has robbed animals of even the impulse to be free. And yet a quartet of poems entitled "Animals of Spring, of Summer, of Fall, and of Winter," imply that human mastery is limited and temporary.[81] In these poems, animals at first appear to be familiar, even tamed, and therefore harmless, yet they hide a dangerous wildness that cannot be controlled.

"The Origin of the Species" imagines the beauty and freedom before man imposed his will on the wild after the fall:

> Imagine
> horse and wind
> in the sun's warm pastures
>
> before the fall. Imagine
> the two of them alone
> adrift in the absolute
>
> beatitude of grass,
> no insect biting,
> no rope or bridle.
>
> In the mornings of that lost
> and long ago beginning,
> nothing broken
>
> or in need of breaking.[82]

Crozier's antipathy to control is apparent in the thoughts her persona expresses in "Santiago Zoo": "Strange what we cage, she thinks, what grace we want worn down, what colours muted, what beauty made smaller than our own."[83] In "Mercy," she makes her position clear: As the wind turns two dead coyotes, "weight and counterweight in a faceless clock," she observes:

> Beauty graces them, even now, death graces them.
> Is it a curse to love the world too much,
> to praise its paws and hooves,
> its thick-furred creatures, each life a fear in me?"[84]

---

81 Uher [Crozier], *Humans and Other Beasts*, 11, 13, 17, 23.

82 Crozier, "The Origin of the Species," in *Apocrypha of Light*, 6.

83 Crozier, "Santiago Zoo," in *Everything Arrives*, 73.

84 Crozier, "Mercy," in *Small Mechanics*, 30.

Her love for, and sympathy with, "thick-furred" and many other kinds of creatures surfaces often in her poems, including "Fear of Snakes,"[85] "Skunks,"[86] "Red-Eared Turtles,"[87] "After the *Origin of Species,*"[88] "The Spirit Fox,"[89] and four meditations in "Summer Small Talk."[90]

Crozier's antipathy to control carries over into the human realm as well, as she explores the bitter fruit of domination and abuse, particularly of women and children, in such poems as "She Makes Me Beautiful,"[91] "The Child Who Walks Backwards,"[92] "Fathers, Uncles, Old Friends of the Family,"[93] "In Praise of Women,"[94] and "The Old Order."[95]

Crozier also mourns the damage inflicted on the environment, both directly and indirectly, by human mastery:

> Nothing can be turned back.
> Words cannot change
> a life that is past,
> make the land whole again
> or call the buffalo home.[96]

In "Study in Grey" she alludes to the effects of pesticides:

> The great horned owl unrolls
> her last long vowel to the tallow moon.
> . . . .
> She has seen her shadow nailed to the barn
> and her young die in eggs that have no shells.[97]

In her poem "In White," Crozier expresses a hopelessness of any escape from the influence of human activity. After flying so far north

---

85 Crozier, *Angels of Flesh*,13.
86 Crozier, *Inventing the Hawk*, 109–10.
87 Ibid., 13–15.
88 Ibid., 121–22.
89 Crozier, *What the Living*, 19–20.
90 Crozier, *Whetstone*, 56–57.
91 Uher [Crozier], *Humans and Other Beasts*, 35–42.
92 Crozier, *The Weather*, 9.
93 Crozier, *Angels of Flesh*, 29–30.
94 Ibid., 139.
95 Crozier, *Everything Arrives*, 27–29.
96 Crozier, "Time to Praise," in *Inventing the Hawk*, 95.
97 Crozier, "Study in Grey," in *The Weather*, 40.

that "[o]nly those pale as winter have survived: / . . . / she is not safe. / Across the moving ice / the white hunter drives his huskies / into her amber eyes."[98]

Crozier frequently gives voice to a yearning for a freedom found in union with the landscape. "I breathe with the wind / I tremble with the earth," she says in "Vertical Man,"[99] and in "Inner Space" she writes, "i look small / and earthbound // but inside / is the sky."[100] She wishes to be transformed into a fox or wild cat in "Midsummer Morning Run,"[101] and becomes a horse in "Change of Life":

> Drenched with sweat, she tosses
> back her hair, thick and golden,
> her own warm light
> falling all around her.[102]

For Crozier, this yearning to be one with the landscape can only be attained in death. We see this sentiment especially in a series of poems in *Crow's Black Joy*, including "Fortress,"[103] "Deep Well,"[104] and "Consummation," in which she writes: "Her eyes were sky and water. / No longer cold no longer quiet / she was motion she was prairie."[105] In her subsequent work, such as "All the Dancing Girls Lie Down,"[106] "The Swimmer,"[107] and "Too Much Brightness," the theme continues: "Soon I'll be / all running light and water."[108]

Di Brandt is equally passionate with regard to domination and mastery, although her major concern lies with abuse of the landscape. In a 2002 interview, she noted that women have a different kind of vulnerability toward environmental pollution than men, suggesting that concern for the environment should be first among the things women

98 Crozier, "In White," in *The Weather*, 40.
99 Uher [Crozier], "Vertical Man," in *Inside Is the Sky*, 25.
100 Uher [Crozier], "Inner Space," in *Inside Is the Sky*, 42.
101 Crozier, *Everything Arrives*, 5.
102 Crozier, "Change of Life," in *Everything Arrives*, 122.
103 Uher [Crozier], *Crow's Black Joy*, 21.
104 Ibid., 43.
105 Ibid., 59.
106 Uher [Crozier], *Humans and Other Beasts*, 78.
107 Crozier, *Inventing the Hawk*, 8–9.
108 Crozier, "Too Much Brightness," in *Everything Arrives*, 41.

should be writing about.[109] Almost all of the poems in *Now You Care* deal with various aspects of this theme. She asks—

> Who shall be fisher king
> over this poisoned country,
> whose borders have become
> a mockery,
> blowing the world to bits[110]

—and implores, "Tell the doctors: / no more chemotherapies! // All our rivers and lakes now glow / in the dark."[111] But sadly, "Now that it's much much too late, / now you care."[112] Other poems decry oil spills ("The twisted golden rope / under oil slicks / drags their broken / wings down"),[113] deforestation and ocean pollution ("the cry of trees / ripped from the earth in huge furrows a cry of oceans / reeling with blood"),[114] acid rain, ozone depletion—

> the man in the pulpit quotes Jesus
> & Shakespeare to prove the world
> is still round a perfect circle in
> God's eye in spite of acid rain & the
> hole above Antarctica ripping the sky
> apart[115]
>
>   let the God shaped
> papyrus shaped hole in our hearts disappear
> the great styrofoam wound in the sky
> weeping be healed[116]

—and species depletion:

---

109 Di Brandt, "*Wild Mother Dancing*: An Interview with Di Brandt," by Clarise Foster, *CV2* 24, no. 4 (Spring 2002): 29, 31.

110 Brandt, "Zone: <le Détroit>," in *Now You Care*, 13.

111 Brandt, "Dog days in Maribor," in *Now You Care*, 34.

112 Ibid., 38.

113 Brandt, "Dreamsongs for Eden," in *Now You Care*, 66.

114 Brandt, "i'm finding myself again in the healed heart," in *Agnes in the Sky*, 13.

115 Brandt, "the man from the pulpit," in *Agnes in the Sky*, 5.

116 Brandt, "small earth trilogy," in *Agnes in the Sky*, 25.

two loons on the lake, this summer, instead of twenty.
one family of ducks. two fireflies in the forest,
tonight, in all these trees. no moths, snakes, frogs, no
cantankerous beetles. no owls.

the falling, silent.[117]

One can sense both the joy in the prairie landscape and the sadness over the loss of its wild "singing":

> One of the wonderful things about growing up on a prairie farm was being able to feel the wildness of the prairie very strongly, as a kind of voice, a singing, all around me. I think it's lost some of that magic, what with all the high-tech farming methods being used now. A lot of the trees are dying. You don't hear the same wild buzzing any more, crickets and frogs and flies and grasshoppers and bees and birds and cicadas.[118]

Her voice is by turns angry, sad, disillusioned, and tentatively but tenaciously hopeful.

Brandt explicitly connects male domination of the land and male domination of women and children in "fathers never leave you":

& their judgements & their flames
circumscribing the world with a
heavy hand cutting down trees in a
northern bush camp to defend their
Word breaking the land & the horses
& the children into stupid submission.[119]

Many of her essays in *Dancing Naked* focus on male subjugation of women, particularly in the context of Brandt's Mennonite upbringing. These essays portray her love of the prairie and her conflicted feelings about her inadvertent participation in Aboriginal displacement, a perspective

117 Brandt, "Earth falling, empty, silent.," in *Jerusalem, beloved*, 51.

118 Di Brandt, "The Sound the Wind Makes: A Sh(e) Mail Interview with Randi Patterson," in *Dancing Naked: Narrative Strategies for Writing Across Centuries* (Stratford: Mercury Press, 1996), 118.

119 Brandt, "fathers never leave you," in *Agnes in the Sky*, 26.

similar to Suknaski's, although Suknaski claims that both his ancestors and Aboriginal peoples were "victimized by the white supremacist."[120]

Like Crozier, Brandt is angered by the loss of wildness in domestication and by the cruelty that often accompanies it. In "Rodeo" she mocks the fiction of "wildness and heroism" in the spectacle of the rodeo, which she says is only "a whisper away / from the fiberglass / horses that greet / tourists in the airport."[121] She writes similarly of the

> ballet
> of hockey arenas:
> modern rituals
> to ease the shame
> of our Puritan
> conquest of
> Nature without grace.
> . . . .
> chickens squawk
> hysterically
> in their wire cages,
> their necks
> permanently calloused
> and bleeding,
> from banging against
> the wires

while in the newly broken farmers' fields, "[t]he decimated buffalo / herds huddle . . . / docile, like cows."[122] She brings these things close to home in "my father's hands," in which she writes: "with his thick / hands my father broke horses broke / prairie into farmland pounded nails / into wood."[123] In a visit to Detroit, she wanders the railroad tracks, on her "usual quest for a bit of wildness," looking for "something untinkered with"—and when she finds it, she feels her "prairie blood surging / in recognition and fellow feeling."[124]

Brandt is keenly aware of the domination and oppression of Aboriginal peoples:

---

120 Andrew Suknaski, *Contemporary Authors*, Vol. 101.

121 Di Brandt, "Rodeo," in *Walking to Mojácar* (Winnipeg: Turnstone, 2010), 136.

122 Ibid., 136, 138.

123 Brandt, "my father's hands," in *Agnes in the Sky*, 55.

124 Brandt, "Zone: <le Détroit>," in *Now You Care*, 16.

Throb of buffalo
herds, drumming
under the earth.
Whiff of sage
in the wind.
Chokecherry
branches, bowing,
heavy with fruit.
Sob of grass.
Wheels rumbling.
Burning tipis,
smoking flesh.
I Thirst Dance,
Ghost Dance,
I Give-Away Dance,
Beg Dance.
'Shot our children
as they gathered
wood.'

Skull Dance.
'A mountain of bones.'[125]

Elsewhere she writes:

we also thanked
the queen and
the Canadian government
for letting us live
in the bountiful prairies
in peace,
neglecting to mention
the First Nations
and their wantonly
slaughtered buffalo herds
who were so drastically
cheated by our
bogus treaties and
thrown into turmoil for
showing us how.[126]

125 Brandt, "St. Norbert in July," in *Now You Care*, 26.

126 Brandt, "The Phoenicians," in *Walking to Mojácar*, 176, 178.

Brandt feels somehow implicated in the injustices done to Aboriginal peoples in that her

> Flemish peasant
> ancestors
> fleeing Russian czars
> found refuge in
> land newly stolen
> from buffalo
> and Métis.[127]

In a remarkable conflation of the experiences of both her ancestors and an Aboriginal woman's ancestors, Brandt writes:

> so, Marie, i've started hearing them, just like you
> said, voices in the landscape, ancestors, yours &
> mine, the spirits of our grandmothers, singing,
> . . . .
> wailing their songs in my ears . . .
> . . . their anger rising like
> flames in prairie wind, remembering dust & buffalo
> skin & white bones, a creaking old ship bulkily
> plowing through ocean waves, the straight horizon,
> blue, grey, white, grey, the children hungry, crying,
> nausea, morning sickness, fainting, & before that,
> before that, before that, remembering, an empty
> field, a black cross, a forest, a digging stick, a willow
> basket, a reedy nest, turtle woman, Ishtar, the Great
> She Bear in the sky.[128]

Brandt also identifies intimately with the landscape: "this earth is my home, my body, my mother, / unafraid & so, unutterably, beautiful."[129]

Jan Zwicky expresses her love for the prairie perhaps most poignantly in *Thirty-seven Small Songs and Thirteen Silences* and in *Songs for Relinquishing the Earth*. The latter volume also reflects her concern about human domination of the environment and the abuse that results. In "Transparence" she laments what seems to her to be an intransigent de-

---

127 Brandt, "The lottery of history," in *Walking to Mojácar*, 124.

128 Brandt, "so, Marie, i've started hearing them," in *Jerusalem, beloved*, 56.

129 Brandt, "blue light, falling around us," in *Jerusalem, beloved*, 32.

sire to control the land: "if we could learn / to let go without leaving then / our real lives might begin."[130] In another poem she denounces "the stupid / gothic grab of land."[131]

One final possible result of an intimate connection to the landscape is a sensitivity to the spiritual in the material world, a topic that I will examine in detail in the chapter "Beyond Paradox: Mystery and Silence." That assessment shows that female poets are indeed sensitive to the spiritual in the landscape. But what about male poets? Does their work confirm the broad contrasts suggested at the beginning of this section? In fact, these contrasts are contradicted. For example, none of the male poets whose work I examine celebrates domination over the land or its peoples, as would have followed from the similar discussion of male/female domination. Even when Suknaski honours his ancestors' struggle to make a living on the prairie, he, like Brandt, writes with a deep sense of the price paid by the original inhabitants for that privilege. Far from supporting domination of the land and its peoples and creatures, male poets express sympathy for the oppressed and concern for environmental damage, although the latter is rarely given the attention and force that characterizes the work of female poets.

Dennis Cooley is one who does: "we are bad housekeepers / the blue eye, once a light house / fuzzy now as the flannel we sleep in / something in its eye, weeps for our harm / we all are in the same boat now;"[132] "the ocean / red with silt // from where the forests were / torrents of green the earth / in torment bleeds away / the water stiff with blood."[133] In a recent unpublished poem, Cooley laments, through the voices of Mrs. Bentley and Paul, that

> the whole world in decreation . . .
> coyotes into wind dissolving
> gophers dip down holes in the earth unbirthing
> owls hawks meadowlarks robins long gone
> through the mirror on the horizon.

130 Zwicky, "Transparence," in *Songs for Relinquishing the Earth*, 37.

131 Jan Zwicky, "Track," in *Robinson's Crossing* (London: Brick Books, 2004), 47.

132 Cooley, "east of eden," in *this only home*, 33.

133 Cooley, "Madagascar," in *this only home*, 61.

Paul lists more than seventy-five prairie plants, "and more / lots more / lost."[134]

The light touch that Cooley employs in "bonnie" does not hide his deep concern for "this only home":

> no its not an orange
> it's many colours
> & we are peeling it
> wearing away the coat
> the abrasions we take to it
> as if we were
> making marmalade
>
> till she's a whole new
> ball game
> this belle of the ball
> blue lady
> till she's lepral
> spectral as moon & as bony
>
> two skulls grinning at each other
> their lonely dance in a darkened ballroom
> there on the dark end &
>
> what will you think
> what about your bonnie lass then
> when she's not up to scratch
>
> will you sing still to her
> will you stand under a saxophone moon
> o come back blue
> lady come back don't
> be blue anymore.[135]

Cooley's use of "lepral," evokes a powerful image of the disintegrating damage inflicted on the planet by human complacency. John Newlove also refers to lepers when he couples his dark view of nature with a critique of human destructiveness:

> these are the locust years that come to everyone,

---

134 Cooley, "the whole world in decreation," e-mail to the author, March 3, 2015.

135 Cooley, "bonnie," in *this only home*, 99.

coming to this speckled, dying planet,
. . . .
but on earth, surrendered, raped, mutilated,
rained upon with acid and rage, stripped bare, buggered,
filled with sand, spat upon by lepers, green.[136]

In general, however, when most of the male poets address domination, they do so as it relates to paternal domination in the family, or in the treatment of Aboriginal people, rather than domination of the landscape. Mandel is reminded of the Holocaust while watching films of cowboys shooting Indians in theatres in Estevan and Regina, and he comments on the darker side of male power and control in "*Grandfather's Painting*: David Thauberger."[137] Newlove's "Ride Off Any Horizon" contains a somber and sympathetic recounting of the injustices done to Poundmaker and Big Bear:

Ride off any horizon
and let the measure fall
where it may –

and damn the troops, the horsemen
are wheeling in the sunshine,
the cree, practising

for their deaths: mr poundmaker,
gentle sweet mr bigbear,
it is not unfortunately

quite enough to be innocent,
it is not enough merely
not to offend –

at times to be born
is enough, to be
in the way is too much –

some colonel otter, some
major-general middleton will
get you, you –

---

136 John Newlove, "Progress," in *Apology for Absence: Selected Poems, 1962–1992* (Erin: Porcupine's Quill, 1993), 194, 198.

137 Mandel, *The Other Harmony*, Vol. 1, 335–36.

indian. It is no good to say,
I would rather die
at once than be in that place –

though you love that land more,
you will go where they take you.[138]

Suknaski's work, especially *Octomi*, *East of Myloona*, and *Silk Trail*, also shows a sensitivity to the plight of Aboriginal people. In "Pacific Western Flight North" he identifies what distinguishes the oppressor from the oppressed:

. . . there was
another people
with their own DREAM
spanning these vast plains
and parkland
. . . touching earth
they yearned for country
and HOME
. . . denied
by those who could not
touch earth.[139]

Cooley, too, portrays the result of Aboriginal oppression:

Sioux Lookout

leave white tongues behind
red tongues
in the mouth
afraid to tell
unable to speak.[140]

Cooley's "the heft of rocks" includes an epigraph from Victor Shklovsky—". . . art exists . . . to make one feel things, to make the stone stony." In this striking poem, Cooley presents a wonderful mix of Aboriginal

138 Newlove, "Ride Off Any Horizon," in *Black Night Window*, 36–37.
139 Suknaski, "Pacific Western Flight North," in *East of Myloona*, 12.
140 Cooley, "in tongues," in *correction line*, 73.

life, profound physical forces, childhood memories, and local landscape, weaving a story of lost days and lost lives:

> there under the grass
> their lives circled
> in smoke & talk
> hundreds and hundreds of them
> dreaming inside hoops of skin & rocks & pictures
> rounded from where they had fallen
> from a far world its cliffs of ice
> & enormous sweeps of snow a few people
> the world turning on its axis
> water turning warmer
>
> the weight of those who stopped here
> just over there they are eating & dancing
> & over smoking fires tanning
> hundreds of years in wind and sun
> thousands passing through they too
> with the buffalo their rivers of flesh
> drifting with the seasons from wooded clefts
> in what we called the souris valley
> & what they named the family did not know.[141]

Tim Lilburn is the only male poet of those I have looked at to dwell on the theme of a close union with the landscape. His plea to "[e]mpty yourself, be alone. / Love the earth as felt and grease, love it, / heavy bread of leafmould, deer shit and moon light,"[142] could stand as a summary of his poetic search for an intimate union with the physical world, a theme that especially pervades his *Moosewood Sandhills, To the River,* and *Kill-site*. The title of Patrick Friesen's first book, *the lands i am,* and a similar sentiment in "passage" ("a voice infolds me / speaking of time I was / land I was")[143] suggest a close association between poet and landscape, but his focus is not so much a union with the land as the elusive and mysterious union of flesh and spirit.

The poetry written by male and female prairie poets does not bear out the oppositional distinctions suggested at the beginning of this sec-

141 Cooley, "the heft of rocks," in *correction line,* 76–77.

142 Lilburn, "From an Anchorage," in *Moosewood Sandhills,* 24.

143 Friesen, "passage," in *bluebottle,* 33.

tion, although there are differences in emphasis and tone. Female poets seem more likely to express their concern over the many forms of domination with more force and edge, seeing the domination of women, children, and land as all emanating from patriarchy. Crozier and Brandt are especially forceful in their opposition to various forms of domination. Crozier expresses sympathy for animals and the wild, and bitterly denounces the abuse of people, especially children, and Brandt displays deep concern for the abuse of the environment more generally. Both speak to the sense of female and environmental vulnerability. Although Cooley and Newlove show environmental concern, and Suknaski and Friesen deal with domination in family and social situations, none of the male poets express the same level of concern expressed by female poets. Poets of both genders frequently tie domination to religious strictness, with its emphasis on male domination. Female poets seem more likely to express their love of landscape through identifying intimately with it. Although Lilburn also expresses similar yearnings, for female poets this is often driven more by a spiritual quest. Brandt and Suknaski feel most keenly the tension in the twin stories of hard-won success and culture-destroying loss as the settler society—of which they are a part—displaced the original inhabitants. Their poetry attempts to honour both strands of the woven story of the prairie.

Although there are differences and similarities of themes among these poets, there is little to suggest that gender has a strong influence on them. The most that can be said is that there are differing emphases on similar themes, with a more overt feminine emphasis on spirituality. One might suspect that personality and conviction are more likely influential, rather than gender—each poet, as one would expect, writing out of his or her emotional reservoir and thus variously transforming the prairie landscape in the process. It is important to hear these gendered voices with their varying and unique emphases in order to fully encompass the meaning of the prairie region.

There are some connections among the perspectives of gender, race, and location. Aboriginal peoples' perspective on landscape resonates most clearly with non-Aboriginal female poets, with their love of the land and common concern over the health of the environment. These two groups express this concern differently, with Aboriginal poets emphasizing abuse of the land as one aspect of a more general non-Aboriginal domination of both peoples and the environment. Native American poet Linda Hogan expresses it this way: "The fear of wilderness, the fear of Aboriginal people, and the fear of not having control are all the same fear."[144] Non-Aboriginal women tend to see abuse of the land more in terms of another expression of male domination. Among Aboriginal poets, the city is "white" domination writ large, a place of danger and disillusionment. Non-Aboriginal prairie poets, men and women alike, also tend to view the city negatively, although more in contrast with the freedom and spirituality of the countryside, rather than as a dangerous place in and of itself. It is surprising, however, that the city does not figure more prominently in what is largely the work of urban-dwelling prairie poets. Friesen's powerful evocation of Winnipeg is the exception, and even his vision of the city has a significant negative component.

RURAL/URBAN PERSPECTIVES

George Melnyk suggests that the "natural" elements of the city landscape leaven the negative view of the city, but this only emphasizes the city's need of leavening.[145] In the previous chapter I explored the largely rural landscape's impact on the work of prairie poets; here, I will turn to the potential impact of the urban landscape on prairie poetry. Urban places account for a miniscule area of the prairie region, and yet more than 80 per cent of the population lives in urban environments. The nine prairie poets I consider currently live, or have lived, in these urban centres, and one would expect the urban experience and urban landscapes to figure in their work. Although Aboriginal poets have roots and, often, homes in rural areas, a majority now live in urban places, and are worth considering in this regard as well. If their urban experience is different from that of non-Aboriginal people, it would be expected that their poetry would express different perspectives and emphases.[146]

Crozier's few references to the city suggest a gloomily controlling landscape. She contrasts garden colours with the grey of the city in

---

144 Linda Hogan, quoted in Akiwenzie-Damm, "We Belong to this Land," 86.

145 George Melnyk, *New Moon at Batoche: Reflections on the Urban Prairie* (Banff: Banff Centre Press, 1999).

146 Interestingly, a recent study has found similarities in the experiences of Winnipeg's Aboriginal population and recent non-Aboriginal newcomers. John Gyepi-Garbrah, Ryan Walker and Joseph Garcea, "Indigeneity, Immigrant Newcomers, and Interculturalism in Winnipeg, Canada," *Urban Studies*, vol. 51, no. 9 (July 2014): 1795-1811.

"Backyard Eden."[147] In "Rapture," she imagines the return of Jesus "descend[ing] to the city" where there is "the fervour of getting on / and off, the signs—their good direction," and wishes instead for him to come "among the chickadees" and where "yellow warblers [are] circling / above his head, flicking like sparks."[148] Here the controlling aspect of the city reaches even to religion, and the "good direction" in the city suggests a rigid fundamentalism that she contrasts with "chatty angels lighting on his palms" in a rural area.

Brandt focuses on the rural environment, but in *Jerusalem, beloved* she inserts a poem that describes the gritty underbelly of Winnipeg, "this city, that i love," in the middle of a series of poems that detail the outrages suffered by Jerusalem and its people.[149] She also expresses a personal ambivalence to the city in an early biographical account of her move from rural Manitoba to Winnipeg.[150]

"The white unceremonious city"[151] figures in several of Mandel's poems, but he rarely treats it as landscape. When he does, however, the images are striking: Edmonton's "powerhouse shrugs the sky (torn / overcoat) over its cold smoky shoulders."[152] City streetlights are

> not sunflowers
> yet they burn on their stems
> like the golden eyes of those other plants
>
> and they bend
> in such an iron complaint
> toward the street's inverted sky.[153]

Sometimes he identifies with the city itself:

> sometimes I think I am a city
> there is a steel furnace in my heart
> roaring with a molten lion's mouth
> and trains rush up and down my arms

147 Uher [Crozier], "Backyard Eden," in *Inside Is the Sky*, 23.

148 Crozier, "Rapture," in *Whetstone*, 28.

149 Brandt, "this city, that i love," in *Jerusalem, beloved*, 11.

150 Di Brandt, "The Poet and the Wild City," *Journal of Mennonite Studies* 20 (2002), 89–103.

151 Mandel, "Noon Hour," in *The Other Harmony*, Vol. 1, 51.

152 Mandel, "The Professor as Bridegroom," in *The Other Harmony*, Vol. 1, 50.

153 Mandel, "Streetlights," in *The Other Harmony*, Vol. 1, 109.

....
and my suburban head is a builder's project
full of unsold homes.[154]

In "Noon Hour," Mandel pictures the working place and pace of the city: "and from the loins of noon / ladies out of offices and banks / spilled like the hot noon wind."[155]

By far the most comprehensive treatment of the city is Friesen's *st. mary at main,* in which he weaves together the highs and lows of Winnipeg's landscape and life with his own sense of futility and longing. Light, both artificial and natural, figures prominently in these mostly bleak poems. The city, seen through the windshield of a car, is low on the land, and flooded with light: "too much light / . . . / earth's matter seared to light."[156]

[S]ometimes there's too much light
or maybe that's not it
sometimes the eyes are too wide open
and all earth's light flares in

sometimes the world is unbearable
the city lit like an explosion
the steel and glass and trees
blurred in blazing auras

even the traffic is silent
and there is no necessity for memory
light pouring through
like the first day.[157]

Even from the air

the city is a diamond
of cold blue lights
the molten copper and heaviness
of a three-quarter moon
hanging from heaven
....

154 Mandel, "Among Those Beings Not This at Least," in *The Other Harmony,* Vol. 1, 98.
155 Mandel, "Noon Hour," in *The Other Harmony,* Vol. 1, 51.
156 Friesen, "through the windshield," in *st. mary at main,* 18.
157 Friesen, "god's stench," in *st. mary at main,* 51.

> the city in its sins
> smoke sagging
> like a still life
> above the frozen red.[158]

Friesen contrasts old-country cities and this new city without a history, with "strong steel rails bend[ing] easily / beneath the seething sun."[159]

> [Y]ou stand there human
> against the horizontal light
> sky fills the streets
> and you drift away
>
> this city is hardly here
> only a tough mirage
> an oasis for nomads
> drawn to its radiant core
>
> light dances like rain
> on a cloudless day
> feels like speed and wired
> all morning long
>
> then it's twilight
> the sun flaring rose
> and brilliant as hallucinations
> over st. james.[160]

This is a "double city / of ghost and muscle," a place where, amid the city's ceaseless change,

> we find our way here for a while
> among the elm and the oak
> wandering through our lives
> trying to leave something behind
> evidence a voice a breath.[161]

---

158 Friesen, "still life," in *st. mary at main*, 57.

159 Friesen, "we don't remember like armenians," in *st. mary at main*, 19.

160 Friesen, "the eye," in *st. mary at main*, 24.

161 Friesen, "forgetting into the city," in *st. mary at main*, 27.

For Friesen, Provencher Bridge, one of Winnipeg's significant structures, becomes a symbolic divide between Aboriginal and non-Aboriginal societies:

> blood is so thick
> the dream of home so deep
> and here we live
> never quite home
> feeling betrayed
> and abandoned
> on both sides of the river
> a mirage of canoes
> slipping through the water
> and the distant shouts
> of barter.[162]

He depicts a similar hopelessness in Vancouver, where the "human city" is a place of "sleazy transactions" no matter where you live—"downtown eastside / or west end.[163] The city is a place of despair: "it's raw in this city hunger and angry jazz in the veins streetlamps without light / . . . / it's all broken down there's no tenderness in the alley no tenderness on broadway."[164] It is also a place of "risk and sudden death / we keep drumming / so we won't perish on the edge of the prairie."[165]

Friesen admits that "this isn't home / it's a city I've come to / without expectations / on my way home."[166] But despite his dark view of the city, one senses that Friesen is like "gwendolyn who never left / though she moved away."[167]

Newlove's perspective on cities is similarly negative. They are "cold and isolate,"[168] "mechanized,"[169] and "concentration camps of the soul."[170] Although colours as "rural as the hairy crocus or urban as a waxy tulip" seduce poets and entice them to sing, Newlove seems to contrast the natural rootedness found in the rural landscape and the ar-

162 Friesen, "provencher bridge," in *st. mary at main,* 36.
163 Friesen, "a voice any voice disappears," in *Earth's Crude Gravities,* 62–64.
164 Friesen, "what's the story Natalya," in *st. mary at main,* 55.
165 Friesen, "backbone beat," in *st. mary at main,* 37.
166 Friesen, "the forks," in *st. mary at main,* 34.
167 Friesen, "umbilical city," in *st. mary at main,* 23.
168 Newlove, "East from the Mountains," in *Moving In Alone,* 50.
169 Newlove, "When I Heard of the Friend's Death," in *Black Night Window,* 63.
170 Newlove, "Like a River," in *Lies,* 51.

tificial, transplanted rootlessness of the city.[171] After describing the city as "[j]ewelly plastic shining in the machine's remove," situated in the "muck of sharp mud, / life's stinging black slime," Newlove calls out: "o Shining creation, when will you die / among the fishbones and the plastic weeds, / and let me lie?"[172] The city is "slow in high / civilization, / lonely as a crow."[173] People in the city are caught "between the locomotive and the fish . . . [t]he flat sea and the prairie / that was a sea contain them." Life in both the city and the rural prairie is full of violence, but in the city people are "wait[ing] to be told" and are engaged in "joyless pleasure," while prairie life is active and natural.[174] Although it might be said that Newlove's dim view of the city is merely a reflection of his dim view of life itself, there is a leavening of lightness in some of his rural depictions that is missing in his descriptions of the city.

Among Aboriginal poets, women seem particularly sensitive to the dangers of the city. Earlier, I pointed out some of the concerns that Aboriginal women have expressed about the city landscape. The city leaves treadmarks on LaRocque's soul with its "cold steel spires / stealing earth and sun / dance," and its rigid streets "all in parallels and perpendiculars." To Halfe, it is "Worm-Heart City;" to Damm, it is a place where "I lose track of the land." Deerchild writes that she was ambivalent about her move to the city; she was excited about potential opportunities, but at the same time was terrified, knowing that "big cities swallow Indian people all the time. You will find their bodies—dead and alive—littered in its greedy streets."[175] In "back on the rez," she clearly and frankly states the two destinies of many Aboriginal women who leave the reserves for the city: either being raped by drugs or men "until you are reborn a lie told over and over," or becoming so successful that the people back on the rez will not have you, considering you "an assimilated whore . . . until / the way back on the rez / is forgotten."[176]

171 John Newlove, "The Green Plain," in *The Night the Dog Smiled* (Toronto: ECW Press, 1986), 21.
172 Newlove, "It is a City," in *Lies*, 30.
173 John Newlove, "The Silence," in *What They Say* (Kitchener: Weed/Flower, 1967), 7.
174 Newlove, "The Engine and the Sea," in *The Cave*, 9.
175 Deerchild, *Manitoba Scene*, www.cbc.ca/manitobascene/books/2011/04/11/post/.
176 Rosanna Deerchild, "back on the rez," *Prairie Fire* 22, no. 3 (Autumn 2001): 85.

Lilburn, Zwicky, Cooley, and Suknaski have little to say in their work about the city or urban life on the prairies. Their poetic focus, where it involves landscape, is clearly on the rural.

The decidedly negative view of the city in the work of these poets, given their urban lives, may seem puzzling. There is no sense of the city as a refuge from the dangers of the wilderness, or as a garrison from the dangers of other people. But of course the landscape has changed: the "wilderness" is no longer wild, and Aboriginal peoples have been put away in their own garrisons in the main. But the city has also changed; once considered a refuge, it now has become wild and unpredictable. It is hardly surprising, then, that the largely negative attitudes toward the city persist in prairie poetry. It is also possible that prairie poets are reacting to the city as an extreme form of cultural and economic imperialism.[177] The small town, in contrast, is cocooned in memory as a home place; consequently, Crozier, Suknaski, and Cooley all speak with nostalgia about Swift Current, Wood Mountain, and Estevan, respectively.

177 Adamson, "Notes from a Dark Cellar," 240.

CHAPTER 4

Paradox: Ambivalence and Ambiguity in Poet/Landscape Relationships

Two paradoxes are better than one; they may even suggest a solution.
—EDWARD TELLER[1]

In the introductory chapter, I noted Yi-Fu Tuan's comment that literature "mediates among the contradictions and polarities of human experience," and I suggested that poets have a particular facility to do so. In this chapter, I wish to develop this idea and illustrate the ways that poets deal with paradox. The byproducts of paradox are tension and ambivalence. Balancing or accepting the tensions involved in a paradox are ways of resolving it, or at least accommodating it. Ambivalence, or uncertainty, is paradox's twin in human thought or action, a credible response to circumstances or ideas that resist comfortable commingling. It is the father in Patrick Friesen's poem who "stands up raising his hands in ambiguity."[2] It is also John Newlove's response to two contrasting landscapes in "Two-Headed Snake;" and Dale Zieroth's in "The Mountains Have Not Yet Entered."[3] Ambivalence appears throughout Dennis Cooley's *the stones*, both in the text and in his line breaks. He notes a poet's audience "which may or may

1 Edward Teller, *Conversations on the Dark Secrets of Physics* (Cambridge, MA: Perseus, 1991), 135.

2 Friesen, "bombed by the sun," in *jumping in the asylum*, 19.

3 Dale Zieroth, "The Mountains Have Not Yet Entered," in *Clearing: Poems from a Journey* (Toronto: Anansi, 1973), 53–54.

not listen,"[4] a key "that may or may / not be there,"[5] a place "where the world began (or / ended(,"[6] and a crypt "in which there is / or is not any / thing at all."[7] He imagines an ambivalent Moses coming down from Mount Sinai,[8] and Big Bear in Stony Mountain Penitentiary, as he "whirled like Lucy / & felt or didn't feel."[9] Ambivalence is Lorna Crozier's red-eared turtle trapped in a cage and "trying to find the one way / out or in,"[10] while in the next poem a "fly tapping on the windowpane / makes the same sound / wanting in or out."[11]

The presence of paradox prevents the reductionist from defining a region by its essence, or by its singularity. To do so, one must otherwise disregard all but a single significant element and then indentify it as the defining characteristic. For example, Deborah and Frank Popper have proposed the concept of the "buffalo commons" as a defining regional metaphor for the North American Great Plains, although even this designation is (positively) ambiguous and paradoxical, as the authors point out.[12]

My own stance in this book is also paradoxical in that I wish to bring together "the loving reductionist urge to understand"[13] and a refusal not to foreclose on anything in my readings—that is, to allow paradox full play. I wish to recognize the importance of not only the scientific, the factual, the "real" of prairie landscape, but also the imaginative and emotional, so that together they might express the full range of observations and reactions to this spare land.[14]

Paradox, whether the essence of the prairie region or at least of central importance to it, is expressed in many ways. I have chosen sever-

4 Dennis Cooley, *the stones* (Winnipeg: Turnstone, 2013), 28.

5 Ibid., 32.

6 Ibid., 43.

7 Ibid., 127.

8 Ibid., 32–33.

9 Ibid., 102.

10 Crozier, "Red-Eared Turtles," in *Inventing the Hawk*, 15.

11 Crozier, "September," in *Inventing the Hawk*, 16.

12 Deborah and Frank Popper, "The Buffalo Commons: Metaphor as Method," *The Geographical Review* 89, no. 4. (October 1999): 491–510.

13 Glen Downie, "Heartland," in *Heartland* (Oakville: Mosaic, 1990), 26.

14 In a sense, choosing paradox as the essence of this region may be a solution to this dilemma, if a solution is possible. Suggesting that paradox (uncertainty, ambiguity, tentativeness) is the essence of the relationship between people and prairie landscape eliminates all the other possible "essences" and is therefore a reductionist claim. However,

al that I feel to be significant—those we encounter in poets' work and that inform geographers' attempts to fully comprehend this paradoxical landscape. I have expressed them as love/hate, life/death, nature/culture, spiritual/material, presence/absence, urge to write/failure of language, moving/remaining, belonging/not belonging, and honouring ancestor settlers/honouring pre-settler Aboriginal peoples. I am well aware that characterizing these elements as opposites suggests an either/or approach that would undermine my general goal of enhancing, rather than restricting, the range of relationships with the prairie landscape. However, I hope to show from the poets' work that these are not so much dichotomies as interactive binaries and that the relationships between them may be more one of tension and ambivalence than of either/or choices.

LOVE/HATE

The prairie landscape has elicited paradoxical perceptions by European explorers and settlers with a long history of ambivalence to its features. It was the "Great Lone Land" to Sir William Francis Butler but also the "Garden of the West" to John Macoun and Charles Horetzky. It is a "harsh and lovely land"[15] and a barren and bountiful land, a land for which the literary motif is survival and the economic motif is progress and prosperity. It is unsurprising, then, that many people live in a paradoxical love/hate relationship with the prairies. If reason or common sense alone prevailed, people who loved the land, or at least found it fruitful, would stay, and those who hated it or found it barren would leave. But the reality is much more complex, and the emotional bonds to the land, paradoxical. Many prairie people persisted when conditions were harsh and hostile; others left when conditions were benevolent. Poets are alert to these contradictions. Aaron Bushkowsky, for example, expresses the first of these tensions in his poem "at the edge of the world":

---

at the same time, it dismisses the possibility of that reductionist stance by stressing the variable and unpredictable nature of the relationship between people and landscape. If the essence of the landscape–poet relationship is paradox, then there can be no core truth, only tentative and ambiguous ones. Paradoxically, then, the statement is both reductionist and non-reductionist—a fitting assessment for poets engaged in the art of paradox.

15 Marshall, *Harsh and Lovely Land*.

wheat with wind dry
with wind dry wheat
wind dry wheat with
dry wheat with wind

ed thinks it over and over
over by the fence
lips dry as the back
of his hands   dry as the sky

thinks it's over
the well's run
dry   wheat with that wind
gets to your eyes   ed says to no one
in particular
                    picks at a barb
with a stick
                    imagines himself
ploughing it all under
losing more topsoil
                         better to leave
it in   ed tells joe
over coffee   every morning
the same subject   wind
taking the top two inches off
to montana
                  ed now getting pushed
and pushed as he walks with the wind
the dry dry wind   down the line
to the edge of the world

can't imagine where else
he'd rather be.[16]

Ed is the exemplar of those prairie people who lived out an intransigent attachment to the land despite the stress of dealing with its harsh realities. Love for the land trumped, or at least co-existed with, the realities of the landscape's dark side. John Newlove reverses this tension in "Kamsack" when, after describing Kamsack as a "[p]lump eastern saskatchewan river town, / where even in depression it's said the wheat

16 Aaron Bushkowsky, "at the edge of the world," in *ed and mabel go to the moon* (Lantzville: Oolican, 1994), 53. This determination in the face of extreme hardship is also seen in Stegner's "Carrion Spring," in *Wolf Willow*, 220–38.

/ went thirty bushels and was full-bodied, / the river laying good black dirt each year," he confesses "but I found it arid, as young men will," and left.[17] The first example illustrates the paradox of remaining in the face of a hostile and barren environment; the second, the paradox of leaving in the face of a lush and fruitful one. Each observer perceives the landscape through his or her own lens, a seeing beyond current realities to some more important, as yet unsatisfied, value or goal.

Newlove, as E. F. Dyck points out, is a binary figure, having both "loathing" and "desire" for the prairies.[18] Newlove expresses these mixed feelings, and the resulting restlessness, in "The Prairie":

> One bred
> on the same earth wishes himself
> something different, the other's
> twin, impossible thing, twining
> both memories, a double meaning,
>
> but cannot be—never
> to be at ease, but always migrating
> from city to city
> seeking some almost seen
> god or food or earth or word.[19]

Newlove's evocation of the prairie landscape reflects these mixed feelings: "I have travelled this road many times, / . . . / beneath a black mass of flat clouds, / dry in a damned and useless land."[20] Elsewhere he writes: "This land waits. It watches. How beautifully desolate / our country is, out of the snug cities, / and how it fits a human."[21]

Yet there are also flashes of the pure joy of the land: "the yellow fields / of bread, the soft green grain in summertime, / wild mustard in the wind."[22] He captures the sights and sounds of a hot summer day beautifully in "The Hero Around Me":

---

17 Newlove, "Kamsack," in *Moving in Alone*, 49.

18 E. F. Dyck, "Place in the Poetry of John Newlove," *Canadian Literature* 122–123 (Autumn/Winter, 1989): 69–91.

19 Newlove, "The Prairie," in *The Cave*, 35.

20 Newlove, "By the Church Wall," in *Moving in Alone*, 56.

21 Newlove, "Driving," in *The Night the Dog Smiled*, 9.

22 Newlove, "The Sun," in *Black Night Window*, 79.

> Fields of grain around me were crystal,
> the sky polished, endless gold and blue,
> and in the still heat a meadowlark
> twisted its sculptured tune around me
> once, quickly, a deft feat of superior magic.[23]

Elsewhere he writes: "This is Spring, soft ashes falling to the ground."[24] Even winter appears to have its attractions:

> I seem to remember those winters.
> The hard-surfaced snow
> would have stretched tightly
> over the low hills, vast pearls
> glowing in the night of five o'clock,
> white lies.[25]

The poem's ending leaves one wondering whether the beauty covers something sinister. This uncertainty appears elsewhere:

> And the land around us green and happy,
> waiting as you wait for a killer to spring,
> a full-sized blur,
> waiting like a tree in southern Saskatchewan,
> remarked on, lonely and famous as a saint.[26]

Newlove suggests his ambivalence toward his home town through a creative line break in "Kamsack," when he speaks of the one companion who loved him (as he loved himself), his dog: "running and barking / away toward the town."[27] Elsewhere he writes longingly: "Give me back the green fat / fields of the place where I learned / to be human."[28] Three poems in close proximity in *Lies*—"The Hero Around Me," "The Sky," and "White Lies"—reflect Newlove's feelings of unrest with regard to the prairies. The first description evokes a state of contentment: "all time stopped, world without end, / and I was as a tree is, loathing no one." In the second, the boundless sky and land stimulates an im-

---

23 Newlove, "The Hero Around Me," in *Lies*, 11.

24 Newlove, "Slow Spring," in *Apology for Absence*, 123.

25 Newlove, "White Lies," in *Lies*, 15.

26 Newlove, "The Green Plain," in *The Night the Dog Smiled*, 22.

27 Newlove, "Kamsack," in *Black Night Window*, 61.

28 Newlove, "Vancouver," in *Moving In Alone*, 49.

pulse to leave. In the third poem one hears his yearning for the prairie despite his rather grim descriptions of it, and he confesses, again with a tinge of sad longing, that "I haven't been home in years."

Prairie poets often internalize their mixed feelings about the physical and cultural elements of the prairie (attractive or unattractive; hospitable or hostile) through feelings of belonging or not belonging, through feeling at home or feeling like an outsider. What happens if one feels like both a foreigner and a homebody while visiting a childhood place, for example? One is either a stranger in a strange homeland or one risks giving in to romanticism and nostalgia. Balance is required.

Eli Mandel is constantly "shifting time and space" as he crosses this "frontier" between belonging and not belonging.[29] He says, "I wish the doctors could do something about my forked tongue."[30]

Mandel pointedly expresses his sensitivity to these polarities in his volume of poetry *Out of Place*. The title itself is ambivalent, suggesting both writing "out of [this] place"—growing out of a strong sense of the prairie—and "out of place," as an outsider. The suite of poems entitled "the double," Part II of that work, focuses on and amplifies this theme. In "instructions: (on the nature of doubles and doubling)," he notes that "you begin to see the difficulties" of living in such a paradoxical place: "the place of no shadows called badlands / the place of shadows called badlands."[31] The paradox is even more complex in "Strange Places":

> the places that we go are strange
> but stranger that we go to place
> our strangeness where we neither
> know we were nor where but only
> that the place we know is neither.[32]

Mandel's feeling of being out of place is accompanied by a sense of being invisible on the prairies, except through his writing. He links his own ambivalence, exquisitely, to that of Andrew Suknaski's:

> Dark Ukrainian boy, I know your home, your young years, lost.

29 "Still, border country is everywhere the same / And crossing frontiers still shifts place and time." Mandel, "Erie Country," in *The Other Harmony*, Vol. 1, 12.

30 Mandel, "Woodbine," in *The Other Harmony*, Vol. 1, 135.

31 Mandel, "instructions: (on the nature of doubles and doubling)," in *The Other Harmony*, Vol. 1, 281.

32 Mandel, "Strange Places," in *The Other Harmony*, Vol. 1, 288.

We write ourselves into existence
on these plains.
Invisible.
Ukrainians.
Jews.[33]

He confesses his ambivalence as he moves back to Regina:

no longer knowing whether I should write poetry,
especially poems about land, about Estevan,
or about why I came back to Regina, Saskatchewan,
this cold winter of 1979 or what I thought
I might find in a city of this kind to write of.[34]

Mandel also expresses contradictory feelings about the prairie itself: "I want to be in a wheatfield / stupid as grain yellowing in the sun," and again, feeling as an outsider, "I want you to open the last door / into the field of orphan wheat / the orient grain the green golden corn."[35] Even the words—"orphan wheat" and "green golden corn"—are ambivalent or contradictory. In "badlands" the land evokes fear, both physically or emotionally:

amid
the endless treachery
that is remembering
. . . .
understand this
simplicity
this land is
treacherous.[36]

But these negative feelings are countered by other statements. He seems to question the significance of place—"the question philosophy of place / of place . . . / the wasted question"—and yet the landscape he sees is home.[37] In "Saskatchewan Surveyor" he appears to be critical of

33 Mandel, "Journal Going Home: Regina 1979," in *The Other Harmony*, Vol. 1, 433.

34 Mandel, "*Grandfather's Painting*: David Thauberger," in *The Other Harmony*, Vol. 1, 335.

35 Mandel, "There is No One Here Except Us Comedians," in *The Other Harmony*, Vol. 1, 97.

36 Mandel, "badlands," in *The Other Harmony*, Vol. 1, 246.

37 Mandel, "The Wind at Djemila," in *The Other Harmony*, Vol. 1, 49.

the landscape—"at a correction line / he reads the wind's grammar // rhetoric falls from trees // in a simple sentence of land / a disappointed syntax"[38]—but in "Locality" he says, "late alone I remembered / it was not Spain but Estevan, / that home, I meant"[39] and the home that he was seeking.[40]

Given such disquiet about a place he yearns for and yet is critical of, it makes sense that Mandel is drawn to the idea of parallel worlds, expressed by Plato, Asimov, and others. Mandel envisions two worlds, exact replicas of each other, and somehow he inhabits both of them. The worlds may represent Mandel's "savage" and "intellectual" selves, yet he writes that "nothing on either prairie changes though the winds blow / across immensities your heart would shrivel to imagine / knowing they pass between the worlds and can be heard to do / so on the road to Wood Mountain."[41] The reference to Wood Mountain clearly alludes to the poetry of Andrew Suknaski, whose "terrible authenticity of voice," Peter Stevens notes, Mandel himself refuses to try to use to bridge the "immensities" between the two worlds.[42]

Then there is Suknaski himself, caught between cultures, caught between histories, alien to his Ukrainian heritage but alien also to the larger Canadian culture, and seeking somehow to belong, to find home in a place neither here nor there. Not surprisingly, his poetry is often structured around binaries, especially in his long poem *Silk Trail.*

Di Brandt expresses her own sense of doubleness in her relationship with her culture and with her family. As a child and a young woman, she felt split as she tried to balance what she was thinking with what her culture was telling her.[43] Her relationship with her father is especially complex in this regard. In commenting on Virginia Woolf's opinion that she was thankful that her father died young, because otherwise she would never have become a writer, she says: "I believe that was true for

---

38 Mandel, "Saskatchewan Surveyor," in *The Other Harmony,* Vol. 1, 188.

39 Mandel, "Locality," in *The Other Harmony,* Vol. 1, 194.

40 Dennis Cooley suggests that Mandel's "recurrent unease" about belonging generally would find expression in uncertainties about the prairie landscape. Dennis Cooley, e-mail to the author, April 2014.

41 Mandel, "the double world," in *The Other Harmony,* Vol. 1, 279.

42 Peter Stevens, "Poet as Critic as Prairie Poet," in Cooley, *RePlacing,* 57–58.

43 Brandt, "Dancing Naked: Narratives Strategies for Writing Across Centuries," in *Dancing Naked,* 32–42.

me too, though I say this out of great love for him, and great grief, who was such an inspiration to me, and such a foe."[44]

LIFE/DEATH

Poets also take up the theme of the paradoxical co-existence of life and death in the prairie landscape. This paradox is experienced by the life which is part of the landscape and by the "life" of the physical landscape itself: change and continuity, destruction and persistence, diminishment and durability, frailty and fixity. John Newlove expresses this paradox in almost ecclesiastical terms: streets full of "sunshine and death."[45]

Crozier engages the antinomies of life and death by transforming them into binaries of a larger whole. As she muses in "Inventing the Hawk," if her persona is inventing hawks, surely someone somewhere is "drawing gophers and mice out of the air."[46] Predator and victim are "companions," as both are essential to the ongoing cycle of life on the prairies. In "Angel of Tigers," Crozier depicts the familiar prairie scene of fields of rippling wheat, but weaves in a potent metaphor: wheat fields, like a great cat, are both beautiful and dangerous:

> The wheat ripples in the wind
> like muscles under the skin
> of a great cat.
>
> Never have the fields
> been so beautiful, so dangerous.
> The beards of wheat flick back and forth,
> even when the air is still.
>
> In the long dry heat everything awaits
> the gazelle-footed touch of the rain.[47]

---

44 Brandt, "So this is the world & here I am in it: Orality and the Book," in *So this is the world*, 210.

45 Newlove, "What They Say," in *What They Say*, 12–14.

46 Crozier, "Inventing the Hawk," in *Inventing the Hawk*, 44.

47 Crozier, "Angel of Tigers," in *Inventing the Hawk*, 53.

The last stanza adds to the sense of beauty and danger by transforming the antinomies of life and death—likening the nourishing rain to the death of a gazelle, which produces life for the "great cat."[48]

To some, the paradox of life and death is a meaningful part of the cycle of life, but to some poets, death is only death. Newlove's "Crazy Riel" couples the meaningless death of frogs and jackfish with the deaths of the great leaders Poundmaker, Big Bear, Wandering Spirit, and Louis Riel.[49] Here death is futile and barren; it produces no complementary life and is only "noise" filling up spaces. Patrick Friesen also is less certain about the eventual benefits of death, describing the paradox of life and death for humans as "carrying the shadow."[50] Death constantly shadows life; the death we fear is only the end of a long process of dying. Coming to terms with this fact and attempting to attribute some meaning to it is the burden of many of Friesen's poems.

For Newlove, the answer appears to be acceptance: "I am grappling, the realization of death / is the realization of life, the spirit / of that wind formidable." Life, taken bit by bit, leads to deterioration, and so he resolves: "Let me swallow it whole and be strong, /. . . . / Let me know it well / and be strong and complete and be saved."[51] Jan Zwicky arrives at a different conclusion: "Everywhere you look / there's beauty, and it's rimed / with death." She asks, "Is the cosmos / laughing at us?" Her response is: "No. It's saying / improvise."[52]

Aboriginal poets and Aboriginal cultures are more apt to celebrate life and death as natural components of the circle of life. Life and death are complementary, not paradoxical.

THE GWENDOLYN PARADOX

What I have called the "gwendolyn paradox" is the experience of moving away from one's "primal" landscape but remaining rooted there in one's imagination, a paradox that is especially acute in poets and other

48 Marilyn Dumont also conflates opposites in "when you walk through my door": "when death and birth join hands / in a round dance circle" and "let there be sound of death and birth at the same time." Dumont, *Really Good Brown Girl*, 34.

49 Newlove, "Crazy Riel," in *Black Night Window*, 18–19.

50 Friesen, *carrying the shadow*.

51 Newlove, "Resources, Certain Earths," in *Moving In Alone*, 74. This poem could serve as an articulation of Newlove's view of life.

52 Jan Zwicky, "Practising Bach," in *Forge* (Kentville: Gaspereau, 2011), 24, 25.

artists whose works grow out of a sense of place. The concept comes from Friesen's "umbilical city," in which he writes: "gwendolyn who never left / though she moved away."[53] Similarly, Brandt quotes Adele Wiseman: "You can leave Manitoba, but you can't leave it behind."[54] Zwicky puts a spin on this paradox by saying, "if we could learn / to let go without leaving then / our real lives might begin."[55] Newlove deals with the duality of belonging in two landscapes in "The Double-Headed Snake," and comes to the conclusion that remembrance

> is a foolish act, a double-headed snake
> striking in both directions, but I
> remember plains and mountains, places
> I come from, places I adhere and live in.[56]

Zieroth, moving from the prairies to British Columbia, similarly attests:

> The mountains have not yet entered
> my dreams and become familiar as the cities
> and the old places where the land
> is flat and the shadows are my own.[57]

Newlove poses the paradox of beauty (whatever makes the adrenalin run), which for him consists of fear and security. He expresses this in landscape terms: there is fear, and hence beauty, in living in either the mountains or the prairies, but there is comfort in thinking about one while living in the other. Newlove offers us a succinct, imaginative expression of the sublime landscape:

> Beauty's whatever
> makes the adrenalin run. Fear
> in the mountains at night-time's
> not tenuous, it is not the cold
> that makes me shiver, civilized man,

---

53 Friesen, "umbilical city," in *st. mary at main*, 23. The reference is to poet Gwendolyn MacEwan. Patrick Friesen, e-mail to the author, January 26, 2014.

54 Quoted in Di Brandt, "That crazy wacky Hoda in Winnipeg: A brief anatomy of an honest attempt at a pithy statement about Adele Wiseman's *Crackpot*," in *So this is the world*, 35.

55 Zwicky, "Transparence," in *Songs for Relinquishing the Earth*, 37.

56 Newlove, "The Double-Headed Snake," in *Black Night Window*, 43.

57 Zieroth, "The Mountains Have Not Yet Entered," in *Clearing*, 53.

white, I remember
the stories of the Indians,
Sis-i-utl, the double-headed snake.

Beauty's what makes
the adrenalin run. Fear at night
on the level plains, with no horizon
and the stars too bright, wind bitter
even in June, in winter
the snow harsh and blowing,
is what makes me
shiver, not the cold air alone.

And one beauty cancels another. The plains
seem secure and comfortable
at Crow's Nest Pass; in Saskatchewan
the mountains are comforting
to think of; among
the eastwardly diminishing hills
both the flatland and the ridge
seem easy to endure.[58]

Armand Ruffo expresses a similar ambivalence as he feeds his cats:

Each morning I feed the cat who lives indoors
along with the one who lives outdoors.
When it is cold one wants in.
When it is warm one wants out.
It's just the way it has been
for as long as I can remember.
Two lives. Two worlds.[59]

After commenting on two examples of the influence of landscape on artists moving from one landscape to another, Edward Chamberlin extends the point and poses some crucial questions: "Most of us could add a dozen more geographies, with different flora and fauna and distinct climates and communities. Do these differences determine habits that are different in kind, or merely in degree? Do they require or inspire

58 Newlove, "The Double-Headed Snake," in *Black Night Window*, 42–43.

59 Ruffo, "It Happens," in *At Geronimo's Grave*, 82.

different languages, and different literatures?"[60] Newlove suggests that indeed they do:

> So you live of the sea;
> and I am the dry acrid land.
>
> You have the sweet fish swimming
> and dull mannerly grain grows in me.
>
> Your blood shines in curving darts;
> I grow in calculated rows.
>
> So I say I love you,
> and you say Why do you hate me?
>
> I speak in a foreign language;
> you don't know what I say.[61]

Marilyn Dumont suggests an even more profound difference: "Have you, my darling ever wanted to / understand the prairie in me like I / want to understand the sea in you?"[62]

Tim Lilburn agrees that we are possessed profoundly by the worlds in which we grew up: "I've often thought how hard it would be to move and have to try to take up another landscape. It would involve learning another language, an extreme and maybe undoable apprenticeship."[63] And yet he, along with Zwicky, Crozier, and Friesen, have done just that, each moving from the prairies to Vancouver Island but continuing to write on prairie themes with prairie voices. Friesen sees the experience of living in different places as an archaeology of place, which he plumbs for poetic material. Crozier mourns the loss of such things as "the blue / snow [that] gives back to morning," which she "once thought dear and permanent," but at the same time she also openly acknowledges the beauty of her new home on the West Coast.[64] She commemorates

60 J. Edward Chamberlin, "*Klahowya Tillicum*: Coming Home to the Stories and Songs of the West Coast," *Journal of Canadian Studies* 46, no. 2 (Spring 2012): 105.

61 Newlove, "Why Do You Hate Me?" in *Lies*, 80.

62 Marilyn Dumont, "having said nothing, yet," in *green girl dreams Mountains* (Lantzville: Oolichan, 2001), 62.

63 Tim Lilburn, "The Provisional Shack of the Ear," interview by Shawna Lemay, in *Where the Words Come From*, ed. Tim Bowling (Roberts Creek: Nightwood, 2002), 181.

64 Crozier, "Names of Loss and Beauty," in *What the Living*, 3.

a new perception of familiar things: "So the birds sound different here. / So the poplars and the wind. . . ."[65]

HONOURING SETTLERS/HONOURING PRE-SETTLERS

Both Brandt and Suknaski are caught in the tension of honouring two histories: settler and Aboriginal—a tension I discussed earlier. Brandt, with her close contact with Aboriginal writers, is particular sensitive to this doubleness. Referring to the section of *Jerusalem, beloved* entitled 'those of us who have daughters,' she notes: It "is predominantly about the prairie landscape, which I recognized more clearly and urgently after my journey to Palestine as also colonized, occupied land."[66] Suknaski, too, is keenly aware of the paradox of his responsibility to honour both his settler ancestors and the Aboriginal peoples on whose land his ancestors settled.[67]

NATURE/CULTURE: WILDERNESS/GARRISON

The shift in prairie poetry—from describing a hostile wilderness against which people were struggling ineffectively, to a vision of the prairie landscape as freeing and restorative—may be due in part to the disappearance of true wilderness in what is now an almost totally humanized landscape. We no longer have to fear the wild, but we have many reasons to escape from the "wild" city to what is left of the wild landscape, tamed as it is and lacking many of the features that once made it fearful. Nonetheless, our relationship with nature remains paradoxical. As I've noted in the previous chapter "Parallax: Race, Gender, and Location," Crozier reverses the normal association of security in the garrison, and chaos and fear in the wild. She celebrates the freedom of the wild and denounces the patriarchal view that sees security in the order and control of the garrison. She takes this reversal back to the Garden of Eden in "Original Sin."

She pictures the Garden of Eden as lush and fruitful, but in its shadows, she realizes it is a place of bondage and of female servitude.[68] Only outside the ordered garden can freedom be found—a place beyond the

---

65 Crozier, *Bones in Their Wings*, 29.

66 Brandt, "Because, because, because," in *Dancing Naked*, 152.

67 Margaret Laurence wrestled with a similar tension in "Sources," *Mosaic* 3, no. 3 1970: 80–84.

68 Crozier, "Original Sin," in *Apocrypha of Light*, 20-21.

control of Adam and his hard naming. It is in the outlier's place, beyond law and order, where poetry and silence are to be found.

Female poets in general have been in the forefront of countering the patriarchal view that led to the garrison/wilderness binary, and the control of nature by celebrated culture. Brandt comments on this departure from mainstream poetry:

> Diana Relke's study, *Greenwor(l)ds*, argues that women poets did not ever buy into [Northrop] Frye's idea of a garrison mentality, and in fact have always celebrated a much more ecopoetically intimate relationship with the land than the men have (postmodernism in that sense arguably has a different meaning for the women than the men, too, in that we came to modernism as first and foremost a liberation into public subjectivity rather than post-industrial alienation and machine-based futurism, as was true for a lot of the men.)[69]

Relke's study of Dorothy Livesay's early poetry confirms the early appearance of this view: "Livesay creates a special role for the woman poet—a role not limited to the articulation of female experience but expanded to include the task of mediating the conflict between culture and nature."[70] She continues, "For Livesay, the tasks involved in transforming this state of mutual alienation into mutual cooperation are twofold. First, she must explode the illusion that culture can possess nature; we may invade it and occupy it but this does not mean that we know it on its own terms. Getting to know nature on its own terms is the second task."[71] What does it mean to know nature on its own terms? Do we shrug off the advances of culture and attempt to unite with nature in some sort of utopian fantasy? What Relke seems to imply, rather, is the importance of being sensitive to nature's limits—of asking, as it were, what will nature allow.

Di Brandt's powerful and evocative essay "The Poet and the Wild City" also reverses the garrison/wilderness dichotomy by contrasting the security of an ordered, controlled rural landscape with life in the

---

69 Di Brandt, e-mail to the author, April 13, 2003. See Relke, *Greenwor(l)ds*, 207–209.

70 Relke, *Greenwor(l)ds*, 143.

71 Ibid., 148–49.

chaotic urban landscape.[72] She becomes the "wild" card in this paradoxical reversal.

STIMULUS TO WRITE/FAILURE OF LANGUAGE

Another paradox is that the poet's urge to write about the prairie landscape co-exists and is in constant tension with the inability of language to adequately and accurately express the paradoxical "truth" about the landscape. John Newlove expresses it this way:

How curiously we deceive ourselves.

There is no consolation to be had anywhere for this.
There is always so much more to be said than can be said.[73]

Elsewhere he writes:

men roaming
as beasts seen through dips
in history, fostered by legend,
invented remembrance. Scenes shake,

the words do not suffice.[74]

Cooley suggests that the difficulty lies in the duplicities of language:

because a word spreads & slides
like cheese whiz
never lines up
with the world (there but for I
go i) & if they did
how would we know
they werent/ lying
slippery as fish
you cant lay a hand on them.[75]

Crozier points out that no matter how perfect the words may be, they fail to faithfully evoke the simple wonders of nature:

---

72 Brandt, "The Poet and the Wild City," 90–91.

73 Newlove, "When I Heard of the Friend's Death," in *Black Night Window*, 63.

74 Newlove, "The Prairie," in *The Cave*, 35.

75 Cooley, "the taboo on saying what you dont," in *Perishable Light*, 55.

you with your perfect words
cannot make the rustling
of wind-rippled wheat
cannot reply to the coyote's howl
cannot call like the meadowlark
from the fenceposts
of your boundaries.[76]

The cowboy poet Brian Brannon comments, perhaps less elegantly, on the failure of language to express his feelings about the landscape: "And though these words do fill my soul, / they'll not to paper come / In such a way, to homage pay / their representing sum."[77]

According to Lilburn, language is an act of creation, and its failure prevents the creation of a perfect, or at least a better, parallel world: "world next / to the world, a garden that would appear if the word were found."[78] Zwicky suggests that her quest for the "perfect word" is linked to another paradox—the tension between the material and the non-material—and if she could find that perfect word she would "nail / mind to the world."[79] The tension between the need to write and the failure of language to fully communicate the poet's feelings is not limited to the prairie poet, of course, but the immensities of space and sky pose unique challenges in this regard. T. E. Hulme, on the other hand, found that the "flat spaces and wide horizons of the virgin prairie" provided a stimulus to write.[80]

My own assessment after examining the poetry arising from this region is that while language may fail, or at least prove inadequate, the landscape never ceases to provide stimuli for poets in their attempts to respond to it. Their efforts, at base, revolve around particular and precise ways of observing local details and fundamental elements of the prairie landscape. It is Crozier's "soul-seeing" in her descriptions of animals;

---

76 Uher [Crozier], "Writing is All But," in *Inside Is the Sky*, 5.

77 Brian Brannon, "The Tchaikazuan," in Mike Puhallo, Brian Brannon and Wendy Liddle, *Can't Stop Rhymin' on the Range* (Surrey: Hancock, 1997), 56.

78 Lilburn, "There is no Presence," in *To the River*, 11.

79 Zwicky, " The Geology of Norway," *Songs for Relinquishing the Earth*, 35.

80 "[T]he first time I ever felt the necessity or inevitableness of verse, was in the desire to produce the peculiar quality of feeling which is induced by the flat spaces and wide horizons of the virgin prairie of Western Canada." T. E. Hulme, quoted by Peter Jones, ed., in his introduction to *Imagist Poetry* (Harmondsworth: Penguin, 1972), 15.

it is Lilburn's "thick looking"[81] and "contemplative attention,"[82] which sees inwardly and clearly what is embedded in the natural world; and it is Zwicky's "ontological attention,"[83] which reveals the symbolic in the material world. This intent observation is not constrained by the material, the concrete. It ranges into and beyond the visible to apprehend what the visible might obscure or represent. This kind of seeing precedes the imaginative transformation and voicing that takes place in the poem.[84] The poetry, then, comes from poets immersing themselves in the experience of intense observation and transforming that perception through imaginative language. The task is not easy. As Mandel says:

> expecting always
> a rocket metaphor
> blazing over an unexplored interior
>
> I find only
> this damp fuse
> of an unlit simile
> lying like a shoelace
> on the familiar sidewalk of my mind.[85]

UTILITY OF POETRY

Adopting a double perspective is key to dealing with paradox, for, as the poet Czesław Miłosz points out, "The purpose of poetry is to remind us / how difficult it is to remain just one person, / for our house is open, there are no keys in the doors, / and invisible guests come in and out at will."[86] Several of the poets whose work I have discussed feel a need to be, in a sense, two people, to adopt some form of doubleness. Crozier often uses the images of a divided self, a lost twin, or a doppelganger to characterize her perspective on life, as well as landscape

---

81 Lilburn, "The Provisional Shack of the Ear," 181.

82 Lilburn, "Poetry's Practice of Philosophy," *Prairie Fire* 23, 3 (Autumn 2002): 33–40.

83 Jan Zwicky, *Wisdom & Metaphor* (Kentville: Gaspereau, 2003), 57 Left.

84 See Lorna Crozier, "Afterword: See How Many Ends This Stick Has," in *Before the First Word: The Poetry of Lorna Crozier*, sel. Catherine Hunter (Waterloo: Wilfrid Laurier Press, 2005), 55–60.

85 Mandel, "Poetic Process," in *The Other Harmony*, Vol. 1, 29.

86 Czesław Miłosz, "Ars Poetica?", *The Collected Poems* (Hopewell: Ecco Press, 1988), 212.

and its creatures.[87] Dyck, as I have noted earlier, describes Newlove as a binary character, and Mandel's well-known obsession with doubleness permeates much of his poetry. Suknaski and Brandt both grapple with the double burden of honouring their ancestors and the Aboriginal culture that their ancestors displaced.

This same double perspective is crucial to the task of regional geographers, who strive to comprehend regions such as the prairies, for we too must learn "the secrets of seeing double" and must have our "binary dreams" if we are to have the "luxury of comparing landscapes."[88] We stand with one foot in the scientific tradition, which provides some basic measures of "reality" and understanding, and the other foot in the artistic tradition, which seeks a reality beyond that which can be quantified. One perspective adds rigour; the other adds imaginative richness and depth. We seek to incorporate both in an analysis that presents the region as a complete entity—a fully realized whole. In our presentation, we want, as Crozier's wants, the words we use to be both tame and wild—domesticated by scientific precision but wild with artistic imagination and emotion.

Erica Jong suggests that a purely scientific view of the world is at best incomplete, and at worst barren: "scientists measure / only what is measurable / & leave out, therefore, the whole world."[89] Denise Levertov imagines John Ruskin's internal tension, raised by his struggle to accommodate both an artistic and a scientific perspective, as he looks at a Yosemite landscape:

> Imagine him in Yosemite. Would loyalties already divided
> —Rock Simple or Rock Wrought,
> strata of mountains, strata of human craft,
> tools of Geology or tools of Art—have split him?
> Would wilderness, legends unknown, or if known offering
> no toe-hold for his mind's expectant footing,
> have swept him wholly into its torrents of non-human grandeur?

---

87 "To be doppelganger, / the soft underside of wings, / the part of cumulus that slides / thin promises of rain across the wheat. // To disappear. To be blue / simply because snow has fallen / and it's the blue hour of the day." Crozier, "Shadow," in *Whetstone*, 22.

88 See notes 4, 5, 6 on page 2.

89 Erica Jong, "Explanations," in *At the Edge of the Body* (New York: Holt, Rinehart & Winston, 1979), 33.

Or wouldn't Art have pulled him back in the end
to layered history felt in the bones,
(even Geology a fraction of that insistence, loved
for its poetry of form, color, textures,
not as a scientist loves it)?
Back to where human hands created
. . . .
Back to where Nature—even the Alps, still so remote,
unsung through so many centuries—

lay in the net or nest of perception,
seen then re-seen, recognized, wrought in myth.[90]

Literature, then, offers a window through which we can see and accommodate both perspectives. Prairie poets, dealing as they do with the paradoxes of prairie landscape and life, can suggest ways of dealing with the enigmas of the prairie region. They underline the need to search for the "between-ness" of the truth about this region, and of recognizing that there is always a tension between knowing and not knowing.[91]

In engaging the paradox of love and hate, poets remind us that the emotional bonds that people make to the prairie landscape are far more complex than a simple correlation between hating and leaving, or loving and staying. They involve ambivalent feelings not only toward the land but toward one's place in that landscape as well—feeling at home or out of place. Similarly, poets treat life and death not as opposites but as intertwined realities, both in landscape and in life, which reflects the inclusiveness of imagination rather than the narrow focus of reason. The paradox of life and death exists constantly in the landscape itself. The landscape is simultaneously being created and destroyed—it is constantly "carrying the shadow," in Friesen's analogy, bearing in itself the seeds of life and death, of birth and destruction. In the end, as Wallace Stegner suggests, "eternity is a peneplain"[92]—a landscape in which life and death, as well as tectonic and erosional forces, are in balance.

Prairie poets point out that the relationship between nature and culture, between country and city, has not only changed through time but has become less clear, become more intertwined as urban values

90 Levertov, "The Faithful Lover," in *Evening Train*, 20–21.

91 Friesen, "Gathering Bones."

92 Stegner, "The Question Mark in the Circle," in *Wolf Willow*, 7.

invade the countryside and as nature is brought into the city. These poets continue to praise the rural landscape and (usually) denigrate what they see as an artificial urban landscape,[93] but they do so while living in an urban environment, a paradox raised at least 15 years ago by Linda Warley, et al.[94]

Wallace Stegner's "question mark in the circle" suggests a relationship between humans and the environment.[95] Humans may be "challenging upright things" in the vast circle of the prairie, but their relationship to the land is enigmatic.[96] After all, they are question marks rather than exclamation marks, bent over, looking at the ground for answers, either in the land or in the memory of the land. Poets can help us make sense of these enigmas. They remind us of the need to see both sides of a paradox and, once we have seen "double," to "swallow [them] whole,"[97] to accept them both as much a part of the prairie landscape as the land and sky. The prairie is a region grounded in myth and memory, as well as mimesis and measurement—a region where story is inextricably intertwined with landscape, where people's relationships to the prairie are paradoxical and ambivalent. Poetry can help us understand these realities.

---

93 George Melnyk argues that the old antinomies of city and countryside should be revised, claiming that the quantity and quality of nature in present-day prairie cities should make for a much more positive view of the city. It is worth noting, however, that "natural" elements are the means of producing this revised perception, not the cityscape itself. George Melnyk, "The Urban Prairie: Between Jerusalem and Babylon," in *New Moon*, 63–115.

94 Linda Warley, John Clement Ball, and Robert Viau, "Introduction: Mapping the Ground," in *Studies in Canadian Literature* 23, no. 1 (1998), https://journals.lib.unb.ca/index.php/SCL/article/view/8270/9333.

95 Stegner, "The Question Mark in the Circle," in *Wolf Willow*, 8.

96 Ibid.

97 Newlove, "Resources, Certain Earths," in *Moving In Alone*, 74.

CHAPTER 5

Beyond Paradox: Mystery and Silence

If paradox is the essence of people's relationship to the prairie landscape, then mystery is a paradox so profound as to be beyond the reach of understanding and language. As psychologist Paul Pruyser says, "mystery is a borderland situation in which something both powerfully reveals and powerfully conceals itself, and its self-concealment is a feature of its essence."[1] In the poets' work I have considered, mystery is most often associated with some form of spirituality; it is the unknown that is experienced but is unseen. It is mystery which apprehends the spiritual, which "powerfully reveals itself" in the vitality of the feelings it provokes, and which is, paradoxically, "self-concealing" by remaining hidden and inexplicable. Acknowledging mystery or spirituality is an essential aspect of being human. Patrick Lane puts it this way: "The spiritual is always at hand, felt, and resonant in us. Of all binding human concerns the spiritual is the greatest because it strives to take us to the past and future of our mortality, that which lies beyond us. The transformation the poet reaches for rests in language and its ability (combined with his craft) to surround that mystery, not explaining it, but articulating its existence."[2]

The poet's pursuit, then, is to articulate the mystery of things not seen but variously encountered, and the connections between imma-

1 Paul Pruyser, *Between Belief and Unbelief* (New York: Harper & Row, 1974), 104.

2 Patrick Lane, "A Brooding Upon the Heart of Things," interview by Russell Thorn-

nence and transcendence, between the numinous and the commonplace, and between the "red heart and the blue wind."[3] My particular concern is with the presence of mystery in the landscape, and the poets I consider most often sense it in the way landscape embodies or connects with some form of spirituality. The terms *spiritual* and *spirituality* are used and interpreted in a variety of ways. Here it is used in a broader way than the conventional religious usage, and refers to a sense of otherness in something or someone transcendently beyond ourselves.

Wind, light, and expanse—three significant elements of the prairie landscape that are often associated with the spiritual—are well represented in the poets' work, but they also consider the spiritual as it exists in the plants and animals of the living landscape of the prairies. In an interview with Elizabeth Philips, Lorna Crozier says:

> I write about common things to get at the uncommon, the spiritual. For me it's finding the numinous in the actual, in the material. . . . The nexus between what you know and what you'll never know, something coming close to you and then dancing away. The poem flickers in the middle of those two movements. Sometimes what's holy is how the light falls on the tomato sitting on your windowsill. It's that small and that fleeting. That simple and that complex."[4]

Crozier's poetry bears this out; in it there is a haunting and expectant sense of spiritual encounters in the landscape. For Crozier, the free spirit is found in wild and untamed (and unnamed) nature—spirituality exists in wildness, although not in the ordinary sense. She writes about the time her Uncle Jack took her, a "city kid," out into nature to find the land's "wild places," where "the spirits of the earth, / if they still exist, / might dwell." This in sharp contrast with "what was broken, / the acres the other uncles fought over / when Grandfather died."[5] The endless land and sky of the prairie landscape is freighted with mystery and spiritual intimations. In an early poem, Crozier uses the image of a horse to portray the spiritual in the landscape:

---

ton, in Bowling, *Where the Words Come From*, 73.

3 Friesen, "anna first dance," in *You Don't Get*, 5.

4 Crozier, "Seeing Distance: Lorna Crozier's Art of Paradox," 152.

5 Crozier, "Time to Praise," in *Inventing the Hawk*, 91–92.

> It is a place
>   that demands
> the dream
>
>   : here a spirit
>   flares its wide nostrils
>   streaks the sky with
>   its mane."[6]

And in "Rebuttal to the Higher Power," the ordinary growth of prairie grass is endowed with hints of the spiritual: "Through hollow stems, grass siphons / the can't-be-seen // and sends it out ignited."[7]

Crozier's Mrs. Bentley observes:

> What's most like the prairie
> is the mind of God, the huge way
> he must have of looking at the world.
> That's why I feel small and scared
> inside myself, and yet at times
> full of wonder.[8]

The paradox of spirit in the material parallels her own paradoxical response of both fear and wonder.

Both cultural and physical landscapes are tinged with the spiritual in her poem "The Dark Ages of the Sea":

> It was a time of farms
> across the grasslands,
> ancient lakes
> that lay beneath them,
> and a faith in things
> invisible, be it water
> never seen or something
> trembling in the air.[9]

Snow, the most common element of the winter landscape, "prays" as the intermediary between the mysteries of life and death: "It closes the gap

---

6 Uher [Crozier], "Sand Hills," in *Crow's Black Joy*, 49–50.
7 Crozier, "Rebuttal to the Higher Power," in *Whetstone*, 40.
8 Crozier, "Wilderness," in *A Saving Grace*, 77–78.
9 Crozier, "The Dark Ages of the Sea," in *Everything Arrives*, 38.

/ between drought and plenty, belief and blasphemy, / the ear and silence."[10]

Allusions to the divine are also bound up with the animal world. Crozier, whose "soul-seeing" is especially evident in her animal poetry, invests familiar creatures with a presence that exists beyond their visible form. In "A Prophet in His Own Country," the ubiquitous gopher, which as the poem's title suggests has no honour on the prairie, twitches beside his hole, "taut with holiness and fright." He is a "dusty Lazarus" going into darkness and rising, again and again, but "[h]e won't tell us / what he's seen."[11] A star-nosed mole "who tunnels through the dark" has a "Damascus road" experience and "thinks he is the chosen one, / all his paths suddenly / diffused with light."[12] Crozier finds prayers in the paw prints in the snow along a fence line and, following the advice of Teresa of Ávila, learns to read them "in poor light and in good."[13] In "The Souls of Animals" she suggests that animal and human souls might not be all that different:

> That's what those bright ones are,
> those people we glimpse with a glow about them,
> an ecstasy. The souls of animals
> crossing from one country to another,
> pausing for a moment among us
> only to rise in glory,
> beasts again.[14]

Animals are endowed with supernatural powers. The spirit fox,

> [p]aws hushed by snow,
> by prairie wool...
> steps just behind you. You feel
> its gaze on the back of your neck
>
> and you're afraid to turn
> into the green flint of its stare
> you know will see too much of you
> and leave nothing out.[15]

---

10 Crozier, "Prayers of Snow," in *Whetstone*, 11.

11 Crozier, "A Prophet in His Own Country," in *Apocrypha of Light*, 13.

12 Crozier, "The Garden at Night," in *Everything Arrives*, 105.

13 Crozier, "How the mind works, works, works," in *Apocrypha of Light*, 75.

14 Crozier, "The Souls of Animals," in *Everything Arrives*, 71–72.

15 Crozier, "The Spirit Fox," in *What the Living*, 20.

Crozier's Mrs. Bentley expresses a somewhat rebellious longing for the old wild gods of the past—horse god, wind god, god of light, rain god—and muses that the rain god

> must be
> female, a four-legged animal
> with soft paws and swishing tail
> for that's what we hear
> when she comes near us
> for her green communion
> with the grass.[16]

The term "communion" both heightens the sense of an earthy spirituality and expresses an intimate spiritual connection. Grass and wind are angel presences in the physical world—"Their feet . . . / interpret each blade of grass, / an exegesis of the earth"[17]—and in the animal world—

> Maybe that was the blessing:
> the cat purring in the shadow
> of the angel's wings,
> the apples on fire
> in their usual way
> in the apple tree
>
> the wind
> touching everything
> at the same time.[18]

A whole suite of poems on angels in Crozier's *Apocrypha of Light* brings a sense of the divine to ordinary, earthly things. The entire volume focuses on the mystical combination of human and divine, of matter and spirit, but Crozier reverses the human/divine dichotomy by elevating humanity and its foibles and reducing the divine to human terms.

Whereas Crozier sees landscape as a place for encountering some form of spirituality, Tim Lilburn sees the possibility of experiencing a vision of God within nature itself, if only a purified desire and a

16 Crozier, "Country Dweller," in *A Saving Grace*, 8–9.
17 Crozier, "The Language of Angels," in *Inventing the Hawk*, 62.
18 Crozier, "Angel of Infinity," in *Angels of Flesh*, 37.

self-emptying humility are focused in a "thick looking"[19] at nature's elements. Lilburn finds everything "odoured with infinity,"[20] in contrast to Zwicky's view that all beauty is "rimed with death."[21] Lilburn's God-infused nature is not silent; landscape speaks in multiple voices:

> Listen to prairie, rasp of root
> curling round bone, clawing.
> Listen to air,
> to wings, spirit cousins, ancestors
> becoming, by centuries' stealth,
> the beat of all God-wanting hearts.[22]

Animals, too, embody this incarnation:

> Two coyotes slouch-jog out of the moth-coloured trees down to the river
> after supper, jive-dekes, weightless as Amway sales talk,
> a garage sale of moves.
> This is the life of light in matter.
> This is the flesh.[23]

He writes that this is "Blake's marriage, / whelping the tigerish heart, this wedding of vagabond light / and beaconed matter, spirit and muscle," and he suggests that the desire to fully participate is like God "cannibalizing" the poet.[24] He unites the seen and unseen in an eloquent plea for us to listen to nature telling us what we really need to know about life:

> I have no doubt the poplars, masters and mandarins of sleep, could give them to us
> chapter and verse, and tell us of all this together, the world, the whole
> seen and unseen, how it's
> ingeniously physical, and how it makes sense, not by doing anything, not by using
> some bloody verb, but just by growing fatter each day with variety
> as when magpies pass a song through the trees at 6:00 am like a basketball
> at a Harlem Globetrotters warm-up.[25]

---

19 Lilburn, "The Provisional Shack of the Ear," 181.

20 Lilburn, "Paradise of the Cells," in *Moosewood Sandhills*, 47.

21 Zwicky, "Practising Bach," in *Forge*, 24, 25.

22 Lilburn, "A Common Language," in *Names of God*, 32.

23 Lilburn, "Solo on Orthodoxy," in *Moosewood Sandhills*, 32.

24 Lilburn, "Grim Invocations: V," in *Names of God*, 76.

25 Lilburn, "Touching an Elephant in a Dark Room," in *Tourist to Ecstasy*, 46.

Lilburn points out that many are blind to the numinous in nature: "they [Byzantine theologians] squint like worms in the blasting light. Yet they fail to see / earth dream itself flame."[26] But can this mystery be fully articulated? Apparently not: "Your tongue curls double / in your mouth and utters, once, *nothing.* / *Mystika nou* / Treasure this unknowing."[27]

Lilburn continues his long exploration in *Moosewood Sandhills,* as with fixed intensity he desires to find that a true vision of nature is indeed a vision of God. He uses the image of deer eating grass in a double paradox, suggesting not only the unity of eater and eaten, but the paradoxical unity of God in the flesh. In the end, Lilburn concludes that it is the desire itself that is critical, and he quotes Gregory of Nyssa, who said that the desire to see God is itself the vision of God.[28]

In Lilburn's long meditation *To the River,* the objective elements of landscape assume mystical proportions. He expresses a persistent desire to see the landscape from the inside out, to somehow get inside the elements, or to arrive at a union of spirit and matter through attentive observation, openness, and humility.

Patrick Friesen also seeks to understand "how to speak once more about the flesh and the spirit / the red heart and the blue wind."[29] His work is energized by the paradox of incarnation—the spirit made flesh. "Spirit suffused in matter, not separate, not inhabiting," he writes. "The physical object alive, not merely technically, not as a vessel, but shot through with light. Not a lamp carrying oil, but a wick on fire. No fire without matter."[30] Friesen's search, "from womb to shambles," is concerned with the mystery of the space—the moment, the silence—that connects supposed opposites. He looks for the place "between touch and ghost."[31] In "st. mary at main" he writes, "we're all silhouettes in the window / trying to make ends meet / body and soul // as they say."[32] Words themselves are a dance between spirit and material—between ephem-

26 Lilburn, "St. Dionysius the Areopagite: Six Letters to Timothy: III," in *Names of God,* 29.

27 Lilburn, "St. Dionysius the Areopagite: Six Letters to Timothy: II," in *Names of God,* 28.

28 Lilburn, "Acknowledgements," in *Moosewood Sandhills,* 68.

29 Friesen, "anna first dance," in *You Don't Get,* 5.

30 Friesen, "Gathering Bones," 14.

31 Friesen, "bluebottle," in *bluebottle,* 9.

32 Friesen, "st. mary at main," in *st. mary at main,* 90.

eral sound and material print: "I love words in the air balanced between mouths and ears I / love the way they're smoke before they're stone."[33]

Friesen seeks to understand this more within himself than in nature, although there are suggestions of this connection with nature in several of his poems. He ends a detailed description of a red-winged blackbird in a willowy marsh with a reference to "the old story of angel / finally happy in the wings / of matter."[34] He muses, "all the words and rhymes are rain or wind a common book of prayer or john donne from the pulpit."[35]

> [O]n the prairies you walk through
> god's breath most of your life
> if that's how you think of it
> and the red tail soars
> and long grasses sway
> and you're never any further
> down the road.[36]

He speaks of many gods, including "those among the aspen / and those in fields of wheat."[37] Landscape elements seem to coexist with, or be connected to, a sense of the divine: "sometimes it's a long wait for water there is rain and there is drought and there is god."[38]

A more extended example is found in the clearing poems of *the breath you take from the lord*, in which Friesen interweaves the physical clearing and its spiritual implications. The clearing is a made thing; it "is not nature the hand has touched it."[39] But it is also a place of spiritual awareness, of the divine just barely seen "out of the corner of your eye," as it were. It is a place of visibility and light, a place that combines an opening of the landscape and an opening of human awareness, a "clearing away" of the bush which conceals, a place where "the air stirs shifting from one silence to another something about to happen."[40] Here "there is room for a mind between the high prairie sky and this scrappy under-

---

33 Friesen, "anna second dance," in *You Don't Get*, 18.
34 Friesen, "columbine," in *Earth's Crude Gravities*, 96.
35 Friesen, "st. michael & all angels," in *st. mary at main*, 50.
36 Friesen, "wind," in *Earth's Crude Gravities*, 30.
37 Friesen, "so many gods," in *Earth's Crude Gravities*, 40.
38 Friesen, "quartet in july," in *Earth's Crude Gravities*, 15.
39 Friesen, "clearing poem 6," in *the breath you take*, 22.
40 Friesen, "clearing poem 1," in *the breath you take*, 12.

growth."[41] Friesen speaks of himself as a man in search of the divine: "you are a man you don't know how else to say it you are a man who has always sought god."[42] In the end, after mysterious and ambiguous sightings and soundings of "the lord," Friesen concludes, "you stand alone next thing to heaven and nothing there but hawk and mind,"[43] left with a sense of motion connecting the flesh with an intimation of something beyond flesh.

Di Brandt's attention to spirituality in the landscape is similar to that of Sharon Butala: both sense a palpable spiritual presence in the landscape. Brandt's connection to the mystery of the land is tied to her love of the prairie landscape and to her identification with the Aboriginal people's experience of the spirit in landscape. She describes one of the pleasures of her childhood as "being able to feel the wildness of the prairie very strongly, as a kind of voice, a singing, all around me," and laments the loss of this kind of "magic."[44] Similarly, she also notes sadly that "the memory of the old time, before the arrival of the white settlers, the old Indian time, is almost gone."[45] She identifies with the old spirits of the Aboriginal peoples in the landscape,[46] but admits that her connection cannot be as intimate as theirs, for their beliefs include past lives as elements of the landscape.[47] She acknowledges "the spirit of the lake" and "the wounded outrage of gulls, herons, / no longer recognized as angels, winged spirit / messengers." This powerful lake god fills her "with awe, & desire," and

> i'm scared, filled to overflowing
> with the great furious roar of this lake, this angry god,
> proud spirit, who in spite of lovers, in spite of prayers,
> chemicals, spirit killers, will not be tamed, or harnessed
> or subdued.
>
> ever.[48]

---

41 Ibid., 11.

42 Ibid.

43 Friesen, "clearing poem 25," in *the breath you take*, 50.

44 Brandt, "'The Sound the Wind Makes,'" 118.

45 Ibid.

46 See for example, Brandt, *Jerusalem, beloved*, 68.

47 Brandt, interview by the author, September 17, 2012.

48 Brandt, "making love to the spirit of the lake," in *Jerusalem, beloved*, 68.

Clearly, for Brandt, there is more at work in the landscape than meets the eye.

The other poets have less to say about the interaction of spirit and material, at least as it relates to the prairie landscape. Andrew Suknaski focuses on Aboriginal myths and spirituality, particularly in *Octomi*, and notes the close connection between spirit and prairie in Aboriginal life:

> manitou
> 'the great spirit'
> as the santees
> of these southern prairie hills knew
> the sioux word
> also meaning
> 'the prairie'
>
> spirit and prairie
> one.[49]

Dennis Cooley alludes to the spiritual in the prairie landscape—"in fall the fields of flax / from the mouth of night / spun over / night into gold // & the sky & the wind / & the spirits spurt"—but this is a limited and relatively isolated example.[50] John Newlove may be thinking of the spiritual when he comments on the restless search for some "almost seen / god or food or earth or word."[51] His "fleshly trees"[52] suggest something beyond mere "tree-life," and he allows for the possibility that trees could have some sort of moral sentience:

> The green trees grow from year to year
> and seem to have no thoughts
> although I hear it said
> they scream when we kill before them.[53]

Eli Mandel's poetry is peppered with religious references but these are unrelated to a spirituality of the landscape.

---

49 Suknaski, "Manitou," in *Octomi*, 7.

50 Dennis Cooley, "Exorcism," in *Soul Searching* (Red Deer: Red Deer College Press, 1987), 21.

51 Newlove, "The Prairie," in *The Cave*, 35.

52 Newlove, "The Last Event," in *The Cave*, 39.

53 Newlove, "Notes From and Among the Wars, 13," in *Lies*, 44.

SILENCE AND ABSENCE

Silence is a response to a variety of experiences. The paradoxes treated in the previous chapter are "contra-dictions." They leave us without words. Mystery has the same effect: "our first reaction to it is silence, muteness, dumbness. It forces us to 'shut up'—at least for a moment."[54] The qualification, of course, is "at least for a moment," for poets do not remain silent for long. In the focused attentiveness that precedes the writing of poetry, there is both the realization that the essence of the thing observed is beyond articulation and poetry's "oceanic thirst" to attempt the impossible.[55] Silence may be the inability of language to express mystery, but as Friesen points out, silence can also be a withholding of words.[56] As the Russian poet Anna Akhmatova demonstrates, this silence can be a powerful form of protest and a way to identify with those who are forced into silence; it is the silence of being.[57] Diana Relke makes a similar point with respect to the way silence appears in women's poetry as a form of protest against patriarchal dominance.[58]

Then there is the silence of the land. If we accept Al Purdy's view, the land is silent until we give voice to it. Newlove expresses a similar view: "Outside / everything is gone; the white / sheer land answers no questions, / but only exists."[59] Other poets disagree. Friesen remembers his time on the prairies as a constant conversation with the landscape. Even in his own silence, motion of mind and wind involved all his senses.[60] Glen Downie opines, "The land is what speaks / and will not be spoken to,"[61] but elsewhere he writes, "The land ignores us all / and goes on breathing / eons in and out."[62] Aboriginal poets, too, would disagree with Purdy: they hold the land's communication in high regard and respond to its wisdom.

---

54 Pruyser, *Between Belief*, 104.

55 "The only reason we like poetry is because it does attempt to deal with the unknowable." Kristjana Gunners, "Meditation on a Snowy Morning: A Conversation With Robert Kroetsch," *Prairie Fire* 8, no. 4 (Winter 1987/88): 54–67. The phrase "oceanic thirsts of poetry" is from Don McKay, "Chickadee Encounter," in *Apparatus* (Toronto: McClelland & Stewart, 1997), 10.

56 Patrick Friesen, "Silence," in *Interim: Essays and Mediations* (Regina: Hagios, 2006), 15.

57 Friesen, "anna first dance," in *You Don't Get*, 4.

58 Relke, *Greenwor(l)ds*, 47.

59 Newlove, "East from the Mountains," in *Moving in Alone*, 50.

60 Friesen, e-mail to the author, March 22, 2014.

61 Downie, "Rubble Creek," in *Heartland*, 48.

62 Downie, "Calling Cards," in *Heartland*, 51.

According to Lilburn, the land only appears silent because people are not listening. As I have noted earlier, Lilburn understands that the land speaks in multiple voices, and several kinds of silence are required to hear its voices and interact with it. Silence and "alert craning"[63] within that silence form a state of deprivation that, for him, precedes writing. Silence as preparation. Silence is also "deference to the otherness of one's experience," a sense that other things can speak for themselves without the poet speaking for them.[64] Silence as respect. Language is insufficient for accessing the soul of nature: "You lie down in the deer's bed . . . the place where / language buries itself."[65] Silence as spiritual humility. As American poet Theodore Roethke says, "The self says, I am; / The heart says, I am less; / The spirit says, you are nothing."[66] An emptiness of the flesh accentuates spiritual acuity. In an early set of poems, Lilburn speaks of silence as having an "eloquent body"; it is "an intense dark, living, personed, / fecund, an intense dark everywhere, / inside things."[67]

Walter Ong points out that in the passionate desire for literacy, some aspects of the oral culture must die in order to take on this new life.[68] Perhaps the leap from literacy to silence is similar in that poets have to (temporarily) abandon words, at least with respect to their self-referential utility, in order to live in the richness and meaning of silence.

Crozier points to the union of spirituality, silence, and landscape by suggesting that the natural elements of air, grass, and earth are interpretations of the unseen and unspoken presence of angels:

> Their marvellous mouths say nothing,
> say nothing. What you hear is
> their silence. It falls through the seven
> celestial spheres, gathers in the dark
> behind the rock they rolled from the tomb.
> Here their wings translate the air.
> Their feet, more beautiful than any Homer knew,
> interpret each blade of grass,

---

63 Lilburn, "The Provisional Shack of the Ear," 180.

64 Ibid.

65 Lilburn, "Contemplation is Mourning," in *Moosewood Sandhills*, 16.

66 Theodore Roethke, "What Can I Tell My Bones?" in *Words for the Wind: The Collected Verse of Theodore Roethke* (Bloomington: University of Indiana Press, 1964), 210.

67 Lilburn, "St. Dionysius the Areopagite: Six Letters to Timothy, I," in *Names of God*, 28.

68 Ong, *Orality and Literacy*, 15.

an exegesis of the earth. Words,
thoughts, senses are all one body,
the body before you that burns.
All flesh these
words, these extravagant mouths,
mute as swans."[69]

In another poem, angels speak "just below / the threshold of your hearing."[70] Crozier also suggests that silence is related to poetry and attends to that which is beyond human control: "and everything Adam couldn't name / fell into poetry and silence."[71] She celebrates the existence of things without words:

Delight in the small,
those that inhabit
only a corner of the mind,
the ones shaped by wind
and a season: . . .
. . . .
. . . delight
in the small, the silent
whose language lies
in their doing and their
undoing, those who turn
to stone to bone to wing
without a shout of praise
find their perfect form
become imago.[72]

Silence is closely related to absence, particularly in Friesen's poetry. He is intrigued by the near simultaneity of presence and absence, which for him is almost a tangible, visible connection: "a person walking away from you, the space where they've been closing in behind them,"[73] or, "how present absence can be you almost smell it sometimes absence

69 Crozier, "The Language of Angels," in *Inventing the Hawk*, 62.

70 Crozier, "Angels of Silence," in *Angels of Flesh*, 59.

71 Crozier, "Original Sin. 2: The Fall of Eve," in *Apocrypha of Light*, 22.

72 Crozier, "Delight in the Small, the Silent," in *The Garden Going On*, 116–117.

73 Friesen, e-mail to the author, July 2004. Also: "each moment there's a hole where she was but it heals each / moment the air rifts then knits together behind her." Friesen, "the silence of angels," in *You Don't Get*, 41.

isn't absence at all / but memory like the wind wears away at the world and though wind remains memory does not."[74] Sometimes presence arises out of absence, as in Friesen's memories of his father's singing, "filling the spaces just when you realized they were there."[75]

In Friesen's clearing poems, discussed earlier, the clearing is an absence in the landscape, but it is also a presence, not only in the sense of a physical opening in the bush, but also as a memory and an apprehension of something beyond what is visible. Brandt's yearning—"i want to go back to the prairies, / to emptiness, words circling around absence, the / straight horizon, home"[76]—alludes to both the absence of prairie (the prairie is absent as home and is also a place of absence and emptiness) and an absence of words to fully embrace it.

It is perhaps not surprising that absence figures significantly in the poetry of the prairies, considering it is a landscape that is often defined in terms of absences, or at least near absences—absence of trees, absence of rain, absence of significant hills, absence of topographical variety, although this last is more a problem of perception than of reality.

We speak of the spaces between words on a page as absences, and we speak of absences in the landscape where human activity has eliminated or reduced the natural elements. We also speak of the silenced voices of those who are oppressed, marginalized, or ignored. The first is to be respected, and the last is to be freed and heard. As Friesen has said, "if it's chosen / silence is not an enemy,"[77] but when it is forced on someone, it needs to be opposed.

UTILITY FOR GEOGRAPHY

Prairie poets, in their search for the transcendent in the prairie landscape, remind us that there is more to landscape than topography and culture's impress. Their probing and articulation open spaces of investigation beyond vision and voice, spaces often ignored in geographic research. Silence may be the proper response to such mysteries, but poets and geographers alike are only temporarily silenced, and we speak with a language not fully adequate in articulating what we dimly perceive.

---

74 Friesen, "give me flesh and give me wine," in *the breath you take*, 75.

75 Patrick Friesen, "pa poem 7: rehearsing for Sunday," in *Unearthly Horses* (Winnipeg: Turnstone, 1984), 23.

76 Brandt, "waking up in Jerusalem," in *Jerusalem, beloved*, 27.

77 Friesen, "silence," in *You Don't Get*, 57.

We search for Zwicky's "perfect word" to "nail / mind to the world."[78] We seek words that are "smoke before they're stone,"[79] so that when the smoke becomes stone—when the experience of the observer becomes words on a page—reading the words will rekindle the imagination and allow the reader to participate in the feelings and emotions of the writer.

Call it what you will—"alert craning," "thick looking"—we need the experience of *being still* in the prairie landscape, absorbing and being absorbed by its visible and invisible insistences,[80] by its paradoxes and its mysteries, by things unknown or not yet understood. On the open prairie, there is a sense of stillness deeper than a lack of movement; it settles on the soul, and even in the ceaseless wind the stillness of the prairie remains calm, fixed, and unchanging. It is the paradox of a deep unmoving in the midst of a ceaseless movement. On the prairie this solid silence is not broken by the individual sounds of bird song or insects, but rather enhanced by them. Friesen suggests that this mystery is motion, and that even in the midst of silence and stillness the landscape itself is in motion, either in the incessant movement of wind or in the larger sense that Downie observed: "breathing / eons in and out." For Friesen, the observing mind is also in motion, flickering between the known and the unknown.[81]

Geographers look at a landscape of materiality, but they also recognize that there are forces at play that are vital yet unseen, forces that are operating silently and often mysteriously. But there is more here than barely perceptible physical forces. We need to be sensitive in apprehending and accommodating the transcendent in our understanding of the prairies, and in recognizing that landscape elements can be "radiant with grace"[82] and can contain the "woman beauty of distances."[83] To do otherwise will result in a diminished and incomplete understanding of the prairie region.

---

78 Zwicky, "The Geology of Norway," in *Songs for Relinquishing the Earth*, 35.

79 Friesen, "anna second dance," in *You Don't Get*, 18.

80 That is, all of those things which *insist* on being there.

81 Friesen, e-mail to the author, March 22, 2014. This perspective is very much like the thrust of non-representational theory, which takes movement as the central concept in its approach to geography. See Nigel Thrift, *Non-Representational Theory: Space, Politics, Affect* (NY: Routledge, 2007), 5.

82 Mark Abley, "Laying Down the Law," in *Essays on Saskatchewan Writing*, ed. E. F. Dyck (Regina: Saskatchewan Writers Guild, 1986), 165.

83 Tim Lilburn, "Inanna," in *From the Great Above She Opened Her Ear to the Great Below* (Ilderton: Brick Books, 1988), 39.

CHAPTER 6

Public Perception: The Influence of Literary and Popular Poetry

The previous chapters have considered one half of the reciprocal poet/landscape relationship: the influence of the prairie landscape on prairie poetry. My approach has been to identify these influences by assessing how the content of the poetry reflects elements of the physical and cultural landscapes, and then to consider the characteristics of the poets themselves (specifically race, gender, and location) that might influence the way they perceive the landscape. Poets describe the landscape imaginatively, and in so doing transform it, in a sense—making it new. I have also considered the more abstract elements of paradox, mystery, and silence as poets respond to and engage with this landscape. In this chapter, I will consider the other half of the relationship: the influence that the reimagining of the prairie landscape by its poets has on public perceptions of the prairies. I will assess that influence by looking at popular (rather than literary) poetry, and by looking at its relative accessibility to the general public, in terms of the number and type of readers, and by how long it remains in print.

First, I want to acknowledge that contrasting "popular" and "literary" poetry is inherently problematic. How, for example, does one distinguish between literary poetry and popular poetry without suggesting, either overtly or unintentionally, that popular poetry is not literary, or even that it does not have literary value? The lack of critical attention to popular poets like Edna Jaques or to cowboy poetry, both of which

I consider below, suggests that many critics hold this view. Conversely, designating one type of poetry as "popular" suggests that literary poetry is not popular, or at least that it is less popular. Both terms are problematic in that they signify both a genre and a quality. Adding to the dilemma is the lack of a clear distinction between the two: some popular poetry bears the stamp of literary poetry in form and quality, and some literary poetry is popular in the sense of being widely appreciated. In any case, I have chosen to use the terms "literary" and "popular" to distinguish between the two kinds of poetry, though I do not distinguish between good and bad poetry. These qualitative distinctions contribute little to my analysis. I will look at two groups of writing as representative of popular poetry—the poetry of Edna Jaques, a prolific and widely popular poet of the 1930s and 1940s, and cowboy poetry, which arises directly out of the ranching life.

LITERARY AND POPULAR POETRY: SOME GENERAL DISTINCTIONS

Literary poets know both the art and craft of making words sing. They combine rhythm, diction, syntax, acute observation, deep feeling, and imagination to transform the ordinary into the extraordinary and to engage readers' emotions and intellect. Popular poetry, by its very nature, is much more audience-driven. Its appeal is to a more general population, which introduces certain constraints on language, theme, and style. It aims to engage readers, but does so by entertaining them and by appealing to what is familiar and presenting it in a sentimental, patriotic, or humourous way, and often by crafting content to suit a particular occasion—such as a wedding, anniversary, or birthday—or a specific activity, like bronc-riding or calf-roping. Literary poets ask their readers to work through a poem in order to recognize the art and craft embedded there, its nuances of feeling, and its play of language and imagination. Popular poets ask their readers to experience and enjoy the ride. Popular poets direct their creative energy more toward finding appropriate rhymes than to an imaginative transformation of material, often sacrificing rhythm and syntax in the effort.[1] The confession of cowboy

1 The back cover blurb of one book of popular poetry, for example, states that the poet "could be counted upon to come up with a poem for any occasion usually with humour and a personal note." Even Mozart recognized this difficulty: "Verses are indeed the most indispensable element for music—but rhyme—solely for the sake of rhyming—the most detrimental." Quoted in C. Day Lewis, *The Lyric Impulse* (Cam-

poet G. T. Burton could well stand for many others: "I told him I didn't know line from verse about poetry. All I knew was rhyme."[2] Popular poets are encouraged in this aspect of their craft by their audience, who regard the ability to make rhymes as a gift, and a sure indication that the work is indeed poetry. It would, however, be a disservice to many talented folk poets to label them as mere "versifiers."

The genesis of much popular poetry is oral performance, and much of it continues to be performed orally. It relies much more on "sounds in the air" than "words on a page." In this sense, popular poetry represents what Robert Kroetsch calls "the great sub-text of prairie literature": the oral tradition. Repetition is more important than improvisation, and the use of rhyme helps fix the poetry in the listener's mind. The emphasis on orality inhibits the type of language play that is more clearly recognizable on the page. As Laurie Ricou notes, popular literature is defined, in part, "by its direct and untutored quality, which makes it easily read and understood."[3] What emerges then, are works that are carefully predictable, with content designed to comfortably support widely held sentiments of home, lifestyle, and landscape. There is little play of language (although the necessity of rhyme often produces considerable originality) or memorable metaphors. Ordinary language bonds poet and audience in the enjoyment of the poem. Cowboy poets create this same bond using "insider" words and phrases that link the specialized world of ranching to a knowledgeable audience. These are generalizations, of course; many popular poems display imaginative and memorable images.

THE POETRY OF EDNA JAQUES

Folk prairie poet Edna Jaques's enormous popularity and prodigious output puts her in a league of her own, [4] though I would argue that her concerns and methods are common to all popular poets. Jaques's poetry ticks all the boxes of popular poetry; it is written for the general public

---

bridge: Harvard University Press, 1965), 27.

2 G. T. Burton, Introductory comments in *Cow Pies and Candle Lights* (Morris Publishing, 1999).

3 Laurence Ricou, "The Meadowlark Tradition: Popular Verse of the Canadian Prairie," in Cooley, *RePlacing*, 161.

4 She was able to say on her 85th birthday that her books of poetry had sold more than 250,000 copies. Edna Jaques, *Uphill All the Way: The Autobiography of Edna Jaques* (Saskatoon: Western Producer Prairie Books, 1977), 242.

above all else. Her verse avoids any pretense of academic erudition, and it seems she has little concern for literary Canadian poetry and her place in it.[5] Only decades after her death did her poetry attract any serious critical attention.[6]

Jaques's methodology is simple. When, for example, she is faced with "so many universal things," she concludes: "I think I'll make a list."[7] And that she does, in almost every poem, listing new things, old things, clean things, peaceful things, remembered things, and things in old trunks, old button bags, old farmhouses, and old barns. She lists the characteristics of old ladies, old mothers, old sisters, old men, old farmers, old ranchers, old pensioners, old preachers, old Ruthenians, and old maids. Her intended audience is equally clear. These poems are written for people who are "reliable and staid," whose thoughts and minds run "in quiet grooves,"[8] and who, like her, love simple and peaceful things. In poetry as in music, she rejects "high falutin piping thin and hollow" and instead longs for "things we know" that "common folk can hear against their hearts."[9] She reinforces this sentiment in poems like "Country Violin Player" and "The Writer," in which she expresses her desire to touch both "dear earthly things" and "dull and commonplace" people with divinity and grace.[10] These sentiments suggest a dedication to communicate simply with ordinary, workaday people (although they might not have appreciated her characterization of them as "dull and commonplace").

Jaques's poems all follow a similar format and use familiar domestic images and language, although occasionally she breaks out of her regular diction and line arrangement. Occasionally she uses rural vernacular speech—in "An Old Man Talks," for example, she uses elided "g"s ("fix-

---

5 Carole Gerson, "Sarah Binks and Edna Jaques: Parody, Gender, and the Construction of Literary Value," *Canadian Literature* 134 (Autumn 1992): 66.

6 See Gerson, "Sarah Binks and Edna Jaques," 62–73; and Candida Rifkind, "Too Close to Home: Middlebrow Anti-Modernism and the Sentimental Poetry of Edna Jaques," *Journal of Canadian Studies* 39, no. 1 (Winter 2005): 90–114. Neither of these are critical reviews of Jaques's poetry per se, but use the slighting of Jaques by literary critics to address other concerns.

7 Edna Jaques, "Universal Things," in *Fireside Poems* (Toronto: Thomas Allen, 1950), 1.

8 Edna Jaques, "I Love," in *Aunt Hattie's Place* (Toronto: Thomas Allen, 1941), 43.

9 Edna Jaques, "To a Violinist," in *Backdoor Neighbors* (Toronto: Thomas Allen, 1946), 13.

10 Edna Jaques, "The Writer," in *Dreams in Your Heart* (Toronto: Thomas Allen, 1937), 26.

in'," "talkin'") and "writ" for written[11]—though it tends to jar with the more ordinary language of the rest of the poem. In "Colors in Nature" she uses a prose-style paragraph format but keeps to regular rhymes.[12]

The "choking realism"[13] noted in the foreword to *Backdoor Neighbors* is, in fact, largely absent in Jaques's work. Although five of her books were written in the midst of the Depression, there are few references to that grim time, and even those few are "mellowed by love and hope . . . faith and charity."[14] The war poems in *Aunt Hattie's Place* tend to express, to borrow Dennis Cooley's phrase, "fatty praises of God, Mother Country and Nature,"[15] but her poems "Reprisal"[16] and "Plymouth"[17] are more realistic treatments of the horrors of war. These and a few from some of her other books stand out as exceptions. In most cases, however, the hard edges of reality are softened by the golden glow of nostalgia or the moral inspiration of national purpose.

Jaques, like other popular poets, is constrained by intention and convention. Her goal to make her poems accessible to "ordinary" folk makes it difficult for her to go beyond well-worn phrases and inspirational sentiments (this is, perhaps, more apparent in reading her complete body of work than in reading single poems periodically). She often uses words like "clean," "sweet," "fresh," "simple," "gay, "friendly hills," "quiet fields," and "crystal cups"—keeping to words and images that will resonate with the experiences and language of her audience.

Despite these limitations, some poems combine deep feeling and apt images. For example, she observes that the love of a craftsman remains in his work;[18] that sparrows are like "hooded friars," with the lawn "a begging bowl for rice and bread;"[19] and that a night-wandering tom cat obeys the urges of "old jungle laws" and "takes on wildness like a fit-

11 Edna Jaques, "An Old Man Talks," in *Hills of Home* (Toronto: Thomas Allen, 1948), 9.

12 Jaques, "Colors in Nature," in *Dreams in Your Heart*, 44.

13 This phrase, as well as the whole foreword, though attributed to Donald Gordon, was written by Jaques. She recounts her brief meeting with Gordon in *Uphill All the Way*, 209.

14 Gordon, "Foreword," in Jaques, *Backdoor Nieghbors.*

15 Dennis Cooley, "RePlacing," in Cooley, *RePlacing*, 10.

16 Edna Jaques, "Reprisal," in *Roses in December* (Toronto: Thomas Allen, 1944), 52.

17 Jaques, "Plymouth," in *Aunt Hattie's Place*, 14.

18 Edna Jaques, "Singing at His Work," in *My Kitchen Window* (Toronto: Thomas Allen, 1935), 25.

19 Jaques, "Sparrows," in *Dreams in Your Heart*, 31.

ted cloak."[20] She compares the Depression landscape of "barren drifted fields" to barren hearts, "where nothing blooms," and finds the latter twice as bare.[21]

Jaques's landscape descriptions tend to be limited to garden, farmstead, and field—carefully controlled landscapes where the pioneer farmer's plow "caressed the furrows."[22] However, a few descriptions convey a deeply-felt sense of landscape and distance: the prairies "sweep to the sky" on a level plain, the wind "goes thundering by," heat ripples a "phantom sea" of ripe wheat, all part of a "vast immensity."[23] She likens the wind to an "old crone whose mind has gone awry," and who scatters "wisps of clouds" in the "upper reaches of the sky.[24] "The mighty forces" of Spring move silently but inexorably to break down "winter's snowy bastions,"[25] while midsummer is the time when the "hot field" sends up the "earthy smell / Of roots and rock."[26] Jaques feels a part of "the taste of wheat upon the prairie wind," the "smell of sage and flax," and "the blue smoke of a smoldering prairie fire."[27]

Although these examples do describe the prairie landscape, it is a landscape whose images and stories are partial and romanticized. The story is old and familiar—that of hardy folk carving out a home from a wild and virgin land, like the eponymous old-timer who loved the prairie and its "unbroken fields" and who gave up his youth in the struggle "to make a home in this new virgin land."[28] These hardy pioneers survived through a combination of tenacity, good humour, the "glowing healthy kinship of the soil,"[29] and the knowledge that they were building the foundation of a nation.[30] Jaques's view of nation is "little homes against the earth" built by men who earn their living from the soil.[31] And beyond

20 Jaques, "Alley Cat," in *Backdoor Neighbors*, 41.
21 Edna Jaques, "Hard Times," in *Prairie Born, Prairie Bred: Poetic Reflections of a Pioneer* (Saskatoon: Prairie Books, 1979), 66.
22 Edna Jaques, "The Pioneer," in *Beside Still Waters* (Toronto: Thomas Allen, 1939), 44.
23 Jaques, "Prairie Bred," in *Prairie Born*, 11.
24 Jaques, "Winds," in *Backdoor Neighbors*, 57.
25 Jaques, "Spring Offensive," in *Roses in December*, 38.
26 Jaques, "Mid Summer," in *Fireside Poems*, 22.
27 Jaques, "Prairie Memories," in *Prairie Born*, 17.
28 Jaques, "Old Timer," in *Aunt Hattie's Place*, 46.
29 Jaques, "Old Farmers Talk," in *Dreams in Your Heart*, 38.
30 Jaques, "Fall," in *My Kitchen Window*, 23.
31 Jaques, "Building a Nation." in *My Kitchen Window*, 52.

all this, these folk are seen as holding the country's future "safe in their calloused hands." They are the guardians of the nation's future.[32]

This story of the land includes nothing of the parallel story of the displacement and diminishment of Aboriginal people, and little, as I have said, of the disillusionment and despair accompanying the Depression years. All we have of the former is a passing reference or two to the "redskins" loitering around a white settlement, "trying to understand the white man's ways,"[33] or watching the building of a log cabin "with angry brooding eyes."[34] She does mention Aboriginal peoples' loss of land and freedom in her autobiography, *Uphill All the Way*: "There were only a few white families; all the rest were Indians, resentful of people coming and taking their hunting ground away and forbidding them to carry guns in the little village."[35] These matter-of-fact statements lack any sense of the profound impact of these losses on Aboriginal peoples.

Curiously, amid the mass of detail about domestic rural landscapes and way of life, Jaques's poems lack a particular sense of place. The theme is more of rural life than the landscape of the prairies, and the details of landscape and farm life are so burdened with a sentimental sweetness that it blurs the clear edges of the landscape. Mandel alludes obliquely to this tendency in "Pictures in an Institution," in which he writes, "the wind-break / on the farm that Barak plowed to dust / makes images would ruin public poetry," suggesting that the reality of the Depression landscape would destroy the rose-coloured images presented by popular poetry.[36] Jaques's lack of precision about place is accentuated by her use of images of prairie, mountain, rural Ontario, and seaside, often in the same poem. Ricou refers to this as the "meadowlark tradition" in prairie poetry: "The prairie, as an identifiable, distinctive landscape makes little impression on the people."[37]

Comparing a section of Lorna Crozier's "Time to Praise"[38] with Jaques's "A Born Farmer"[39] dramatizes the difference between a roman-

32 Jaques, "Homesteaders," in *Beside Still Waters*, 64.
33 Jaques,"Old Age," in *Fireside Poems*, 23.
34 Jaques, "Rail Fences," in *Fireside Poems*, 69.
35 Jaques, *Uphill All the Way*, 107.
36 Mandel, "Pictures in an Institution," in *The Other Harmony*, Vol. 1, 125–26.
37 Ricou, "The Meadowlark Tradition," 163–64.
38 Crozier, "Time to Praise," in *Inventing the Hawk*, 90.
39 Jaques, "A Born Farmer," in *My Kitchen Window*, 16.

ticized and a realistic view of farm life. Jaques's farmer gazes at a field bordered by "singing pine" with a creek that "hug[s] the ragged timber-line" and an orchard whose limbs "are alive with song." Every part of the farmstead, from the "sweet-scented cattle" to the "old good things of earth," is loved. Crozier, on the other hand, contrasts the romanticized view of shepherds and shepherdesses sitting in fragrant meadows rhapsodizing about the rural landscape with the real farm work of cleaning the barn, mending fences, hauling feed and water, and a host of other chores. Romanticized images and repeating lists of familiar details of rural life in general do not enhance an awareness and understanding of place.

Jaques does pick up on several themes that appear in the literary poetry I have been considering. In keeping with these other poets, she too prefers the rural landscape and rural life to that of the city. The city is a place of the "clamouring crowd," whereas the farmer "walk[s] the very aisles of light."[40] She contrasts walking "on stony pavements . . . / In hard hot leather shoes with stilted heels" with walking on "the cool, clean ground" and the feel of wet grass.[41] Several poems—"City Dweller"[42] and "Land Hunger,"[43] for example—show city people wishing to escape the constraints of city life and longing for a bit of country. It is in the country, after all, where children have healthy tans that reflect "the shining wholesomeness of country places."[44] Moreover, it is outside in "sun and wind and rain" that "you'll find the answer to all life."[45] And although she loves Toronto,[46] when she talks of Canada she does so primarily of rural Canada, hardly mentioning the cities.[47] She does appear to favour small towns over sparsely populated places, however: "Not for me the lonely ways / Bush or wide unpeopled plain." It is somewhat difficult to reconcile her dislike for "the lonely ways" and the "waving miles of growing grain" with her enthusiasm for the rural farm life, which appears often in her other poems.[48]

40 Jaques, "The Old Farmer," in *My Kitchen Window*, 58.
41 Jaques, "My Body A Servant," in *Dreams in Your Heart*, 27.
42 Jaques, "City Dweller," in *Backdoor Neighbors*, 63.
43 Jaques, "Land Hunger," in *Roses in December*, 35.
44 Jaques, "Small Things," in *Dreams in Your Heart*, 23.
45 Jaques, "To City People," in *Hills of Home*, 12.
46 Jaques, "Life in Toronto," in *Aunt Hattie's Place*, 78.
47 Jaques, "This Is Canada," in *Backdoor Neighbors*, 35.
48 Jaques, "Not For Me," in *Dreams in Your Heart*, 29.

As with the literary poets, Jaques also expresses a strong connection between women and the landscape. In "Eve Created," she describes Eve's "vital body fertile as the earth / . . . // One with the sea and earth."[49] It is a description that is echoed in other poems that deal with women in general. In "Motherhood," for example, she claims that all women are "fertile and rich as the sod" and "eager for birth," becoming "eternally one / with the tides and the earth."[50] In "The Immigrant," she finds this same connection in an immigrant woman who "is kin to this brown earth" and in whom is "the motherhood of all things glad for birth."[51] This is a different sort of kinship than that understood by academic female poets. For Jaques, this identification leads naturally to the idea that a woman would find her highest calling in domestic life: "A fire to tend . . . a little mouth to feed."[52] The woman who must work outside the home, who has been denied the place of domesticity, Jaques feels, longs for all the pleasures and contentedness of a domestic life.[53]

Jaques alludes to one component of prairie life absent from the poetry of the other writers I have considered: that of the ranch. Jaques longs "for cattle bawlin' in the night," for "roundup time and spring," and cowboy songs.[54] She wonders if cowboys and their songs, which carry "[a]cross the prairie dusk," will be a part of the life to come.[55] And she identifies the rancher's fear of the inevitable changes coming to his way of life: "Sensing—far off—an eager happy band / Of settlers coming in to claim the land."[56] It is telling that she reserves this looming loss for ranchers, and not for the First Peoples in the region who lost so much more than a way of life. In fact this lapse may reflect the central element that makes her writing "popular" rather than "literary" poetry: it merely perpetuates the settler perspective of a prairie history in which Aboriginal peoples played little part. Like her poetry, her view of Aboriginal peoples lacks the deep critical engagement with landscape and history that literary poetry exhibits.

---

49 Jaques, "Eve Created," in *My Kitchen Window*, 42.

50 Jaques, "Motherhood," in *Beside Still Water*, 87.

51 Jaques, "The Immigrant," in *Dreams in Your Heart*, 60.

52 Jaques, "Another Day," in *Dreams in your Heart*, 40.

53 Jaques, "Working Woman Wishes," in *Roses in December*, 77.

54 Jaques, "Prairie Born," in *Aunt Hattie's Place*, 39.

55 Jaques, "Paradise," in *Hills of Home*, 74.

56 Jaques, "Old Rancher," in *Roses in December*, 23.

COWBOY POETRY

Cowboy poetry, like other popular poetry, originated in the spoken word; it was read aloud for specific occasions and never reached beyond the listening audience. Grounded in the oral tradition, it is meant to be heard, not read.[57] It was only when it began to be picked up by newspapers that it started to reach a large audience, and the best of that was reproduced in small books. No academic journals existed for this kind of poetry, so there was never any "professional" criticism of it, in terms of what was considered good and bad writing. The only criterion was the audience's approval.

Cowboy poetry is focused on a particular part of the southern grassland's cultural landscape and on its distinct way of life, and it has become immensely popular. Cowboy "gatherings" began in Elko, Nevada, in 1984, and have spread across ranching country. Dozens of them now draw scores of performers and hundreds of listeners. The oral tradition remains, and today cowboy poets are as likely to promote their poetry through recordings as through books. These poetry gatherings often restrict performances to those who are working or who are in some way involved in the cattle industry, which gives the poetry an authenticity and freshness that adds to its appeal. Unlike most other popular poetry, many cowboy poems enjoy a long life. Many of the standard poems were written in the heyday of the open range and have been heard and read for well over 100 years.

Cowboy poetry is largely traditional, with strict adherence to rhyme and metre, although many poems are better at preserving the former than the latter. As Mike Puhallo says, "any B.S. artist can be a star / if he can make those damn lies rhyme."[58] In "Scotch Holiday," Doug Richards sets out to make a "rhyme" about "where people go."[59] His friends reinforce the need to follow the rhyming tradition. When they tell him to include a group greeting in his poem "Welcome Home," they also tell him to be "sure to make it rhyme."[60] Although most written, and almost all oral, cowboy poetry sticks close to these traditional demands, some

57 Hal Cannon, ed., introduction to *Cowboy Poetry: A Gathering* (Salt Lake City: Peregrine Smith, 1985).

58 Mike Puhallo, "Cowboy Poet?" in Mike Puhallo and Wendy Liddle, *Meadow Muffins: Cowboy Rhymes and Other B.S.* (Surrey: Hancock, 1999), 8.

59 Doug Richards, "Scotch Holiday," in *Listen to Her Rodeo* (Moosehorn: Ramshead, 1993), 65.

60 Richards, "Welcome Home," in *Listen to Her Rodeo*, 68.

cowboy poets experiment with more open forms and unrhymed lines, as Brian Brannon does in "Wapiapi Gap." His description of a winter landscape in the foothills uses a more open, unrhymed format: "Moonlight lays a scintillating carpet of diamonds / On a blanket of deep powdery snow / That somehow, gives an impression of warmth."[61] Jake Conkin's "When the Land Belonged to God" similarly departs from rhymed lines.[62] Many of the Canadian poems in Ted Stone's anthology of cowboy poems are more open than the traditional form. Neil Meili's "The Lonely Men," for example, is a moving depiction of a time when single settlers and their "dark little houses still dotted the prairie," and how the "long and difficult transplanting" loosened their roots "until one by one they broke off / like tumbleweeds / and were gone."[63] Meili's "Round-Up," however, echoes Ed's sentiment in Aaron Bushkowsky's "at the edge of the world," when after a long, hard day's work the cowboy still feels that "[t]here's no place you'd rather be."[64] Doris Bircham also uses an open form to describe the landscape that drew her family back to the ranching country of the foothills after trying several other prairie locations.[65] Only here, she says, can one "feel each season's heartbeat" as the wind "fill[s] each empty space."[66] Similar departures from the traditional use of rhyme and format can be found as early as 1984, with Paul Zarzyski's *The Make-Up of Ice*,[67] which challenges a hard and fast distinction between popular and literary poetry.

As with Jaques, cowboy poets also touch on some of the same concerns raised by literary poets. But unlike Jaques, the ones considered here echo the literary poets in decrying the "progress" that has impoverished Aboriginal peoples and changed the old ways of rural living. Conkin's poem, discussed above, voices these concerns, as does his "Cowboy's Lament," in which he longs for the range as it was before the "whiteman's selfish

---

61 Brian Brannon, "Wapiapi Gap," in Mike Puhallo, Brian Brannon, and Wendy Liddle, *Can't Stop Rhymin' on the Range* (Surrey: Hancock, 1997), 51.

62 Jake Conkin, "When the Land Belonged to God," in *Silk 'n' Silver and other things too!* (Sundre: Buckaroo Jake Productions, 1991), 36.

63 Neil Meili, "The Lonely Men," in *Riding the Northern Range*, ed. Ted Stone (Red Deer: RDC Press, 1993), 119.

64 Meili, "Round-Up," in Stone, *Riding the Northern Range*, 117–18.

65 It appears that no distinction is made between male and female poets under the general rubric of "cowboy" poetry.

66 Doris Bircham, "On the Move," in Stone, *Riding the Northern Range*, 147.

67 Paul Zarzyski, *The Make-Up of Ice* (Athens: The University of Georgia Press, 1984).

intrusion": hip-high grass, sparkling streams, antelope, and buffalo.[68] Puhallo's "Dan George" speaks respectfully of the Coast Salish chief and expresses support for the idea of white and Aboriginal equality.[69] Both examples are a contrast to the stereotypical idea that "progress" by the settler society necessitated the removal of the Aboriginal population and improved the land and the quality of life. Some early changes in ranching were made in response to severe weather rather than progress. Puhallo's "Since 1888" depicts the changes resulting from the big "die" of that year: having to put up corrals and fences on the range "so cattle wouldn't stray. / They put in fields and water works / to winter cows on hay."[70] In "The Valley," he paints a vivid picture of a part of the range that has stood against the changes brought by progress. Beginning with a "vale of tranquility, / beauty and charm," the poem ends with a plea to anyone who would bring progress to "please stay away!"[71]

As do many of the literary poets, the cowboy poet has a rather dim view of urban life. In "The Valley," Puhallo speaks of "urban strife," and in "Song of the Night Owl" he pities the "urban folk" who "flee indoors" and who, "with doors bolted tight . . . / [,] abandon the streets" to the outcasts of society.[72] In "Reality," Richards writes of the changing ranch country, and of those from the city whom he pities, who are rearranging the rural landscape with their acreages and dirt bike trails. He is sympathetic, however, for he "understands what it must be like / Having to spend your life in the city."[73] Similarly, Tom King's "Serenity" pities the city people who have to live with grime and a fast-paced life.[74]

The cowboy poet, too, expresses a love for the wild and an understanding that using it requires cooperation and respect, rather than control. As with the literary poets, Brannon, in "A Name Taking," affirms the Aboriginal peoples' tradition of caring for the land—Mother Earth—and suggests that non-Aboriginal people should take up the same task: "Respect is a thing we should learn well / before we trespass

68 Conkin, "Cowboy's Lament," in *Silk 'n' Silver*, 54.

69 Mike Puhallo, "Dan George," in Mike Puhallo, Brain Brannon, and Wendy Liddle, *Rhymes on the Range* (Surrey: Hancock, 1995), 54–55.

70 Puhallo, "Since 1888," in Puhallo et al., *Rhymes on the Range*, 35.

71 Puhallo, "The Valley," in Puhallo and Liddle, *Meadow Muffins*, 31.

72 Puhallo, "Song of the Night Owl," in Puhallo et al., *Can't Stop Rhymin'*, 38.

73 Richards, "Reality," in *Listen to Her Rodeo*, 28.

74 Thomas A. King, "Serenity," in *From a Cowboy's Office Window!: Cowboy Poetry* (Sundre: Akita, nd), 47.

on his land."[75] Likewise, Puhallo sums up what all who use the land—cowboys, farmers, guides, and trappers—need to recognize: that "the earth does not belong to us / we belong to her.[76]

What is curiously missing, or is at least uncommon, in these poems are descriptions of the ranching landscape. Those that do describe it tend to use well-worn phrases. They also tend to describe the mountains and valleys of the foothills of Alberta or the interior grasslands of the Cariboo and Chilcotin regions of British Columbia—only a few speak of the ranching country of the grasslands of southern Saskatchewan and southeastern Alberta. There is no question that there is feeling behind these depictions, but there is little imaginative use of language. Like the literary poets, however, language sometimes fails them in expressing these feelings. Brannon admits such a failure when he confesses that although "these words do fill my soul," he cannot get them down on paper.[77] Detailed descriptions of landscape may be scarce but there is some suggestion that the impact of its elements produce rugged people, people of "twisted rawhide and barb wire."[78]

Despite the popular notion of "cowboy and Indian" enmity, each group's poetry shares similar characteristics, although perhaps this is not surprising in light of the close contact of ranchers and Aboriginal people. For both, their poetry has its genesis in the oral tradition, with an emphasis on repetition and memory, and continues in that tradition alongside print publication. Both cowboy poets and Aboriginal poets focus more on the life of their respective groups than on the landscapes in which that life is, or was, lived. And both lament the changes that have diminished their original way of life. While both groups have experienced change, there are vast differences in the impact of those changes on each group, as Montana poet Wallace McRae points out with exquisite irony and understatement in his book of stories *Stick Horses*,[79] as well as in his poem "A Conversation with Albert."[80] Ranchers have indeed experienced

75 Brian Brannon, "A Name Taking," in Mike Puhallo, Brian Brannon and Wendy Liddle, *Still Rhymin' on the Range* (Surrey: Hancock House, 1996), 53.

76 Puhallo, "Children of the Soil," in Puhallo et al., *Still Rhymin'*, 56.

77 Brannon, "The Tchaikazuan," in Puhallo et al., *Can't Stop Rhymin'*, 56.

78 Mike Puhallo, "Courage," in Mike Puhallo and Wendy Liddle, *Rhymes & Damn Lies* (Surrey: Hancock House, 2006), 57.

79 Wallace McRae, *Stick Horses* (Layton, Utah: Gibbs Smith, 2009).

80 Wallace McRae, "A Conversation with Albert," in Stone, *Riding the Northern Range*, 49–50.

changes to their traditional way of life and have lost much of their land, but they have maintained a version of that tradition in today's society. Aboriginal peoples, on the other hand, have lost much of their traditional lands, their free-ranging lifestyle, and in some cases their languages, and hence important aspects of their culture, and today they seek to reassert themselves alongside a culture that has impoverished them.

Cowboy poets spin their poetry from their lives on the range or at the rodeo, whether recounting recent experiences full of action or humour, glorifying life on the range, or lamenting the changes to it. This contrasts markedly from literary poets, whose poetry focuses on field rather than range and arises from the memory of that life rather than from active participation in it.

IMPACT ON PUBLIC PERCEPTION

Short of sampling public opinion, there is no way to measure how or how much either popular or literary poetry influences public perceptions of the prairie landscape. What I can do, however, is suggest which form has the greater *potential* to influence public perception, although even that poses some difficulties. I will assume that the following variables are at work.

1. Accessibility. To be influential, one could argue, poetry must be accessible to the general public, both in availability (readings, mass media, bookstores, etc.) and in language (easily understood). Presumably, greater access to one kind of poetry or the other ensures greater potential for its influence on the public. Although accessibility alone, either in availability or in language, does not guarantee a wide readership, limited accessibility would certainly inhibit readership and, therefore, influence. As William New points out, writers who use vernacular language to represent a particular class of people may not be read by the very people they purport to represent in their writing.[81]

2. Popularity. Widespread acceptance and enjoyment of one kind of poetry or the other should correlate positively with readership, which, like accessibility, would broaden its influence.

81 New, *Land Sliding*, 213.

3. Longevity. The lifespan of a poem would be expected to affect the number of people influenced by it. The longer a poem is popular in print or in use, the more people will read it and be influenced by it.

4. Readership.[82] Assessing the influence of readership is more complex. It might be said that readers of a certain kind will gravitate to writers of similar interests: rural people might tend to read rural poets, women might be likely to read female poets, literary people might be drawn to literary poets, and so on. If this is the case, some groups of readers may have a much greater potential than others to shape the perception of people beyond their own group, even if their readership may not be as large. Dennis Cooley, for example, points out that professors or teachers of English, through their contact with students, may influence an exponentially larger group beyond the classroom.[83] It is likely also that the attention they give to the poetry would be more focused, and therefore more likely to shape students' perceptions. The kind of readership also affects the longevity of the work. Textbooks used by university professors and high school teachers ensure that literary poetry is used year after year. In contrast, popular poetry is more ephemeral, despite being read by a much greater number of people when it is issued. In many cases it is spoken or read, and then put away or forgotten. Much popular poetry that appears in newspapers or regional periodicals is read today and replaced tomorrow with a new poem. Even the most popular prairie poet, Edna Jaques, is read by few today. Some of her poetry has been kept alive by recent anthologies of her best work, but most is long out of print. Some cowboy poems, as I earlier noted, are an exception, being kept alive over decades by repetition in the oral tradition. Assuming this framework provides a way to assess potential influence, I will apply it to the two bodies of work examined here.

---

82 I have been helped greatly in this section by correspondence with Dennis Cooley.

83 "The folks who do that teaching often are those who mediate the writing nationally and internationally. When they talk about it, write about it, edit it, anthologize it, criticize it, theorize it—and do so with colleagues across Canada and in other countries—that poetry gains greater exposure and currency, which in turn can be amplified in those extended communities. The more widespread and educated audience can in turn generate a still larger readership. We might be looking at an audience, actual or potential, that is larger than what might at first blush seem to be the case." Dennis Cooley, e-mails to the author, January 2014; June 2014.

What is the potential for Jaques's work to influence public perception? The simple answer is that it is enormous. Jaques sold more than 250,000 copies of her books, each one a bestseller by almost any standard. Her poems appeared daily or weekly in several widely read newspapers over a period of several decades, and she read her poems to many thousands more in cities, towns, and small rural communities across Canada. If readership and poetry reading attendance determine potential, Jaques's influence should be massive.

Cowboy poetry also has huge potential to influence public perception. As I have noted earlier, it has hundreds of practitioners and thousands of readers/listeners over a wide swath of the prairies. It is accessible both in terms of availability (through the gatherings, as well as the recordings sold at them) and language (through speaking in the language of the ordinary person). It is also long lived: repetition, humour, and nostalgia have kept some poems in circulation for more than 100 years. It would seem that in terms of attraction and accessibility, popular poetry has the potential to influence far more people than literary poetry, although the issues of focus and longevity noted earlier must be considered in assessing literary poetry's influence.

Perhaps the most critical question, however, is what *kind* of influence does popular poetry wield? What is the perception of prairie landscape conveyed in the poems and in live presentations? Is it the kind of influence that might be expected to change perception or to reinforce it? Jaques's poetry was written to engage rural people and is replete with ideas, images, and sentiments familiar to those people. Her poetry gave the rural landscape and rural life value, both personally and nationally. The farmer was no longer engaged in a personal battle with the wild, but was part of a movement that would ensure the stability and prosperity of a nation. In Jaques's writing, rural values had an additional physical and moral shine, and the work of women in the home was elevated to a national necessity. The tremendous popularity of her poetry is evidence that it connected with rural people of the prairies, and that it resonated with and confirmed or elevated their own beliefs about their work and the land. The transformation that her writing portrayed was not in the perception of the landscape but in the change in the land itself, from virgin wilderness to fertile productivity. Any negative elements in this transformation—loss of species, loss of soil, loss of land by Aboriginal peoples—were lost in the glory of human triumph over the challenges of nature. Her poetry was not meant to challenge the status quo but to reinforce it. Cowboy poetry is focused on the theme of ranching, either describing current activities or engaging in a nostalgia for the past. It, too, looks to reinforce a particular way of life, and not to challenge it.

These are not new ideas—nearly 25 years ago, Laurie Ricou noted that the impulse of popular verse "is to reinforce existing attitudes rather than to create new ones."[84] It reinforces not only the "domestic order," which Ed McCourt blamed for hindering the development of a regional prairie folklore,[85] but also the stereotypical features of prairie life and landscape. Popular poetry is written to reinforce public perception, not to reimagine it. Don Gayton suggests that literary poets may be equally unlikely to change societal perceptions because their individual bonds to (or in this case, reimaginings of) the landscape are not shared by the society in which the poet lives.[86]

To conclude. There is no way to determine which kind of poetry is changing or has changed public perceptions of the prairies. The most I can do is to speculate on the *potential* of each group to change public perception. Given popular poetry's great reach, owing to its accessibility, acceptability, and longevity, whatever messages it carries will be widely disseminated. Literary poetry has a much more limited readership, although individual members may influence large numbers of students in universities and high school classes, and do so over long periods of time. Its potential influence, therefore, might be much larger than the number of readers alone might suggest. On the surface, however, it would seem that popular poetry has greater potential to influence public perceptions.

Yet, as I have noted, the *kind* of influence is as important as its potential. Literary poetry seems more likely to change perceptions, because it reconceives the prairie landscape and expresses this reimagined landscape with evocative and memorable language. Popular poetry is directed toward a much more general readership and it connects with it by using common language and images. It would, consequently, reinforce existing and widely held perceptions and images. It would fail

84 Ricou, "The Meadowlark Tradition," 67.

85 Mandel, "Romance and Realism," 200.

86 Gayton, *Landscapes of the Interior*, 75.

to produce changes in perception for the same reason it is distinct from literary poetry, that is, in Arthur Adamson's terms, for failing to move beyond the descriptive to the imaginative.[87]

It is one thing to affirm that art is a change agent in public perception; it is quite another to suggest the specific ways in which those changes are connected to the art. This is certainly true of poetry in that we are dealing with a branch of the arts—especially literary poetry, which is not widely appreciated in the rural prairies. However, it is probably less important to determine the specific impact of prairie poetry on public perception as to note the effect of art generally on the public mind. Even if the re-visioning or reimagining of the prairies by prairie poets does not effect major changes in the public perception of the prairies, it may do what all good art does: enlighten or enlarge commonly held perceptions, add nuance to stereotypical images of the prairie, confirm a deep emotional attachment to the prairie, and multiply the bonds by which prairie people are committed to this landscape, both in how they appreciate it and how they value it.

87 Adamson, "Notes From a Dark Cellar."

CHAPTER 7

"Shaping a World Already Made": Geography and Poetry

"Art is made to disturb. Science reassures."
—GEORGES BRAQUE[1]

Our minds are in motion, turning observation into memory, "flickering between the known and the unknown"[2]—seeking pattern and purpose in what we observe, shaping instant images and experiences into the flow of life. "Shaping a world already made"[3] is one expression of this shaping and identifies two factors fundamental to the poet/landscape relationship, which serve as the framework of this book: the act of "shaping" and the "world already made." The "world already made" is the foundational component of the poet/landscape interaction: the physical landscape of land and sky, creatures and cover—unshaped by human culture. Although a hypothetical concept (because any landscape, once seen, becomes a cultural artifact, perceived and assessed through the lens of human experience),[4] we normally consider the physical landscape, however perceived, as an assumed, objective reality. This is the view used in the

1 Georges Braque, *Le Jour et la Nuit: Cahiers 1917–52* (Paris: Gallimard, 1988).

2 Patrick Friesen, e-mail to the author, March 22, 2014.

3 Dudek, "At Lac en Coeur," in Newlove, *Canadian Poetry*, 79.

4 This idea is beautifully expressed in P.K. Page's "Cook's Mountain": "By naming them he made them. / They were there / before he came / but they were not the same. / It was his gaze / that glazed each one." *The Hidden Room: Collected Poems, Volume Two* (Erin: The Porcupine's Quill, 1997), 115.

chapters dealing with the influence of the prairie landscape on poetry and the way in which it serves as the object of our intentional and perceptual shaping.

The way in which we shape this landscape, or transform the "world already made," into a cultural landscape marked by human endeavour and activity, with buildings and boundaries, is a major area of geographical investigation. The line that follows "shaping a world already made"—"to a form that I require"—stresses intentional shaping, motivated by human need, desire, and aspiration. Marlene Cookshaw expresses the same sentiment: "The land shapes itself from our desire / While we hang in a funnel of life / Breathing, mouths open to the sun."[5]

Non-Aboriginal shaping of the physical landscape began through controlling the land and its Aboriginal inhabitants. Treaties established control over the land, reservations established spatial control over the people, and residential schools established control over Aboriginal culture. People who once pursued a hunting and gathering lifestyle were moved onto reserves, encouraged to be sedentary agriculturalists, and forced to abandon their culture. These actions paved the way for widespread shaping by the new settler society.

For many of the first settlers, shaping the land was motivated by a desire for familiarity. Carrying with them memories of home, they sought out, or set out to recreate, a physical landscape that resembled their recently abandoned homelands.[6] They began to replicate a familiar cultural landscape with the form and pattern of fields and farmsteads shaped by old-country tradition. Railroads and later roads accelerated and modified the shaping by replacing tradition and survival with economic goals, aided by the nation-building ambitions of the federal government and the economic motivations of the Canadian Pacific Railway. The shaping reached its zenith as farm consolidation and urban opportunity fuelled a migration of rural people to urban places, reducing the "world already made" to a landscape of human artifice. Popular prairie poetry tends to reinforce themes of control and conquest—heralding as heroes the hardy, persistent rural pioneers who transformed a wild and unpro-

5 Marlene Cookshaw, "Everything Necessary," in *Double Somersaults* (London: Brick Books, 1999), 80.

6 "remembering / the sacrifice / it took / to turn horizon / and forest / into something / of remembered / steppes." Suknaski, "Tulova/1979," in *In the Name of Narid*, 45.

ductive landscape into tidy farms and cozy villages—while ignoring the consequences to native plants and animals, and to Aboriginal peoples. Literary poetry, however, challenges these themes, imaginatively transforming the physical landscape into an emotional landscape, lamenting or condemning the diminishment and destruction of prairie life, including that of Aboriginal peoples.

The marks of intentional shaping that humanized the physical landscape are obvious; the shaping in the mind that makes the "world already made" more than an objective reality are less obvious, but no less real. All who observe and interact with this landscape shape it by giving it meaning, according to a host of personal variables.

Our perception of the prairies is usually shaped by elements seen at two scales: the general—the grand panorama of plain, sky, and horizon—and the detailed elements close at hand; the middle ground is usually ignored.[7] The monumental in the prairie landscape evokes fear and an awesome beauty; the local evokes intimacy and a comfortable beauty. The two comprise a sublime landscape, by turns fearsome and comfortingly familiar.

Some elements in the physical landscape endure, some change. It could be said, however, that even the enduring elements are in motion, because desire and experience change our perceptions of them and the meanings we attach to them. Even so, some perceptions of the prairies are fixed in the public mind: endless flat land covered with grass or grain, a vast sky, and a distant and receding horizon. Any variety in the landscape is swallowed up by these stereotyped images engraved on people's mind. The real complexity of the landscape gives way to a few elements easily remembered and communicated. Popular poetry tends to replicate these familiar images to appeal to its readers, thus reinforcing the stereotypes. This gives stereotypical images a permanence in the public's mind that is difficult to dislodge. Prairie poets help us to disrupt these stereotypes with imaginative vision and evocative language, both expressing the complexity and richness of the landscape.

Regional geographers, too, aim at exploding stereotypes by attempting to reveal the full range and variety of prairie landscapes, as well as the conflicted complexity that marks our interaction with them. Poetry and other imaginative sources contain message images that can unseat

---

7 John Warkentin, e-mail to the author, April 9, 2014.

the stereotypical images and assist geographers through the variety of visions and voices that cohere in the prairie landscape. Poets also invest the physical landscape with symbolic significance. Rivers, for example, are not just occasional areas of topographical relief, nor just arteries of transportation or barriers; they are symbols of change, of the impossibility of reliving the past, of movement, memory, and loss.

The central concern of most of the preceding chapters is reciprocal shaping: the shaping of prairie poetry by the "world already made," the physical landscape, and the ways in which prairie poetry might shape people's perception of the prairie landscape. Arthur Adamson suggests that this influence goes beyond the poems that deal specifically with landscape:

> Because of the inherent connection between earth and vision we may say: even a poet who wrote only of interior visions and never of outward landscape would be writing of the earth through those visions. The flower may not look like the roots, but from them it derives its life. Similarly, regional visions derive their life from the landscape. This is the meaning of regionalism. The regional voice *is* the landscape. Without it there is no art.[8]

After pointing out that remembered places are the stuff of poetry, Robert Kroetsch goes on to say: "The idea of landscape is incredibly complicated emotionally. It's no accident that a lot of poets work out of that notion of a place as a reality, as a metaphor, as a story, as a myth."[9] Although the poets discussed in this book express the influence of prairie landscape on their work in diverse ways, they are unified by three common themes: a love of the prairie landscape, a concern about the impact of humans on the elements of that landscape, and a concern for the First Peoples on the prairies. As I have shown, the impact of the prairie landscape on individual poets is mediated by more general factors of race, gender, and location, although not necessarily in ways one would expect.

8 Adamson, "Notes from a Dark Cellar," 224.

9 Kroetsch, "Uncovering Our Dream World," 31.

It is worth considering what kind of language we use to express our experience with landscape and to communicate it to others. Geographers use two modes of analysis and expression: the scientific and the humanistic, and they have long grappled with the challenge of combining them, particularly in the last several decades. The "world already made" is the natural focus of scientific investigation, with forms and processes amenable to precise measurement. We need the reassurance of the scientific perspective to help us understand the processes that mould the physical landscape and monitor the changes that are invisible to the eye, and that give us a comforting sense of order and purpose. Geographers need precise measurement and analysis with words that are clear, precise, and unbiased. Geographers today realize, just like John Newlove, that the weather gets into our words—vagaries of mood, circumstance, and background disturb and undermine such objective goals.[10] Scientists strive to understand and describe the landscape as an objective reality. To rely solely on this approach, however, is to ignore the fact that the landscape is perceived and experienced differently by each individual. Frederick Niven captures this idea in his novel *The Flying Years*, when he describes the reaction of the Munro family to the new landscape of southern Manitoba:

> As for the Settlement: each of them on arrival promptly observed it in a different way, and in that difference you have all three measured and weighed. Mrs. Munro saw the houses as alien, they being built of logs. Munro saw them as not altogether strange, they being thatched; and Angus saw them as romantic, they being of log with thatch. The lack of a mountain-side on which to rest their eyes was dreadful to Mrs. Munro, to Mr. Munro odd, to Angus novel and exciting.[11]

Another expression of the scientific approach is what Jan Zwicky calls "the sickness, clumsy need / To wrestle with the pattern, make one

10 "The weather gets in my words / and I want them dry." Newlove, "The Weather," in *The Night the Dog Smiled*, 78.

11 Frederick Niven, *The Flying Years* (London: Collins, 1935), 18.

blueprint / To explain all bricks."[12] This is similar to what Glen Downie calls "the loving reductionist urge to understand."[13] Geographers often find the reductionist impulse tempting, because the complexity of the world and our interaction with it begs for patterns and systems to make sense of it. We seek pared-down, law-like generalizations that create the simple, noncomplex bricks that we feel able to explain. In *Wisdom & Metaphor*, Zwicky notes that reductionism understands connectedness as sameness.[14] In "Imagination and the Good Life," she goes on to connect this feature of reductionism to the pursuit of "essences" stripped of "accidents."[15] Throughout her work, she argues that it is not necessary to characterize understanding in this way; rather, it is also possible to characterize it as resonance—a relation that sees connection as an echoing of internal relations that preserve the uniqueness of individual things.

This resonance, Zwicky says, is not created by the poet, but discovered. In his gritty novel *The Narrow Road to the Deep North*, Richard Flanagan describes Dorrigo Evans visiting the wife of one of the soldiers who died under his command. In the course of their conversation, she relates her experience with a visiting friend who believes every room has a note of resonance. She starts "warbling away, up and down," trying to find that note. "And suddenly one note came back to us, just bounced back off the walls and rose from the floor and filled the place with this perfect hum. This beautiful sound. Like you've thrown a plum and an orchard comes back at you."[16] Surely this is what poets do. They throw out the resonant image, revealed by "ontological attention"[17] and carefully reimagined, and the whole prairie, in all its resonant richness and emotional power, comes back at us. This is an important concept for geographers, for it

12 "Yet still the sickness, clumsy need / To wrestle with the pattern, make one blueprint / To explain all bricks. / But system is a gift / Of art, its essence transcendental. / The most that we can hope / Is steadiness of soul, courage / To render with exactness what is set before us, / Love what must / each time we grasp it / vanish." Jan Zwicky, *Wittgenstein Elegies* (Ilderton: Brick Books, 1986), 61.

13 Downie, "Heartland," in *Heartland*, 26. Their ideas are similar, but not identical, in that Zwicky believes the urge to understand is indeed basic. What she does not believe is that all understanding is reductionist in form.

14 Zwicky, *Wisdom & Metaphor*, 105 Left.

15 Jan Zwicky, "Imagination and the Good Life," in *Alkibiades' Love* (Montreal: McGill-Queen's, 2015), 262–82.

16 Richard Flanagan, *The Narrow Road to the Deep North* (New York: Knopf, 2014), 277.

17 Zwicky, *Wisdom & Metaphor*, 57 Left.

allows us to view and feel the multiple and complex connections that give the region its integrity—that "perfect hum" that preserves variety instead of eliminating it through the search for a blueprint to define the essence of a region. The geographer interested in the workings of a region must be immersed in the totality of that region's experience, not just in the elements that yield themselves to accounting procedures. The restless desire for reductionism conflicts with the appeal and scope of the imagination.[18]

Where the scientist seeks monumental truths in the landscape, the poet deconstructs the landscape to produce the rich variety of voices and images that express the variety of truths that lie hidden in the land's paradoxes and ambiguities. As C. Day Lewis opines, "The truth of poetry is a thing which transcends sincerity, and disposes or suppresses facts for its own purpose. It has nothing to do with the equally valid but prose truth of science."[19] The Aboriginal poet Garry Gottfriedson sees truth as communal. The same could be said about the truth of landscape. It is communal in that certain perceptions and patterns of activity are common to a region; they resonate with its inhabitants. In this sense, the story of landscape is "our" story. But it is also "my" story in that each encounter and perception of the prairie is personal. There are common elements, but the whole is comprised of a universe of individual observations and experiences. The Aboriginal perspective on landscape is important because it views the landscape communally, as a nurturing Earth Mother that is important and essential to each person. Aboriginal truth comes out of an intimate relationship with the landscape. The non-Aboriginal perspective tends to be fragmented by various agendas: economic, aesthetic, and environmental, but the truth is that non-Aboriginal people, as much as Aboriginal peoples, rely on developing a relationship with the landscape, as well as on recognizing both our dependence on it and our interdependence with it. Barry Lopez suggests that we need to be tutored by the landscape[20]—to be shaped in our appreciation of its worth as well as in understanding the activities it will allow without serious consequence.

---

18 For a powerful response to reductionism in all its applications, see Wendell Berry, *Life is a Miracle: An Essay Against Modern Superstition* (Washington: Counterpoint, 2001).

19 Day Lewis, *The Lyric Impulse*, 25.

20 Barry Lopez, "Foreword," *Heart of the Land: Essays on Last Great Places*, ed. Joseph Barbato and Lisa Weinerman (New York: Pantheon, 1994), xiii–xxi.

Although the scientific perspective provides broad generalizations about the processes and patterns of human activity, the complexity of the cultural landscape is not so easily subjected to scientific scrutiny. It is created by forces which reflect human desire and whim; to attempt to derive objective and repeatable patterns from it results in stripping away the very variety that makes it a living landscape. The intangible parts of the landscape, the paradoxes and mysteries and ambiguities that abound in it, are beyond the purview of scientific methodology. The artistic vision, however, embraces paradox and ambiguity. It relishes the rich variety of human experience and emotion that give meaning to both the physical and cultural landscapes. Prairie poets disrupt our preconceptions of the prairie landscape; they challenge our tendency to see ordinary things as ordinary. Gary Geddes, commenting on Zwicky's poetics, puts it this way: "If, as I believe, poetry is our first language, it has its own grammar, which is, rather, a code, not for making things fuzzy or difficult or ornate, but for descrambling reality, . . . so that we are forced to look at it anew."[21]

J. Nicholas Entrikin, in a paper[22] and later in a book-length study,[23] argued for the "between-ness" of place, a vantage point for viewing place on the mid-point between the extremes of a purely objective, scientific view and a purely subjective, personal view, with narrative as the approach most receptive to a combination at the mid-point. Yi-Fu Tuan's path and garden analogy for combining the scientific and artistic perspectives, which I discussed in the opening chapter, is another approach. I would suggest a double vision of sorts, an approach that fully appreciates the contributions of a scientific perspective but which stresses the use of poetry, with its engagement with paradox and mystery, to reach the same middle perspective. This would allow geographers to look for "the good / lands beyond the eye."[24] Openness to both forms of expression counters Mandel's explanation of

21 Gary Geddes, "Jan Zwicky," in *15 Canadian Poets x 3*, ed. Gary Geddes (Don Mills: Oxford, 2001), 552.

22 J. Nicholas Entrikin, "The Betweenness of Place," in *Reading Human Geography*, eds. Trevor Barnes and Derek Gregory (Los Angeles: Arnold, 1997), 299–314.

23 J. Nicholas Entrikin, *The Betweenness of Place: Towards a Geography of Modernity* (Baltimore: John Hopkins University, 1991).

24 Lilburn, "In Paradiso," in *Moosewood Sandhills*, 56.

seeing double—"you begin to see the difficulties."[25] Instead, we begin to see the possibilities.[26]

Poets offer geographers another kind of doubleness as well: combining the act of intently observing with a forgetting of oneself by being open to the mystery and paradox that exist in the landcape. Zwicky says, "From lyric's perspective, the self does not exist—what exists are moments of emptied, utterly open attention and address."[27] This is similar to Tim Lilburn's "contemplative attention." One must open one's self to the landscape in such a way as to feel it and experience it, not just to see it.[28] One could say that this openness is sensational, in that it appeals to all the senses. Perhaps a landscape can only enter you in this way if you experience it as a child, which would explain its persistent influence on artists throughout their lives. This kind of memory is sharpest when created in childhood. Adult receptivity is coloured or contaminated by a lifetime of being trained out of such innocence. As scholars, we are trained to be objective; total immersion in a landscape would rob us of the ability to see it objectively—to see it as it really is, without our own subjective impressions. The artist, however, strives to immerse herself in it with all her senses open to what the landscape means, or could mean. Imagination, not reason, directs the senses.

The humility that marks the poet's work, especially evident in Lilburn's poems, is appropriate to our work as geographers. As Dennis Cooley notes, "writing is scarcely able then to deliver satisfactorily 'true'

---

25 Mandel, "instructions: (on the nature of doubles and doubling)," in *The Other Harmony*, Vol. 1, 281.

26 It would seem that the challenge of uniting art and science is not for geographers alone. C. Day Lewis notes that behind the artistic impulse of the lyric poet is always the nagging sense of conflict with science. He comments on attempts by poets to avoid this conflict, saying, "he cannot revert to the relative sophistication of his ancestors without feeling that he has falsified modern knowledge or failed it: he cannot include such knowledge and write a simple lyric poem." So we have poets bothered by a scientific perspective that is in conflict with their imaginative impulse, and geographers with a nagging sense of an imaginative world lying behind or beyond the landscape they so carefully measure. Day Lewis, *The Lyric Impulse*, 23.

27 Jan Zwicky, "Lyric, Narrative, Memory," in *A Ragged Pen: Essays on Poetry & Memory* (Kentville: Gaspereau, 2006), 94.

28 "When places are actively sensed, the physical landscape becomes wedded to the landscape of the mind, to the roving imagination, and where the latter may lead is anybody's guess." Basso, *Wisdom Sits in Places*, 107.

accounts or 'accurate' perceptions of the place, and we are forever held in a position of duplicate culture."[29]

Tim Lilburn speaks of the "seeing ear,"[30] as does Lorna Crozier: "The task: to see clearly / so that even the ear becomes a kind of eye / taking you beyond the small circle / of your sight."[31] But we also need the "hearing eye" that looks at a landscape and hears the many voices involved in its making—voices that are repressed, marginalized, distorted, or forgotten. In our approach to landscapes, we need to hear the Aboriginal voice. Rich in their respect for the landscape that has been their home for generations, Aboriginal poets emphasize the joy and satisfaction they have in an intimate connection with the land, and they decry the damage being done to the land. It is a sentiment we see expressed in the recurring phrase "all my relations." Although Aboriginal poetry expresses a much more organic and holistic relationship with the land, many of the non-Aboriginal poets share the Aboriginal peoples' concern for the land, and recognize that the often unchecked abuse of the environment is caused by their own culture. We should also be attuned to the female voice, which reinforces our need to respect the land and which mourns the damage done to and the diminishment of its components. It also extends and emphasizes antipathy to oppression and domination in whatever form they occur. As geographers, and as a society, we should avoid the general attitude that people have toward nature, which Richard Jefferies describes as the landscape surrounding them but not entering them.[32] We are slow to learn the land's lessons, but listening to its many voices promises hope for the future.

Geographical writing demands the full range of scientific and humanistic acuity. Perhaps we need a new language, creating a new narrative to express a love of the land, as Linda Hogan suggests.[33] Barry Lopez agrees with and extends this sentiment: "It is not just words my colleagues are after but ways to make love clear, to adumbrate a mor-

---

29 Dennis Cooley, "Documents in the Postmodern Long Prairie Poem," in *History, Literature and the Writing of the Canadian Prairies*, eds. Alison Calder and Robert Wardhaugh (Winnipeg: University of Manitoba Press, 2005), 185.

30 Lilburn, "Poetry's Practice of Philosophy."

31 Crozier, "To See Clearly," in *Whetstone*, 18.

32 Blythe on Richard Jefferies' view of humans and nature in *Characters and their Landscapes*, 11.

33 Linda Hogan, "Creations," in Barbato and Weinerman, eds. *Heart of the Land*, 105.

al relationship with the land, often through vulnerability rather than blindness to the divine. Such a language would make it possible to speak of reciprocity and tenderness."[34] This is not the language of science—cold, objective, stripped of the colours of the imagination; this is the language of deeply observed and considered experience and emotion full of the lunge and reach and surprise of imagination. This is a language deeply rooted in a love for the prairie. The language of science cannot bear the imaginative weight of the observations and depictions of poets. Poets use focused observation and inventive language; the first undergirds the second, and the second makes the first indelible. Their work can stimulate geographical expression.

In his most recent book, Yi-Fu Tuan encourages a more "romantic" geography, rather than one that results in the prosaic pieces that characterize much geographical research. He encourages a geography of robust expression and recognition of paradox in its search for the sublime landscape. Tuan uses binaries to structure his approach to the sublime landscape: light and dark, order and chaos, mind and body, spirit and matter, culture and nature. Each of these paired elements can be and has been viewed as both good and bad. For Tuan, landscapes that are characterized by these paradoxical values are sublime.[35] In my approach I also view these antinomies as binaries, but I see them rendered by poets as parts of a larger whole. Prairie poets, in love with landscape and language, help us to see the prairies as a sublime landscape, by turns attractive and menacing. Poets reconstitute familiar scenes and elements with evocative imagery, broaden our perceptions, and give us a new vocabulary with which to express the sublime.

The geography of the prairies is not just about those elements that can be measured and tabulated; it is about peoples' perceptions of those elements and their reactions, in action and emotion, to them. Equally, the geography of the prairies is not just about external space and distance. It is also about the spaces we make in our minds and emotions for the voices of prairie people, and how intimately or distantly we connect to them, especially those whose voices are marginalized in mainstream writing. Omitting these interior geographies of the mind not only renders such geographies partial and misleading, it renders them poorer for

---

34 Lopez, "Foreword," xv.

35 Tuan, *Romantic Geography*.

the loss of the rich resources of the imagination that artists contribute to our understanding of regional geography.

The poetry of Glen Downie has become an important tool in the training of medical students by enlarging their understanding of, and reaction to, critically ill patients.[36] I am convinced that prairie poetry can, in much the same way, enlarge and enrich our understanding of the prairie landscape and give us a language with which to articulate feelings that we may otherwise find difficult to express. German literary scholar Wolfgang Iser identifies this process as a coming together of text and (the reader's) imagination. Reading, he says, "activates our own faculties, enabling us to recreate the world it presents."[37] Prairie poetry can do for geography what Dorothy Livesay claimed the documentary long poem does for history: "Such poems record immediate or past history [or landscape, for geography] in terms of the human story, in a poetic language that is vigorous, direct, and rendered emotionally powerful by the intensity of its imagery."[38]

In his perceptive essay on the Canadian prairie long poem, Dennis Cooley points out that document, or "fact-simile," is the source for many long poems, and as such is not only used in a new, literary way, but it retains a "residue" of its original source, at times investing the original with a new literary value. Similarly, I hope the imaginative depth that poetry brings to regional geography will not only stand alongside the scientific perspective—in a sense filling out or adding to what might be lacking in a strictly scientific perspective—but will invest the scientific perspective itself with a newly discovered imaginative resonance.

In the end, the task of the poet and the cultural geographer are similar: to encompass *reality*, a reality "at once flesh and spirit, fact and invention, the language of poetry and the continuously vital poem."[39]

---

36 "Glen Downie's poems have been powerful tools in the teaching of medical students. His perceptions and insights have opened their minds to their lives in medicine, and to the experience of patients." T. J. Murray, quoted on back jacket, Glen Downie, *Wishbone Dance: New and Selected Medical Poems* (Toronto: Wolsak and Wynn, 1999).

37 Wolfgang Iser, "The Reading Process: A Phenomenological Approach," *New Literary History*, Vol. 3, No. 2, On Interpretation: I (Winter, 1972): 284.

38 Quoted in Cooley, "Documents," 176.

39 William H. New, "Introduction," *Articulating West: Essays on Purpose and Form in Modern Canadian Literature* (Toronto: New Press, 1972), xxii.

I suppose all of this is more an appeal than an argument—an appeal to listen to the words of the prairie image-makers as they reveal a region not only of landforms and lists, of science and certainty, but also of myth and memory, of passion and paradox. If we do, we may write of the prairies with less certainty, but with greater understanding and with greater humility in the face of paradox and mystery. We may arrive at a truly romantic geography that recognizes and expresses the sublime contradiction of this "harsh and lovely land."[40] Or in the words of Lorna Crozier:

> If we don't know the taste of the earth where we live, if we can't lay our hands on the ground, how do we keep connected to that earth and its creatures? Is poetry that speaks of concerns outside of the corporate, urban world, old-fashioned, blind to reality, sentimentally nostalgic? Or is it reminding all of us what we need to remember to live passionately linked to place and to the past?[41]

---

40 Marshall, *Harsh and Lovely Land.*

41 Crozier, e-mail to the author, January 21, 2007.

Permissions

Images

The maps that appear in the introduction are courtesy of Peel's Prairie Provinces (peel.library.ualberta.ca), a digital initiative of the University of Alberta Libraries.

Poems

The author acknowledges and thanks the poets, the representatives of the poets, and the publishers of the poetry of the long passages reproduced in this book for granting permission to reprint them.

RITA BOUVIER

Excerpts from "*Epikwetamapiya*" and "Conversation with Peter Gzowski." Excerpted from *Blueberry Clouds* by Rita Bouvier. Copyright © 1999 Rita Bouvier. Reprinted by permission of Thistledown Press.

DI BRANDT

Excerpts from "Wake up: Four quartets," "Zone <le Detroit>," "Dreamsong for Eden," and "St. Norbert in July." Excerpted from *Now You Care* by Di Brandt. Copyright © 2003 Di Brandt. Reprinted by permission of Coach House Books.

Excerpts from "prairie hymn," "the man from the pulpit," "fathers never leave you," "I'm finding myself again in the healed heart," and "my father's hands." Excerpted from *Agnes in the Sky* by Di Brandt. Copyright © 1990 Di Brandt. Reprinted by permission of Turnstone Press.

Excerpts from "waking up in Jerusalem," "little poet, how i found you again," "there is only this lake, this wind," "this is it! i've found it at last! nirvana, the Elysian fields, heaven," "earth falling empty, silent" and "so, Maria, i've started hearing them." Excerpted from *Jerusalem, beloved* by Di Brandt. Copyright © 1995 Di Brandt. Reprinted by permission of Turnstone Press.

Excerpts from "Rodeo," "The Phoenicians," and "The lottery of history." Excerpted from *Walking to Mojácar* by Di Brandt. Copyright © 2010 Di Brandt. Reprinted by permission of Turnstone Press.

AARON BUSHKOWSKY

Excerpt from "at the edge of the world." Excerpted from *ed and mabel go to the moon* by Aaron Bushkowsky. Copyright © 1994. Reprinted by permission of Aaron Bushkowsky.

BRUCE CHESTER

Excerpt from "Hungry Moon." Excerpted from *Gatherings* 2 Theytus Books. Copyright © 1991. Reprinted by permission of Theytus Books Ltd.

BILL COHEN

Excerpt from "Lonely Metaphors are Story-less Figures." Excerpted from *Gatherings* 10 Theytus Books. Copyright © 1999. Reprinted by permission of Theytus Books Ltd.

DENNIS COOLEY

Excerpts from "in tongues" and "the heft of rocks." Excerpted from *correction line* by Dennis Cooley. Copyright © 2008 by Dennis Cooley. Reprinted by permission of Thistledown Press.

Excerpts from "this only world," "night prairie," "east of eden," "Madagascar," and "bonnie." Excerpted from *this only home* by Dennis Cooley. Copyright © 1992 Dennis Cooley. Reprinted by permission of Turnstone Press.

Excerpt from "Jan/us." Excerpted from *Leaving* by Dennis Cooley. Copyright © 1980. Reprinted by permission of Turnstone Press.

Excerpts from *Country Music* by Dennis Cooley. Copyright ©2004 Dennis Cooley. Reprinted by permission of Kalamalka Press.

Excerpts from "swept," "every year my dad drew lines," and "littoral." Excerpted from *sunfall* by Dennis Cooley. Copyright © 1996 Dennis Cooley. Reprinted by permission of Dennis Cooley.

Excerpts from "III" and "IV." Excerpted from *Fielding* by Dennis Cooley. Copyright © 1983 Dennis Cooley. Reprinted by permission of Dennis Cooley.

Excerpt from "Exorcism." Excerpted from *Soul Searching* by Dennis Cooley. Copyright © 1987 Dennis Cooley. Reprinted by permission of Dennis Cooley.

Excerpts from *the bentleys* by Dennis Cooley. Copyright © 2006 Dennis Cooley. Reprinted by permission of The University of Alberta Press.

Excerpts from "winter is when snakes," "in spring trees," "auguries of innocence," "prairie vernacular," "the taboo on saying what you don't," and "on the way to estevan (thanksgiving saturday /85)." Excerpted from *Perishable Light* by Dennis Cooley. Copyright © 1988 Dennis Cooley. Reprinted by permission of Dennis Cooley.

LORNA CROZIER

Excerpts from "The Photograph I Keep of Them," "Delight in the Small, the Silent," "Angel of Infinity," "The Day of the Animals," "Angel of Tigers," "The Dark Ages of the Sea," "Country Dwellers," and "The Origin of the Species." Excerpted from *The Blue Hour of the Day: Selected Poems* by Lorna Crozier. Copyright © 2007 Lorna Crozier. Reprinted by permission of McClelland & Stewart, a division of Random House of Canada Limited, a Penguin Random House Company.

Excerpt from "Genesis." Excerpted from *Small Mechanics* by Lorna Crozier. Copyright © 2011 Lorna Crozier. Reprinted by permission of McClelland & Stewart, a division of Random House of Canada Limited, a Penguin Random House Company.

Excerpts from "Shadow," "Rebuttal to the Higher Power," "Winter Day," "Summer Small Talk 4. Karl Marx Observes the Flowers." Excerpted from *Whetstone* by Lorna Crozier. Copyright © 2005 Lorna Crozier. Reprinted by permission of McClelland & Stewart, a division of Random House of Canada Limited, a Penguin Random House Company.

Excerpts from "Vertical Man," "Inner Space," and "Writing is All But." Excerpted from *Inside Is the Sky* by Lorna Uher (Crozier). Copyright © Lorna Uher. Reprinted by permission of Lorna Crozier.

Excerpts from "Drumheller," "Consummation," and "Sand Hills." Excerpted from *Crow's Black Joy* by Lorna Uher (Crozier). Copyright © 1978 Lorna Uher. Reprinted by permission of Lorna Crozier.

Excerpts from "Time to Praise," "The Language of Angels," and "On the Seventh Day." Excerpted from *Inventing the Hawk* by Lorna Crozier. Copyright © 1992 Lorna Crozier. Reprinted by permission of Lorna Crozier.

Excerpts from "Burial, Partridge Hill," "Wilderness," and "All the Room You Need." Excerpted from *A Saving Grace: The Collected Poems of Mrs. Bentley* by Lorna Crozier. Copyright © 1996 Lorna Crozier. Reprinted by permission of Lorna Crozier.

Excerpts from "As the line moves. The leap! Thrashing there," "There is no road without you," and "Original Sin 2. The Fall of Eve." Excerpted from

Apocrypha of Light by Lorna Crozier. Copyright © 2002 Lorna Crozier. Reprinted by permission of Lorna Crozier.

Excerpt from "Garden in Winter" from *The Garden Going on Without Us* by Lorna Crozier. Copyright © 1985 Lorna Crozier. Reprinted by permission of Lorna Crozier.

Excerpt from "All the Dancing Girls Lie Down." Excerpted from *Humans and Other Beasts* by Lorna Uher (Crozier). Copyright © 1980 Lorna Uher. Reprinted by permission of Lorna Crozier.

Excerpts from "Too Much Brightness" and "Night." Excerpted from *Everything Arrives at the Light* by Lorna Crozier. Copyright © 1995 Lorna Crozier. Reprinted by permission of Lorna Crozier.

Excerpts from *Bones in their Wings* by Lorna Crozier. Copyright © 2004 Lorna Crozier. Reprinted by permission of Lorna Crozier.

Excerpts from "Angels of Silence," and "Lines for the Earth." Excerpted from *Angels of Flesh, Angels of Silence* by Lorna Crozier. Copyright © 1988 Lorna Crozier. Reprinted by permission of Lorna Crozier.

Excerpts from "The Older Sister: Everything Yearns" and "Summer's End, Saskatchewan." Excerpted from *What the Living Won't Let Go* by Lorna Crozier. Copyright © 1999 Lorna Crozier. Reprinted by permission of Lorna Crozier.

BETH CUTHAND

Excerpts from "Four Songs for the Fifth Generation," "Horse Dance to Emerald Mountain," "He." Excerpted from *Voices in the Waterfall* by Beth Cuthand. Copyright © 1987 Beth Cuthand. Reprinted by permission of Beth Cuthand.

KATERI AKIWENZIE-DAMM

Excerpts from "I lose track of the land." Excerpted from *Gatherings 2*, Theytus Books. Copyright © 1991. Reprinted by permission of Theytus Books Ltd.

MARILYN DUMONT

Excerpts from "one season turns away," "We come to repeat ourselves," "my life, a sweet berry." Excerpted from *that tongued belonging* by Marilyn Dumont. Copyright © 2007 Marilyn Dumont. Reprinted by permission of Marilyn Dumont.

Excerpts from "Liquid Prairie," "not just a platform for my dance," "The White Judges," and "recovery." Excerpted from *A Really Good Brown Girl* by Marilyn Dumont. Copyright © 1996 Marilyn Dumont. Reprinted by permission of Marilyn Dumont.

Excerpt from "On the Surface." Excerpted from *Prairie Fire*. Copyright © 2001. Reprinted by permission of Marilyn Dumont.

CONNIE FIFE

Excerpts from "For Our Sons and Daughters" and "Mt. Douglas Beach." Excerpted from *Poems for a New World* by Connie Fife. Reprinted by permission of Ronsdale Press.

Excerpt from "Stains." Excerpted from *An Anthology of Canadian Native Literature* edited by D. Moses and T. Goldie. Copyright © 1998. Reprinted by permission of Connie Fife.

PATRICK FRIESEN

Excerpts from "thorkkelson glass," "big dave meets stephane grappelli," "the moon in the streets," "god's stench," "still life," "the eye," "provencher bridge," "forgetting into the city," "st. mary at main," and "st. michael & all angels." Excerpted from *st. mary at main* by Patrick Friesen. Copyright © 1998 Patrick Friesen. Reprinted by permission of J. Gordon Shillingford Publications Inc.

Excerpts from *A Broken Bowl* by Patrick Friesen. Copyright © 1997 Patrick Friesen. Reprinted by permission of Patrick Friesen.

Excerpt from "terrain." Excerpted from *the lands i am* by Patrick Friesen. Copyright © 1976 Patrick Friesen. Reprinted by permission of Patrick Friesen.

Excerpts from "wind," "columbine," and "summer dream." Excerpted from *Earth's Crude Gravities* by Patrick Friesen. Copyright © 2007 Patrick Friesen. Reprinted by permission of Patrick Friesen.

Excerpts from "light in june," "first river," and "give me flesh and give me wine." Excerpted from *the breath you take from the lord* by Patrick Friesen. Copyright © 2002 Patrick Friesen. Reprinted by permission of Patrick Friesen.

Excerpts from "fingerprint," "poem for a dog," and "small town." Excerpted from *carrying the shadow* by Patrick Friesen. Copyright © 1999 Patrick Friesen. Reprinted by permission of Patrick Friesen.

LOUISE HALFE

Excerpts from "Listen: To the Story" and "*ê-kwêskît* Pandora." Excerpted from *The Crooked Good* by Lousie Halfe. Copyright © 2007 Louise Halfe. Reprinted by permission of Coteau Books.

Excerpts from "Roots and Wings" and "Bone Lodge." Excerpted from *Bear Bones & Feathers* by Louise Halfe. Copyright © 1994 Louise Halfe. Reprinted by permission of Coteau Books.

Excerpts from *Blue Marrow* by Louise Halfe. Copyright © 1998 Louise Halfe. Reprinted by permission of Coteau Books.

EMMA LAROCQUE

Excerpts from "When I First Came to the City" and "The Geese Over the City." Excerpted from *Our Bit of Truth: An Anthology of Native Canadian Literature* edited by Agnes Grant. Copyright © 1990. Reprinted by permission of Emma LaRocque.

Excerpts from "Progress" and "Nostalgia." Excerpted from *Native Writers and Canadian Writing* edited by William New. Copyright © 1996. Reprinted by permission of Emma LaRocque.

DENISE LEVERTOV

Excerpt from "The Faithful Lover." Excerpted from *Evening Train*. Copyright © 1992 by Denise Levertov. Reprinted by permission of New Directions Publishing Corp.

TIM LILBURN

Excerpts from "Poverty" and "Marriage and Agriculture." Excerpted from *To the River* by Tim Lilburn. Copyright © 1999 Tim Lilburn. Reprinted by permission of McClelland & Stewart, a division of Random House of Canada Limited, a Penguin Random House Company.

Excerpts from "Discipline of Secrecy" and "Solo Orthodoxy." Excerpted from *Moosewood Sandhills* by Tim Lilburn. Copyright © 1994 Tim Lilburn. Reprinted by permission of Tim Lilburn.

Excerpts from "Spirit of Agriculture," "Touching an Elephant in a Dark Room," "Contemplation is Mourning," "Restoration," and "From an Anchorage." Excerpted from *Tourist to Ecstasy*. © 1989 Tim Lilburn. Reprinted by permission of Tim Lilburn.

Excerpts from "A Common Language," "Grim Invocations IV," "Grim Invocations V," "St. Dionysius the Areopagite: Six Letters to Timothy, I," and "St. Dionysius the Areopagite: Six Letters to Timothy, II." Excerpted from *Names of God*. Copyright © 1986 Tim Lilburn. Reprinted by permission of Tim Lilburn.

ELI MANDEL

Excerpts from "Val Marie," "Fair in Town," "Poems and Chorus from the Four Winds," "returning from war," "Narrative Poem" "Ancestral Voices Prophesying War," "*Grandfather's Painting*: David Thauberger," "Mary Midnight," "Two Dog Poems," "Street Lights," "Strange Places," "Journal Going Home: Regina 1979," "badlands," "Poetic Process," "Blizzard," "Beach at Miraflores," "Pictures in an Institution," "Envoi," "Wabamun," "near Hirsch a Jewish cemetery," "From the North Saskatchewan," "Hippolytus," "the double world," "birthmark," "Saskatchewan Surveyor," "The Dialogue of Last Mountain Lake," "Canto," "Estevan Saskatchewan," "Orpheus in the Underworld," "the hoffer colony," "doors of perception," and "the return." Excerpted from *The Other Harmony: The Collected Poetry of Eli Mandel*. Copyright © 2000 Eli Mandel. Reprinted by permission of the Estate of Eli Mandel, Anne Mandel Trustee.

JOHN NEWLOVE

Excerpts from "Why do you Hate Me," "The Sky," "The Hero Around Me," "White Lies," "Progress," "Kamsack," "East from the Mountains," "Indian Women," "The Double-Headed Snake," "Ride Off Any Horizon," "The Pride," and "The Prairie." Excerpted from *A Long Continual Argument: The Selected Poems of John Newlove* edited by Robert McTavish. Copyright © 2007 The Estate of John Newlove. Reprinted by permission of Chaudiere Books.

Excerpt from "If You Would Walk." Excerpted from *Lies* by John Newlove. Copyright © 1972 John Newlove. Reprinted by permission of The Estate of John Newlove, Susan Newlove Trustee.

ARMAND RUFFO

Excerpts from "Chant for Mother and Child," "Paleo Song,"and "Mandate." Excerpted from *Opening in the Sky* by Armand Ruffo. Copyright © 1994 Armand Ruffo. Reprinted by permission of Armand Ruffo.

GREGORY SCOFIELD

Excerpt from "Divided." Excerpted from *Kipochkân: Poems New and Selected* by Gregory Scofield. Copyright © 2009 Gregory Scofield. Reprinted by permission of Nightwood Editions, 2009, www.nightwoodeditions.com.

ANDREW SUKNASKI

Excerpt from "Narayan." Excerpted from *The Land They Gave Away* by Andrew Suknaski. Copyright © 1982 Andrew Suknaski. Reprinted by permission of The Estate of Andrew Suknaski.

Excerpts from "Indian Site on the Edge of Tonita Pasture" and "Wood Mountain Almanac." Excerpted from *Wood Mountain Poems* by Andrew Suknaski. Copyright © 1976 Andrew Suknaski. Reprinted by permission of The Estate of Andrew Suknaski.

Excerpt from "Pacific Western Flight North." Excerpted from *East of Myloona* by Andrew Suknaski. Copyright © 1979 Andrew Suknaski. Reprinted by permission of The Estate of Andrew Suknaski.

Excerpt from "Manitou." Excerpted from *Octomi* by Andrew Suknaski. Copyright © 1976 Andrew Suknaski. Reprinted by permission of The Estate of Andrew Suknaski.

JAN ZWICKY

Excerpts from "Highway 879," "Driving Northwest," "Beethoven: Op. 95," and "Beethoven: Op. 127, Adagio." Excerpted from *Songs for Relinquishing the Earth* by Jan Zwicky. Copyright © 1998 Jan Zwicky. Reprinted by permission of Brick Books.

Excerpts from "Small Song: Prairie" and "Study: August Fields." Excerpted from *Thirty-seven Small Songs and Thirteen Silences* by Jan Zwicky. Copyright © 2005 Jan Zwicky. Reprinted by permission of Gaspereau Press.

Bibliography

Abley, Mark. "Laying Down the Law." In Dyck, *Essays on Saskatchewan Writing*, 163–168.

Adamson, Arthur. "Notes from a Dark Cellar: Ruminations on the Nature of Regionalism and Metaphor in Mid-Western Canadian Poetry." In Cooley, *RePlacing*, 223–241.

Akiwenzie-Damm, Kateri. "We Belong to This Land: A View of 'Cultural Difference.'" In *Literary Pluralities*, edited by Christl Verduyn, pp. 84–91. Peterborough: Broadview, 1998.

———. *See also* Damm, Kateri.

Andrews, Malcolm. *Landscape and Western Art*. Oxford: Oxford University Press, 1999.

Banting, Pamela. *Fresh Tracks: Writing the Western Landscape*. Victoria: Polestar, 1998.

Barbato, Joseph, and Lisa Weinerman, eds. *Heart of the Land: Essays on Last Great Places*. New York: Pantheon, 1994.

Barnes, Trevor, and Derek Gregory, eds. *Reading Human Geography: The Poetics and Politics of Inquiry*. London: Arnold, 1997.

Basso, Keith. *Wisdom Sits in Places: Landscape and Language among the Western Apache*. Albuquerque: University of New Mexico Press, 1996.

Berry, Wendell. *Life is a Miracle: An Essay Against Modern Superstition*. Washington, DC: Counterpoint, 2001.

Bifford, Darren, and Warren Heiti, eds. *Chamber Music: The Poetry of Jan Zwicky*. Waterloo: Wilfrid Laurier University Press, 2015.

Bircham, Doris. "On the Move." In Stone, *Riding the Northern Range*.

Blouet, Brian, and Merlin Lawson, eds. *Images of the Plains: The Role of Human Nature in Settlement*. Lincoln: University of Nebraska Press, 1975.

Blythe, Ronald. *Characters and their Landscapes*. New York: Harcourt, Brace and Jovanovich, 1984.

Bouvier, Rita. *Blueberry Clouds*. Saskatoon: Thistledown, 1999.

———. nakamowin'sa *for the seasons*. Saskatoon: Thistledown, 2015.

Bowering, George. *Changing on the Fly: The Best Lyric Poems of George Bowering*. Vancouver: Raincoast, 2004.

Bowling, Tim, ed. *Where the Words Come From: Canadian Poets in Conversation*. Roberts Creek, BC: Nightwood, 2002.

Brandt, Di. *Agnes in the Sky*. Winnipeg: Turnstone, 1990.

———. *Dancing Naked: Narrative Strategies for Writing Across Centuries*. Stratford: Mercury Press, 1996.

———. *Jerusalem, beloved*. Winnipeg: Turnstone, 1995.

———. "A New Genealogy of Canadian Literary Modernism." In Brandt and Godard, *Wider Boundaries of Daring*, 1–25.

———. *Now You Care*. Toronto: Coach House, 2003.

———. "The Poet and the Wild City." *Journal of Mennonite Studies* 20 (2002): 89–103.

———. *Questions I Asked My Mother.* Winnipeg: Turnstone, 1987.

———. *So this is the world & here I am in it.* Edmonton: NeWest, 2007.

———. "'The Sound the Wind Makes': A Sh(e) mail Interview with Randi Patterson." In Brandt, *Dancing Naked,* 110–126.

———. *Walking to Mojácar.* Winnipeg: Turnstone, 2010.

———. "*Wild Mother Dancing*: An Interview with Di Brandt." By Clarise Foster. *CV2* 24:4 (Spring 2002): 28–32.

Brandt, Di, and Barbara Godard, eds. *Wider Boundaries of Daring: The Modernist Impulse in Canadian Women's Poetry.* Waterloo: Wilfrid Laurier Press, 2009.

Brosseau, Marc. "Geography's Literature." *Progress in Human Geography* 18, no. 3 (1994): 333–353.

Bruce, Todd, and Robert Budde. "Cooley Dreams His Way Into the World: A Conversation." *Prairie Fire* 19, no. 1 (Spring 1998): 47–65.

Burton, G. T. *Cow Pies and Candle Lights.* Morris Publishing, 1999.

Bushkowsky, Aaron. *ed and mabel go to the moon.* Lantzville: Oolichan, 1994.

Calder, Alison, and Robert Wardhaugh. "When is the Prairie?" In Calder and Wardhaugh, *History, Literature, and the Writing of the Canadian Prairies,* 3–24.

Calder, Alison, and Robert Wardhaugh, eds. *History, Literature, and the Writing of the Canadian Prairies.* Winnipeg: University of Manitoba Press, 2005.

Campbell, Maria. "'You Have to Own Yourself': An Interview with Maria Campbell." By Doris Hillis. *Prairie Fire* 9, no. 3 (Autumn 1988): 44–58.

Cannon, Hal, ed. *Cowboy Poetry: A Gathering.* Salt Lake City: Peregrine Smith, 1985.

Chamberlain, Paul G. "Work in Progress on the Dasein of the Shakespearean Landscape." *Western Geography* 3 (1993): 85–108.

Chamberlin, J. Edward. "*Klahowya Tillicum*: Coming Home to the Stories and Songs of the West Coast." *Journal of Canadian Studies* 46, no. 2 (Spring 2012): 99–121.

Chester, Bruce. "The Hungry Moon." *Gatherings: The En-owkin Journal of First North American Peoples* 2 (1991), 47.

Cohen, Bill. "Lonely Metaphors Are Story-less Figures." *Gatherings: The En'owkin Journal of First North American Peoples* 10 (1999): 82.

Conkin, Jake. *Silk 'n' Silver and other things too!.* Sundre: Buckaroo Jake Productions, 1991.

Cooke, Nathalie. "Lorna Crozier and Her Works." In Lecker et al., *Canadian Writers and Their Works,* Vol. 11, 75–155.

Cookshaw, Marlene. *Double Somersaults.* London: Brick Books, 1999.

Cooley, Dennis, ed. *the bentleys.* Edmonton: University of Alberta Press, 2006.

———. *correction line.* Saskatoon: Thistledown, 2008.

———. *Country Music: New Poems.* Vernon: Kalamalka, 2004.

———. *Dedications.* Saskatoon: Thistledown, 1988.

———. "Documents in the Postmodern Long Prairie Poem." In Calder and Wardhaugh, *History, Literature and the Writing of the Canadian Prairies,* 175–211.

———. "Eli Mandel and His Works." In Lecker et al., *Canadian Writers and Their Works,* Vol. 10, 187–277.

———. *Fielding.* Saskatoon: Thistledown, 1983.

———. *Inscriptions: A Prairie Poetry Anthology*. Winnipeg: Turnstone, 1992.
———. *Irene*. Winnipeg: Turnstone, 2000.
———. *Leaving*. Winnipeg: Turnstone, 1980.
———. *Passwords: Transmigrations between Canada and Europe*. Edited by Hans Braun, Wolfgang Klooss, and Markus Müller. Kiel: l&f Verlag, 1996.
———. *Perishable Light*. Moose Jaw: Coteau, 1988.
———. *Soul Searching*. Red Deer: Red Deer College Press, 1987.
———. *the stones*. Winnipeg: Turnstone, 2013.
———. *sunfall: New and Selected Poems, 1980–1996*. Concord: Anansi, 1996.
———. *this only home*. Winnipeg: Turnstone, 1992.
———. "RePlacing." In Cooley, *RePlacing*, 9–20.
———, ed. *RePlacing*. Downsview: ECW Press, 1980.
———. "The Vernacular Muse in Prairie Poetry." In *The Vernacular Muse*, 167–222. Winnipeg: Turnstone, 1987.
Costello, Bonnie. "The Soil and Man's Intelligence: Three Contemporary Landscape Poets." *Contemporary Literature* Vol 30, no. 3 (1989): 412–433.
Crozier, Lorna. "Afterword: See How Many Ends This Stick Has." In *Before the First Word: The Poetry of Lorna Crozier*, selected by Catherine Hunter, 55–60. Waterloo: Wilfrid Laurier Press, 2005.
———. *Angels of Flesh, Angels of Silence*. Toronto: McClelland & Stewart, 1988.
———. *Apocrypha of Light*. Toronto: McClelland & Stewart, 2002.
———. *Bones in Their Wings: Ghazals*. Regina: Hagios, 2003.
———. *Everything Arrives at the Light*. Toronto: McClelland & Stewart, 1995.
———. *The Garden Going On Without Us*. Toronto: McClelland & Stewart, 1985.
———. Introduction to Crozier and Hyland, *A Sudden Radiance*, xv–xxi.
———. *Inventing the Hawk*. Toronto: McClelland & Stewart, 1992.
———. *man from elsewhere*. Saskatoon: Jack Pine Press, 2013.
———. "The Real Truth, The Poetic Truth: An Interview with Lorna Crozier." By Doris Hillis. *Prairie Fire* 6, no. 3 (Summer 1985): 4–15.
———. *A Saving Grace: The Collected Poems of Mrs. Bentley*. Toronto: McClelland & Stewart, 1996.
———. "Seeing Distance: Lorna Crozier's Art of Paradox." Interview by Elizabeth Philips. In Bowling, *Where the Words Come From*, 139–158.
———. *small beneath the sky*. Vancouver: Greystone, 2009.
———. *Small Mechanics*. Toronto: McClelland & Stewart, 2011.
———. *The Weather*. Regina: Coteau, 1983.
———. *What the Living Won't Let Go*. Toronto: McClelland & Stewart, 1999.
———. *Whetstone*. Toronto: McClelland & Stewart, 2003.
———. *See also* Uher, Lorna.
Crozier, Lorna, and Gary Hyland, eds. *A Sudden Radiance: Saskatchewan Poetry*. Regina: Coteau, 1987.
Cuthand, Beth. *Voices in the Waterfall*. Vancouver: Lazara, 1989.
Damm, Kateri. "i lose track of the land." *Gatherings: The En-owkin Journal of First North American Peoples* 2 (1991): 29.

———. *See also* Akiwenzie-Damm, Kateri

Dansereau, Pierre. "Introduction." *Inscape and Landscape*, np. Toronto: CBC, 1973.

Davey, Frank. "A Young Boy's Eden: Notes on Recent 'Prairie' Poetry." In *Reading Canadian Reading*, 213–229. Winnipeg: Turnstone, 1988.

Day Lewis, C. *The Lyric Impulse*. Cambridge: Harvard University Press, 1965.

Deerchild, Rosanna. "back on the rez." *Prairie Fire* 22, no. 3 (Autumn 2001): 85.

———. *Manitoba Scene*. CBC online. www.cbc.ca/manitoba/scene/books/2011/04/11/post/

Deloria, Philip J. *Playing Indian*. New Haven: Yale University Press, 1998.

Douaud, Patrick C., and Bruce W. Dawson, eds. *Plain Speaking: Essays on Aboriginal Peoples and the Prairie*. Regina: Canadian Plains Research Center, 2002.

Downie, Glen. *Heartland*. Oakville: Mosaic, 1990.

———. *Wishbone Dance: New and Selected Medical Poems*. Toronto: Wolsak and Wynn, 1999.

Dudek, Louis. "At Lac en Coeur," In *Canadian Poetry: The Modern Era*, edited by John Newlove, 78–79. Toronto: McClelland & Stewart, 1977.

———. *The First Person in Literature: Six Talks for CBC Radio*. Toronto: CBC Publications, 1967.

Dumont, Marilyn. *green girl dreams Mountains*. Lantzville: Oolichan, 2001.

———. "On the surface." *Prairie Fire* 22, no. 3 (Autumn 2001): 193.

———. Poetry Reading. Paper presented at "The Last Best West or Just Like the Rest: Interrogating Western Canadian Identities" Conference, Kamloops British Columbia, September 13, 2007.

———. *A Really Good Brown Girl*. London: Brick, 1996.

———. *that tongued belonging*. Wiarton, ON: Kegedonce, 2007.

Duncan, James, and David Ley, eds. *Place/Culture/Representation*. New York: Routledge, 1993.

Dyck, E. F., ed. *Essays on Saskatchewan Writing*. Regina: Saskatchewan Writer's Guild, 1986.

———. "Place in the Poetry of John Newlove." *Canadian Literature* 122–123 (Autumn-Winter, 1989): 69–91.

Entrikin, J. Nicholas. "The Betweenness of Place." In Barnes and Gregory, *Reading Human Geography*, 299–314.

———. *The Betweenness of Place: Towards a Geography of Modernity*. Baltimore: Johns Hopkins University Press, 1991.

Fairbanks, Carol. *Prairie Women: Images in American and Canadian Fiction*. New Haven: Yale University Press, 1986.

Ference, Ermeline."Alberta Ranching and Literature." In *Frontier Calgary: Town, City, and Region, 1875–1914*. edited by A. W. Rasporich and Henry Klassen, 71–86. Calgary: University of Calgary; McClelland & Stewart West, 1975.

Fife, Connie, ed. *The Colour of Resistance: A Contemporary Collection of Writing by Aboriginal Women*. Toronto: Sister Vision Press, 1993.

———. *Poems for a New World*. Vancouver: Ronsdale, 2001.

———. "Stains." In Moses and Goldie, *Anthology of Canadian Native Literature*, 433.

Flanagan, Richard. *The Narrow Road to the Deep North*. New York: Knopf, 2014.
Foster, Clarise. Online review of Di Brandt's *Now You Care, Globe and Mail*, April 17, 2004.
Friesen, Patrick. "An Interview with Patrick Friesen." By Clarise Foster. *CV2* 24:3 (Winter 2002): 14–15.
———. *bluebottle*. Winnipeg: Turnstone, 1978.
———. *the breath you take from the lord*. Madeira Park: Harbour, 2002.
———. *A Broken Bowl*. London: Brick Books, 1997.
———. *carrying the shadow*. Vancouver: Beach Holme, 1999.
———. *a dark boat*. Vancouver: Anvil Press, 2012.
———. *Earth's Crude Gravities*. Madeira Park: Harbour, 2007.
———. "Gathering Bones." *Poetry Canada Review* 14, no. 4 (1994): 14–15.
———. *Interim: Essays and Mediations*. Regina: Hagios, 2006.
———. *jumping in the asylum*. Toronto: Quattro, 2011.
———. *the lands i am*. Winnipeg: Turnstone, 1976.
———. *st. mary at main*. Winnipeg: The Muses, 1998.
———. *Unearthly Horses*. Winnipeg: Turnstone, 1984.
———. *You Don't Get to Be a Saint*. Winnipeg: Turnstone, 1992.
Frye, Northrop. *The Bush Garden: Essays on the Canadian Imagination*. Toronto: Anansi, 1971.
———. *Divisions on a Ground: Essays on Canadian Culture*. Toronto: Anansi, 1982.
Gayton, Don. *Landscapes of the Interior: Re-Explorations of Nature and the Human Spirit*. Gabriola Island: New Society Publishers, 1996.
Geddes, Gary, ed. *15 Canadian Poets x 3*. Toronto: Oxford, 2001.
Gerson, Carole. "Sarah Binks and Edna Jaques: Parody, Gender, and the Construction of Literary Value." *Canadian Literature* 134 (Autumn 1992): 62–73.
Glacken, Clarence. *Traces on the Rhodian Shore: Nature and Culture in Western Thought from Ancient Times to the End of the Eighteenth Century*. Berkeley: University of California Press, 1967.
Glickman, Susan. *The Picturesque and the Sublime: A Poetics of the Canadian Landscape*. Montreal: McGill-Queens University Press, 1998.
Gottfriedson, Gary. *Whiskey Bullets: Cowboy and Indian Heritage Poems*. Vancouver: Ronsdale Press, 2006.
Grant, Agnes, ed. *Our Bit of Truth: An Anthology of Canadian Native Literature*. Winnipeg: Pemmican Publications, 1990.
Gunners, Kristjana."Meditation on a Snowy Morning: A Conversation With Robert Kroetsch." *Prairie Fire* 8, no. 4 (Winter 1987–88): 54–67.
Gyepi-Garbrah, John, Ryan Walker and Joseph Garcea."Indigeneity, Immigrant Newcomers, and Interculturalism in Winnipeg, Canada." *Urban Studies*, vol. 51, no. 9 (July 2014): 1795-1811.
Halfe, Louise. *Bear Bones & Feathers*. Regina: Coteau, 1994.
———. *Blue Marrow*. Regina: Coteau, 2004.
———. *The Crooked Good*. Regina: Coteau, 2007.
Hogan, Linda. "Creations." In Barbato and Weinerman, *Heart of the Land*, 92–109.

Iser, Wolfgang. "The Reading Process: A Phenomenological Approach." *New Literary History*, vol. 3, no. 2, On Interpretation: I (Winter, 1972): 279–299.

Jaques, Edna. *Aunt Hattie's Place*. Toronto: Thomas Allen, 1941.

———. *Backdoor Neighbors*. Toronto: Thomas Allen, 1946.

———. *Beside Still Waters*. Toronto: Thomas Allen, 1939.

———. *Dreams in Your Heart*. Toronto: Thomas Allen, 1937.

———. *Fireside Poems*. Toronto: Thomas Allen, 1950.

———. *Hills of Home*. Toronto: Thomas Allen, 1948.

———. *My Kitchen Window*. Toronto: Thomas Allen, 1935.

———. *Prairie Born, Prairie Bred: Poetic Reflections of a Pioneer*. Saskatoon: Western Producer Prairie Books, 1979.

———. *Roses in December*. Toronto: Thomas Allen, 1944.

———. *Uphill All The Way: The Autobiography of Edna Jaques*. Saskatoon: Western Producer Prairie Books, 1977.

Johnie, Curtis "Shingoose". "Reservation Blues – A Song." *Gatherings: The En-owkin Journal of First North American Peoples* Vol. 2 (1991): 55.

Jones, D. G. *Butterfly on Rock*. Toronto: University of Toronto Press, 1970.

Jones, Peter, ed. *Imagist Poetry*. Harmondsworth: Penguin, 1972.

Jong, Erica. *At the Edge of the Body*. New York: Holt, Rinehart & Winston, 1979.

Keahey, Deborah. *Making it Home: Place in Canadian Prairie Literature*. Winnipeg: University of Manitoba Press, 1998.

Keith, W. J. *Literary Images of Ontario*. Toronto: University of Toronto Press, 1992.

King, Thomas A. *From a Cowboy's Office Window!: Cowboy Poetry*. Sundre, AB: Akita, nd.

Kingsolver, Barbara. *Animal Dreams*. New York: HarperCollins Perennial, 1990.

Kittredge, William. "The Good Rain: Stegner and the Wild." In *Wallace Stegner, Man and Writer*, edited by Charles E. Rankin, 39–42. Albuquerque: University of New Mexico Press, 1996.

Kizuk, R. Alexander. "Desert Words: Eli Mandel's Poetry." Online review of *The Other Harmony: The Collected Poetry of Eli Mandel*, edited by Andrew Stubbs and Judy Chapman. *Canadian Poetry* 49 (2001): 113. http://www.canadianpoetry.ca/cpjrn/vol49/kizuk.ht.

Klein, A. M. "Writing in Canada." In *Literary Essays and Reviews*. Edited by Usher Caplan and M. W. Steinberg. Toronto: University of Toronto Press, 1987.

Kneale, James. "The Poem That Responds to London: Writing Landscape." Paper presented at the Writing Landscape Symposium, March 2007.

Kolodny, Annette. *The Lay of the Land: Metaphor as Experience and History in American Life and Letters*. Chapel Hill: University of North Carolina Press, 1975.

Kreisel, Henry. "The Prairie: A State of Mind." In Mandel, *Contexts of Canadian Criticism*, 254–266.

Kroetsch, Robert. *Completed Field Notes: The Long Poems of Robert Kroetsch*. Edmonton: University of Alberta Press, 2000.

———. "Effing the Ineffable." In Dyck, *Essays on Saskatchewan Writing*, 143–144.

———. *A Likely Story: The Writing Life*. Red Deer: Red Deer College Press, 1995.

———. "On Being an Alberta Writer: Or, I Wanted to Tell Our Story." In *The New Provinces: Alberta and Saskatchewan, 1905–1980: 12th Western Canada Studies Conference*, edited by Howard Palmer and Donald Smith, 217–227. Vancouver: Tantalus, 1980.

———. "Uncovering Our Dream World: An Interview with Robert Kroetsch." By Robert Enright and Dennis Cooley. In Cooley, *RePlacing*, 21–32.

Kuffert, Len, ed. *The Prairies Lost and Found*. Winnipeg: St. John's College Press, 2007.

Lane, Patrick. "A Brooding Upon the Heart of Things." Interview by Russell Thornton. In Bowling, *Where the Words Come From*, 62–74.

———. "The Poetry of Andy Suknaski." In Cooley, *RePlacing*, 90–99.

LaRocque, Emma. "Conversations on Metis Identity." *Prairie Fire* 7, no. 1 (Spring 1986): 19–24.

———. "The Geese Over the City." In Grant, *Our Bit of Truth*, 341.

———. "Nostalgia." In New, *Native Writers and Canadian Writing*, 132.

———. "'Progress.'" In New, *Native Writers and Canadian Writing*, 137.

———. "When I First Came to the City." In Grant, *Our Bit of Truth*, 341.

———. *When the Other Is Me: Native Resistance Discourse, 1850–1990*. Winnipeg: University of Manitoba Press, 2010.

Lecker, Robert, Jack David, and Ellen Quigley, eds. *Canadian Writers and Their Works*. Poetry Series, 12 vols. Toronto: ECW Press, 1983–.

Lent, John. *Frieze*. Saskatoon: Thistledown, 1984.

Levertov, Denise. *Evening Train*. New York: New Directions, 1992.

Lewis, G. Malcolm. "The Recognition and Delimitation of the Northern Interior Grasslands during the Eighteenth Century." In Blouet and Lawson, *Images of the Plains*, 23–44.

Ley, David, and Marwyn Samuels, eds. *Humanistic Geography: Prospects and Problems*. Chicago: Maaroufa Press, 1978.

Lilburn, Tim. "Afterword: Walking Out of Silence." In *Desire Never Leaves: The Poetry of Tim Lilburn*, edited by Alison Calder, 41–48. Waterloo: Wilfrid Laurier Press, 2007.

———. *Assiniboia*. Toronto: McClelland & Stewart, 2012.

———. *From the Great Above She Opened Her Ear to the Great Below*. Ilderton: Brick Books, 1988.

———. *Kill-site*. Toronto: McClelland & Stewart, 2003.

———. *Moosewood Sandhills*. Toronto: McClelland & Stewart, 1994.

———. *Names of God*. Lantzville: Oolichan, 1986.

———. *Newton, Force at a Distance, Imperialism*. Hong Kong: The Chinese University Press, 2013.

———. "Poetry's Practice of Philosophy." *Prairie Fire* 23, no.3 (Autumn 2002): 33–40.

———. "The Provisional Shack of the Ear." Interview by Shawna Lemay. In Bowling, *Where the Words Come From*, 174–183.

———. *To the River*. Toronto: McClelland & Stewart,1999.

———. *Tourist to Ecstasy*. Toronto: Exile Editions, 1989.

Livesay, Dorothy. *Collected Poems: The Two Seasons*. Toronto: McGraw Hill Ryerson, 1972.

Locher, Frances C., ed. "Andrew Suknaski." *Contemporary Authors 101*. Detroit: Gale Research, 1981, 492–493.

Lopez, Barry. "Foreword." In Barbato and Weinerman, *Heart of the Land*, xiii–xxi.

Lundy, Randy. "Poetry and the Prairie: Writing, *Aboriginality*, and the Land." In Douaud and Dawson, *Plain Speaking*, 77–88.

Mandel, Eli, ed. *Contexts of Canadian Criticism: A Collection of Critical Essays*. Chicago: U of Chicago Press, 1971.

———. "Interview with Eli Mandel, March 16/78." By David Arnason, Dennis Cooley, and Robert Enright. *Essays on Canadian Writing* 18/19 (Summer/Fall 1980): 70–90.

———. "Introduction." In Mandel, *Contexts of Canadian Criticism*, 3–25.

———. *The Other Harmony: The Collected Poetry of Eli Mandel*. Edited by Andrew Stubbs and Judy Chapman. 2 vols. Regina: Canadian Plains Research Center, 2000.

———. "Romance and Realism in Western Canadian Fiction." In *Prairie Perspectives 2*, edited by A. W. Rasporich and H. C. Klassen, 197–211. Toronto: Holt, Rinehart and Winston, 1973.

———. "Writing West: On the Road to Wood Mountain." In Dyck, *Essays on Saskatchewan Writing*, 145–158.

Marshall, Tom. *Harsh and Lovely Land: The Major Canadian Poets and the Making of a Canadian Tradition*. Vancouver: University of British Columbia Press, 1979.

Martel, Yann. *Life of Pi*. Toronto: Knopf Canada, 2000.

McKay, Don. *Apparatus*. Toronto: McClelland & Stewart, 1997.

McRae, Wallace. *Stick Horses*. Layton, Utah: Gibbs Smith, 2009.

———. "A Conversation with Albert." In Stone, *Riding the Northern Range*, 49–50.

Meili, Neil. "The Lonely Men." In Stone, *Riding the Northern Range*, 119.

———. "Round-Up." In Stone, *Riding the Northern Range*, 117–118.

Melnyk, George. *New Moon at Batoche: Reflections on the Urban Prairie*. Banff, AB: Banff Centre Press, 1999.

Miłosz, Czesław. *The Collected Poems*. Hopewell, NJ: Ecco Press, 1988.

Mitchell, W. O. *Who Has Seen the Wind*. Toronto: Macmillan, 1947.

Moore, G. T. and R. G. Golledge, ed. *Environmental Knowing: Theories, Research, and Methods*. Stroudsburg: Dowden, Hutchinson & Ross, 1976.

Morton, W. L. "Seeing an Unliterary Landscape." In special issue "Manitoba in Literature." *Mosaic* 3, no. 3 (Spring 1970): 1–10.

Moses, Daniel David, and Terry Goldie, eds. *An Anthology of Canadian Native Literature in English*. 2nd Edition. Toronto: Oxford, 1998.

Murphy, Rex. *Points of View*. Toronto: McClelland & Stewart, 2003.

New, William. "Introduction." *Articulating West: Essays on Purpose and Form in Modern Canadian Literature*, xi–xxvi. Toronto: New Press, 1972.

———. *Land Sliding: Imagining Space, Presence, and Power in Canadian Writing*. Toronto: University of Toronto Press, 1997.

———, ed. *Native Writers and Canadian Writing.* Vancouver: University of British Columbia Press, 1990.

Newlove, John. *A Long Continual Argument: The Selected Poems of John Newlove.* Edited by Robert McTavish. Ottawa: Chaudiere Books, 2007.

———. *Apology for Absence: Selected Poems, 1962–1992.* Erin, ON: Porcupine's Quill, 1993.

———. *Black Night Window.* Toronto: McClelland & Stewart, 1968.

———, ed. *Canadian Poetry: The Modern Era.* Toronto: McClelland & Stewart, 1977.

———. *The Cave.* Toronto: McClelland & Stewart, 1970.

———. *Lies.* Toronto: McClelland & Stewart, 1972.

———. *Moving in Alone.* Toronto: Contact Press, 1965.

———. *The Night the Dog Smiled.* Toronto: ECW Press, 1986.

———. *What They Say.* (Kitchener: Weed/Flower, 1967).

Niven, Frederick. *The Flying Years.* London: Collins, 1935.

Nolan, James. *Poet-Chief: The Native American Poetics of Walt Whitman and Pablo Neruda.* Albuquerque: University of New Mexico Press, 1994.

Ong, Walter. *Orality and Literacy: The Technologizing of the Word.* New York: Routledge, 1982.

Ortner, Sherry. *Making Gender: The Politics and Erotics of Culture.* Boston: Beacon, 1996.

Pacey, Desmond. "The Canadian Imagination." In Pacey, *Essays in Canadian Criticism*, 234–240.

———, ed. *Essays in Canadian Criticism, 1938–1968.* Toronto: Ryerson, 1969.

Page, P. K. *The Hidden Room: Collected Poems, Volume Two.* Erin: The Porcupine's Quill, 1997.

Palmer, Howard, and Donald Smith, ed. *The New Provinces: Alberta and Saskatchewan, 1905–1980: 12th Western Canada Studies Conference.* Vancouver: Tantalus, 1980.

Popper, Deborah, and Frank Popper. "The Buffalo Commons: Metaphor as Method." *The Geographical Review* 89:4 (October 1999): 491–510.

Pruyser, Paul. *Between Belief and Unbelief.* New York: Harper & Row, 1974.

Puhallo, Mike and Wendy Liddle. *Meadow Muffins: Cowboy Rhymes and Other B.S.*. Surrey: Hancock House, 1999.

———. *Rhymes and Damn Lies.* Surrey: Hancock House, 2006.

Puhallo, Mike, Brian Brannon, and Wendy Liddle. *Can't Stop Rhymin' on the Range.* Surrey: Hancock, 1997.

———. *Rhymes on the Range.* Surrey: Hancock, 1995.

———. *Still Rhymin' on the Range.* Surrey: Hancock, 1996.

Quantic, Diane. "Afloat on the Sea of Grass: Transforming the Myth." In *The Nature of the Place: A Study of Great Plains Fiction.* Lincoln: University of Nebraska Press, 1995.

Rees, Ron. *New and Naked Land: Making the Prairies Home.* Saskatoon: Western Producer Prairie Books, 1988.

Relke, Diana. *Greenwor(l)ds: Ecocritical Readings of Canadian Women's Poetry.* Calgary: University of Calgary Press, 1999.

Richards, Doug. *Listen to Her Rodeo.* Moosehorn, MB: Ramshead, 1993.

Ricou, Laurence (Laurie). "Circumference of Absence: Land and Space in the Poetry of the Canadian Plains." In *Man and Nature on the Prairies,* edited by Richard Allen, 66–76. Canadian Plains Study 6. Regina: Canadian Plains Research Center, 1976.

———. "The Meadowlark Tradition: Popular Verse of the Canadian Prairie." In Cooley, *RePlacing*, 161–168.

———. *Twelve Prairie Poets*. Ottawa: Oberon, 1976.

———. *Vertical Man/Horizontal World: Man and Landscape in Canadian Prairie Fiction*. Vancouver: University of British Columbia Press, 1973.

Rifkind, Candida. "Too Close to Home: Middlebrow Anti-Modernism and the Sentimental Poetry of Edna Jaques." *Journal of Canadian Studies* 39, no. 1 (Winter 2005): 90–114.

Roethke, Theodore. *Words for the Wind: The Collected Verse of Theodore Roethke.* Bloomington: University of Indiana Press, 1964.

Rose, Gillian. "Looking at Landscape: The Uneasy Pleasure of Power." In Barnes and Gregory, *Reading Human Geography*, 266–276.

Ruffo, Armand. *At Geronimo's Grave*. Regina: Coteau, 1991.

———. *Grey Owl: The Mystery of Archie Belaney*. Regina: Coteau, 1998.

———. *Opening in the Sky*. Penticton: Theytus, 1994.

Salter, C. L. and W. J. Lloyd, *Landscape in Literature*. Resource Papers for College Geography 76–3. Washington, DC: Association of American Geographers, 1977.

Schlottmann, Antje. "Limited Language/Linguistic Limitations: A Reply to the Reviews." *Acme* 4, no. 2 (2005): 270–277.

Scofield, Gregory. *Kipocihkân: Poems New and Selected*. Madeira Park: Nightwood, 2009.

Skelton, Robin, ed. *Poetry of the Thirties*. London: Penguin, 1964.

Sorensen, Sue, ed. *West of Eden: Essays on Canadian Prairie Literature*. Winnipeg: CMU Press, 2008.

Spender, Stephen. "The Landscape near an Aerodrome." In Skelton, *Poetry of the Thirties*, 82-83.

Stegner, Wallace. "The Question Mark in the Circle." In *Wolf Willow: A History, A Story, and A Memory of the Last Plains Frontier*. New York: Viking, 1962.

Stevens, Peter. "Poet as Critic as Prairie Poet." In Cooley, *RePlacing*, 54–69.

Stone, Ted, ed. *Riding the Northern Range: Poems from the Last Best-West*. Red Deer: RDC Press, 1993.

Strohmayer, Ulf. "On Not Taking Language for Granted" *Acme* 4, no. 2 (2005): 249–253.

Suknaski, Andrew. *East of Myloona*. Saskatoon: Thistledown, 1979.

———. *the ghosts call you poor*. Toronto: Macmillan, 1978.

———. *In the Name of Narid*. Erin, ON: The Porcupine's Quill, 1981.

———. *The Land They Gave Away*. Edmonton: NeWest, 1982.

———. *Leaving*. Seven Persons, AB: Repository, 1974.

———. *Montage for an Interstellar Cry*. Winnipeg: Turnstone, 1982.

———. *Octomi*. Saskatoon: Thistledown, 1976.

———. *Phillip Well*. Prince George: Caledonia Writing Series, 1973.
———. *Silk Trail*. Toronto: Nightwood Editions, 1985.
———. *Wood Mountain Poems*. Toronto: Macmillan, 1976.
Thrift, Nigel. *Non-Representational Theory: Space, Politics, Affect*. NY: Routledge, 2007.
Tuan, Yi-Fu. "Literature and Geography: Implications for Geographical Research." In *Humanistic Geography: Prospects and Problems*, edited by David Ley and Marwyn Samuels, 194–206. Chicago: Maaroufa Press, 1978.
———. "Literature, Experience, and Environmental Knowing." In Moore and Golledge, *Environmental Knowing*, 260–71.
———. *Romantic Geography: In Search of the Sublime Landscape*. Madison: University of Wisconsin Press, 2013.
Turner, Frederick. *Beyond Geography: The Western Spirit Against the Wilderness*. NY: Viking, 1980.
Uher, Lorna. *Crow's Black Joy*. Edmonton: NeWest, 1978.
———. *Humans and Other Beasts*. Winnipeg: Turnstone, 1980.
———. *Inside Is the Sky*. Saskatoon: Thistledown, 1976.
———. *See also* Crozier, Lorna.
Verduyn, Christl, ed. *Literary Pluralities*. Peterborough: Broadview, 1998.
Wardhaugh, Robert, ed. *Toward Defining the Prairies: Region, Culture, and History*. Winnipeg: University of Manitoba Press, 2001.
Warley, Linda, John Clement Ball, and Robert Viau."Introduction: Mapping the Ground." *Studies in Canadian Literature*. 23:1 (1998). https://journals.lib.unb.ca/index.php/SCL/article/view/8270/9333
West, Elliott. "Stegner, Storytelling, and Western Identity" in *Wallace Stegner, Man and Writer*, edited by Charles E. Rankin, 61–71. Albuquerque: University of New Mexico Press, 1996.
Wiebe, Rudy. "Passage by Land." In *Personal Fictions*, selected by Michael Ondaatje, 227. Toronto: Oxford, 1977.
Williams, William Carlos. *Selected Poems*. New York: New Directions, 1985.
Woodcock, George. Introduction to Lecker et al., *Canadian Writers and their Works*. Vol. 11: 5–13.
Wright, Charles. *Appalachia*. New York: Farrar, Straus and Giroux, 1999.
Yates, J. Michael. *Parallax: Poems*. Surrey, BC: Sono Nis, 1971.
Zarzyski, Paul. *The Make-Up of Ice*. Athens: The University of Georgia Press, 1984.
Zieroth, Dale. *Clearing: Poems from a Journey*. Toronto: Anansi, 1973.
Zwicky, Jan. *Alkibiades' Love: Essays in Philosophy*. Montreal: McGill-Queen's, 2015.
———. *Forge*. Kentville: Gaspereau, 2011.
———. "Lyric, Narrative, Memory." In *A Ragged Pen: Essays on Poetry & Memory*, 87–105. Kentville: Gaspereau, 2006.
———. *Robinson's Crossing*. London: Brick Books, 2004.
———. *Songs for Relinquishing the Earth*. London: Brick Books, 1998.
———. *Thirty-seven Small Songs and Thirteen Silences*. Kentville: Gaspereau, 2005.
———. *Where Have You Been*. Ilderton, ON: Brick Books, 1982.
———. *Wisdom & Metaphor*. Kentville: Gaspereau, 2003.
———. *Wittgenstein Elegies*. Ilderton: Brick Books, 1986.

Index

Page numbers in italics refer to maps.

D

H

I

J

K

L

Q

R

S

Z

ABOUT THE AUTHOR

Carl Tracie is an Emeritus Professor of Geography, Trinity Western University, with a life-long interest in the physical and cultural landscapes of the prairies, and the literature that has arisen from and about that region. He lives, with his wife Darlene, in Abbotsford, British Columbia.